25—

THE
BUDGET
DEFICIT

The Causes, the Costs, the Outlook

Leonard Jay Santow, Ph.D.

New York Institute of Finance

LIBRARY OF CONGRESS
Library of Congress Cataloging-in-Publication Data

Santow, Leonard Jay.
     The budget deficit : the causes, the costs, the outlook / Leonard
Jay Santow.
         p.   cm.
     Includes index.
     ISBN 0-13-085085-3 : $24.95
     1. Budget deficits--United States. 2. Taxation--United States.
3. Deficit financing--United States. 4. Cash management--United
States.   I. Title.
HJ2051.S24 1988
339.5'23'0973--dc19   88-10161
                                                                 CIP

339.5 23
S23b

This publication is designed to provide accurate and authoritative information in regard to the subject matter covered. It is sold with the understanding that the publisher is not engaged in rendering legal, accounting, or other professional service. If legal advice or other expert assistance is required, the services of a competent professional person should be sought.

From a Declaration of Principles Jointly Adopted by a Committee of the American Bar Association and a Committee of Publishers and Associations

Printed in the United States of America

10 9 8 7 6 5 4 3 2 1

New York Institute of Finance
(NYIF Corp.)
70 Pine Street
New York, New York 10270-0003

Contents

List of Charts and Tables   *vii*

A View from the Top   *xi*

Acknowledgments   *xix*

Introduction   *xx*

In a Nutshell   *xxiii*

I. The Deficit Explosion—Its Timing, Causes, Blame, Costs, and Outlook

1. When did the budget deficit problem begin?   2

2. What caused the massive increase in the budget deficit from
   FY-74 to FY-86?   5

3. What has happened to tax receipts since FY-74?   *14*

4. What expenditure areas deserve primary attention from
   FY-74 to FY-87?   *25*

5. Is there a story to tell about each of the four major spending
   categories?   *30*

6. Are there nondefense areas where large cutbacks in outlays
   are possible?   *39*

7. Can major savings be made in the defense budget?   *42*

8.   Should the Reagan administration receive most of the credit for substantially slowing the growth of government outlays? *44*

9.   Is there a ''party-in-power'' factor which correlates with the deficit increase since FY-74? *47*

10. How obvious were the official budget estimating errors when they were made, and immediately thereafter? *54*

11. What is the budget deficit outlook in the years ahead? *55*

12. What price is the United States paying for its huge budget deficit? *62*

II. Tax Reform and Tax Receipts—More Work Is Needed

13. What were the prerequisites used in designing the 1986 Tax Reform Act, and were they the proper ones? *69*

14. Can the budget deficit be reduced substantially without a major increase in receipts? *72*

15. If receipts-raising measures are necessary, why haven't they been instituted? *74*

16. What type of revenue-raising measure would make the most sense? *78*

17. Should the government offer some form of amnesty to those who either do not report, or underreport, their income? *81*

III. Deficit Financing and Cash Management—How It Is Done and How It Can Be Improved

18. Has the Treasury's debt management approach changed significantly since FY-74? *87*

19. How will Treasury financings from 1974 through 1987 affect future debt management? *98*

20. Who were the primary domestic purchasers of Treasury debt from CY-74 to CY-87, and can they be counted on in the future? *105*

21. Have foreigners bought a large amount of Treasury debt issues since 1974? *109*

22. Will foreigners continue to buy large amounts of Treasury obligations? *123*

23. Does it make sense for a nation, such as Japan, with huge official dollar reserves, to invest mainly in U.S. Treasury bills? *130*

24. Whatever happened to the argument that private borrowers would be crowded out by Treasury borrowings? *140*

25. Should individual investors play a much larger role in financing the deficit? *142*

26. Should the Treasury consider offering new maturities in its marketable debt obligations? *144*

27. Should bill financing as a portion of the total financing be expanded? *146*

28. How can the Treasury improve the steadiness of its cash flow? *147*

29. Can the Treasury's financing pattern be changed so as to improve cash management? *160*

30. Has the growth of the government securities market kept pace with the growth of Treasury debt financing? *165*

31. How useful is the debt ceiling from a public policy perspective? *172*

IV. The Budget Document and Process—Practicality Counts

32. Should budget outlays be subdivided—one for capital goods and one for operations—with only operations used in computing the deficit? *176*

33. Should a two-year rather than a one-year budget be used? *178*

34. Is the submission of the budget approximately eight months before the start of the fiscal year the most logical time to do so? *180*

35. Should the president have the power to use a line-item veto to delete segments of legislation? *183*

36. Should a nongovernment/nonpartisan body be established whose specific task is estimating budget deficits? *184*

37. Is there a price to be paid for using the current Gramm-Rudman-Hollings (GRH) approach? *185*

38. Is there a better way, under Gramm-Rudman-Hollings, to improve mandated expenditure reductions? *188*

39. Would a balanced-budget amendment be an improvement over Gramm-Rudman-Hollings? *190*

40. Is it possible to devise a budget amendment that makes sense? *191*

41. Have official forecasts of appropriations and outlays accurately predicted turning points in spending? *193*

42. How can the budget deficit be so large when both Congress and the administration claim they are "saving" so much money? *195*

43. Can government accounting remove expenditures merely by placing them off budget? *196*

44. Besides off-budget items, are there other ways the government can be less than straightforward in its budget reporting? *199*

V. *Budget Concepts Questioned, Budget Relationships Analyzed*

45. Is fiscal "policy" truly a policy? *204*

46. Is the federal budget document and process similar to those in the corporate world? *207*

47. Should fiscal policy be used for countercyclical purposes such as stimulating the economy? *210*

48. Can it be proven a relationship exists between large budget deficits and high interest rates? *213*

49. What are some important relationships to consider when forming budgetary policies? *219*

50. Is there a direct relationship between the United States' budget and trade deficits? *226*

Appendix *229*

Index *243*

Charts and Tables

I-1.1   Officially Estimated Versus Actual Budget Figures   *3*

I-2.1   Deficits—Actuals Versus Estimates   *6*

I-2.2   Increase in Receipts and Expenditures—FY-74 Through FY-87   *7*

I-2.3   Receipts—Actuals Versus Estimates   *10*

I-2.4   Expenditures—Actuals Versus Estimates   *12*

I-3.1   Budget Receipts   *15*

I-3.2   Selected Receipts Categories—Actuals Versus Estimates, FY-74 Through FY-87 (table)   *16*

I-3.3   Selected Receipts Categories—Actuals Versus Estimates, FY-74 Through FY-87 (chart)   *17*

I-3.4   Social Security Taxes—Payments and Ceilings   *20*

I-3.5   Major Tax Refunds—Actuals Versus Estimates—FY-74 Through FY-87   *24*

I-4.1   Budget Expenditure Components   *26–27*

I-4.2   Major Expenditure Categories—Actuals Versus Estimates—FY-74 Through FY-87 (table)   *28*

I-4.3   Major Expenditure Categories—Actuals Versus Estimates—FY-74 Through FY-87 (chart)   *29*

I-5.1   Health and Human Services—Actuals Versus Estimates   *31*

I-5.2   Increases in HHS Spending Compared with Advances in the Consumer Price Index (CPI)   *32*

I-5.3   National Defense   *35*

I-8.1   Federal Expenditures Related to Interest Rates and the CPI   *45*

I-9.1   Political Profile   *48*

I-9.2   Economic Assumptions Versus Actuality   *50–51*

I-9.3   GNP Current Dollar Growth—Assumptions Versus Actuality   *52*

I-11.1   Tax-Take   *60*

III-18.1   Marketable Treasury Debt Outstanding   *88*

III-18.2   Maturity Distribution of Marketable Debt Held by Private Investors   *89*

III-18.3   Treasury Offerings of Notes and Bonds for Cash by Maturities Beginning in 1974   *90–93*

III-18.4   Nonmarketable Treasury Debt Outstanding   *96*

III-18.5   Nonmarketable Treasury Debt Outstanding as of 12/31/87   *97*

III-19.1   Marketable Note and Bond Maturities 1988 Through 2017   *99*

III-19.2   Estimated Offerings, Maturities, and Net Increases in Notes and Bonds—1988 Through 2017   *101*

III-19.3   Estimated Marketable Note and Bond Maturities and Financings—1988 Through 2017   *102–104*

III-20.1   Estimated Ownership of Marketable Securities   *106*

III-21.1   Foreign Holdings of Marketable Treasury Issues—Dollar Amounts and Percentage of Marketable Debt Outstanding   *110*

III-21.2   Annual Japanese Purchases of Treasury Coupon Issues—Japanese Compared with U.S. Data   *111*

III-21.3   Foreign Holdings of Treasury Bills, Certificates, Notes, and Bonds   *113*

III-21.4   Foreign Holdings of Marketable Notes and Bonds Versus Holdings of Bills and Certificates   *114*

III-21.5   Breakout of Foreign Holdings of Treasury Securities   *115*

III-21.6   Holdings of Notes and Bonds by Official and Nonofficial Institutions   *116–117*

III-21.7   Breakout by Countries of Major Holdings of Treasury Notes and Bonds   *117*

III-21.8   Short-Term Treasury Obligations Owned by Foreign Official Institutions and Unaffiliated Foreign Banks   *118*

III-21.9   Major Holders of Foreign Exchange Reserves   *121*

III-23.1   Dollar Versus Yen, Japanese Exports to United States, and Japanese Purchases of U.S. Treasury Notes and Bonds   *131*

III-23.2   Dollar Versus Deutsche Mark, German Exports to United States, and German Purchases of U.S. Treasury Notes and Bonds   *132*

III-23.3   Deutsche Mark (DM) and Yen Versus the Dollar   *133*

III-23.4   German and Japanese Exports to the United States   *134*

III-23.5   Important Interest Rate Relationships—U.S. Treasury Bonds Compared with Japanese and German Treasury Bonds   *135*

III-23.6   Treasury Bill and Bond Yields—United States Compared with Other Countries   *136*

III-23.7   Japanese Foreign Debt Market Investments by Country   *137*

III-23.8   Hypothetical Central Bank Portfolio of 2-, 3-, 4-, and 5-Year Maturities   *139*

III-28.1   Current System—Nonwithheld Income Tax Payment Pattern   *149*

III-28.2   Proposed System—Nonwithheld Income Tax Payment Pattern   *150*

III-28.3   Approximate Monthly Receipts/Expenditures if the FY-87 Budget Were in Balance   *151*

III-28.4   1987 Treasury Cash Balance   *154–155*

III-28.5   1987 Treasury Tax and Loan Balance at Commercial
           Banks   *156–157*

III-28.6   1987 Treasury Balance at the Federal Reserve   *158–159*

III-29.1   Marketable Treasury Financing—July Through September
           1987   *162–163*

III-29.2   Recommendations as to Timing of Note and Bond Offerings *164*

III-30.1   Number of Reporting Dealers Compared with 30-Year Bond
           Performance   *166*

III-30.2   Dealer Positions and Transactions   *167*

III-31.1   Debt Ceiling Changes   *173*

III-31.2   Debt Ceiling—End of Each Fiscal Year—
           1974 Through 1987   *174*

IV-34.1   Budget Submission Information   *181*

IV-41.1   Estimated Appropriations and Outlays Compared with
          Actual Outlays   *194*

V-48.1   Correlation Between Deficits and Interest Rates   *217*

V-48.2   3-Month and 20-Year Treasury Issues   *218*

V-49.1   Important Budget Relationships   *220–221*

V-49.2   Gross Private Savings Compared with Marketable Treasury
         Debt   *222*

V-49.3   Receipts, Outlays, and Deficits as a Percentage of Nominal
         GNP   *224*

V-50.1   U.S. Budget and Trade Deficits   *227*

A-1   Actuals and Estimates for Deficits, Fiscal Years 1975 and
      1976   *231*

A-2   Actuals and Estimates for Deficits, Fiscal Years 1982 and
      1983   *235*

A View from the Top

Henry Kaufman
Albert M. Wojnilower

Henry Kaufman

The Federal budget reflects the social, political and economic priorities of our nation. Together with monetary policy, the budget today serves as an important tool for stabilizing the economy. Actually, this role of the budget is of relatively recent vintage. For most of our history, the budgetary position of the U.S. was quite modest. Deficits advanced only in war times. Federal income taxes as a source of revenue came into being only in this century. For that matter, monetary policy was also quite rudimentary until the Federal Reserve System was legislated in 1913.

The use of the Federal budget as a tool for influencing the economy was mainly due to John Maynard Keynes, who saw fiscal policy as an important vehicle for overcoming the world depression in the 1930s and for transmitting countercyclical influences on economic behavior. While the teachings of Keynes have been hotly debated, it should also be noted that his prescriptions were not fully followed. Our policy makers have often rushed to incur budget deficits in periods of economic slack, but they have been very tardy in reducing and eliminating the deficit when the economy approached full resource utilization.

Countercyclical fiscal policy has often helped to end recessions and speed economic recovery. The most prominent examples have been the Kennedy round of tax cuts and those initiated by President Reagan early in this decade. When the budgets had to be used to restrain the economy, fiscal action has generally been very tardy. This was quite evident during the Viet Nam War and, of course, during the last few years. This extraordinary difference between fiscal accommodation and restraint should not be surprising. It is a failing and reflects our political and social immaturity. Naturally, it is far more pleasant to have taxes cut instead of raised or to be beneficiary of Federal expenditures than to have them reduced or eliminated.

The biggest explosion in the Federal budget deficit has taken place in this decade as a consequence of large tax cuts and increases in defense spending as other expenditures were not sufficiently reduced. Moreover, the much heralded view of growing out of the deficit that comforted so many when it was promulgated did not materialize. As a result, we now have a large structural budget deficit which will be difficult to eliminate. Indeed, most initiatives lately are aimed at reducing the deficit, and even though we are reaching full employment, actions under these circumstances to eliminate the deficit altogether are missing.

Some in recent years have claimed that budget deficits do not matter. I do not share this view. To be sure, monetary policy can neutralize fiscal policy, but this is hardly the way an economy should be managed. Moreover, the Government through its budget competes for limited resources with the private sector and this influences private behavior initiatives.

Most importantly, the huge Federal budget deficits have changed the structure of our credit markets. Today, the U.S. Government market overwhelmingly dominates. This was not always true. If you asked two decades ago, "How is the bond market doing?," the answer would have dealt with the price movement of utility or industrial bonds. Today, the response always centers on Governments. Today, the size of the U.S. Government bond market is much larger than other markets. All new issues in other markets are priced off Governments. The Government market's resiliency is enhanced by a highly developed options and futures market and, of course, by open market transactions of the Federal Reserve. Moreover, U.S. Treasury financing has been highly routinized and issues are available all along the yield curve.

Consequently, a focus on and monitoring of budgetary developments is essential for market participants. Seasoned and cyclical budgetary trends need to be recognized. The impact of Treasury financing on other markets must be analyzed. This is why this book, written by a premier analyst in the field, will be invaluable.

Albert M. Wojnilower

It is a privilege to be invited to comment in this space. Len Santow and I have been professional and personal friends for some three decades. As respects the Federal budget, Dr. Santow is the outstanding diagnostician: the nonpareil analyst and interpreter of the real-life statistical, economic, and political dimensions of the budget as it emerges year after year. And although he is not primarily an accountant or economic theoretician, one cannot accomplish the insights he has accomplished without great expertise in these disciplines.

This volume contains many eminently sensible proposals for reform—such as requiring a 60% Congressional majority on spending bills programs, granting capital gains tax benefits but only on assets held over two years, and adjusting Treasury cash management practices—with which I concur in principle and mostly also in detail. In addition, however, Dr. Santow's work seems to me to lend support to certain broad viewpoints of mine that he may not share. It is his generosity that allows me to summarize these heterodox views here.

Given the apparently universal consensus in favor of balanced budgets, why do we have such a persistent deficit? The stereotypical rhetoric asserts that we have deficits because the poor, there being so many of them, are able to compel the voting of redistributive expenditures, and because civil servants, wishing to feather their nests, promote and indulge in wasteful spending. Dr. Santow's data shows that it is middle-class and business "welfare," rather than subsidies to the poor, that create and perpetuate the deficit. Military expenditures have increased, to some extent reflecting "interservice rivalry" and "questionable weaponry" decisions—but in any event benefiting constituencies that are hardly in dire financial need. Social security outlays have soared, but poor people benefit less because they do not live as long as richer ones. Interest outlays have ballooned, but these tend to flow to the affluent. Farm subsidies have burgeoned but, their difficult plight notwithstanding, farmers are hardly part of the welfare class, nor have small farmers been treated particularly generously. Finally, Dr. Santow cites the major role of the 1981 tax reduction in widening the budget gap. Quite apart from the controversy as to which income groups these tax cuts benefited most, the fact remains that poor people pay little tax, so that their tax savings could not have had much impact on the total deficit increase.

The moral is that our budgetary situation reflects and suits the balance of interests in this country. The deficit represents one method—not the best, but far from the worst—of peaceably reconciling politically powerful claims. It is comfortable to point the finger at a convenient and helpless scapegoat, but in truth the enemy is us.

For decades we have been warned of nameless disasters to be visited on us if we failed to rectify our deficit ways. No such disasters have occurred. Nor did we reap any of the promised rewards when we reduced the deficit. In fiscal 1987 the deficit unexpectedly plunged from $221 billion to $150 billion. Interest rates went up, not down; the trade deficit widened; and the dollar fell. (It is now conventional to argue that budget deficit reduction is needed to bolster the dollar. As recently as two years ago, the conventional wisdom was the opposite, that deficit reduction was needed to bring the dollar down.) This lack of relationship between budgetary shifts and broader economic developments was not surprising, since it only repeated what happened several times before. Indeed our last year of budget surplus, fiscal 1969, was a year of accelerating inflation, rising interest rates, and a weakening currency situation.

Probably the main explanation for the short-run impotence of fiscal policy is that, at least in the United States, monetary policy is ever so much more powerful. Although his wording is guarded, Dr. Santow may well agree that monetary policy far outweighs fiscal policy in its significance for business fluctuations and forecasting.

None of this should be taken to denigrate the longer-range significance of fiscal decisions. In a 4½-trillion-dollar economy, it is a serious matter how a trillion dollars a year is to be spent. Even so, however, it is far from being the ultimate determinant of our welfare. Of the trillion dollars, "only" $400 billion or so is being spent on goods and services ($300 billion of this on defense); the rest essentially reflects transfers among ourselves. Consumers spend much more, over $3 trillion. More importantly, law and regulation, especially tax law, play a critical role in setting private sector incentives—but the consequences show up mainly in private budgets, not the Federal budget. Many a businessman has commented, accurately and ruefully, that "What is so expensive isn't what we have to pay the government, but what the government makes us spend."

This highlights the artificiality and self-serving character of the division so many commentators make between the public and private sector. In the budget process, we decide what instrumentalities to use to carry out those collective objectives on which we have already agreed. We have determined, for example, to support the elderly. We do so through Social Security and Medicare, but could accomplish the same objective differently by legislating severe penalties on next-of-kin who fail to support their elderly relatives appropriately. It is not clear *a priori* which way is more efficient, taking all the ramifications into account. The choice is a political one. Even if no legal sanctions were imposed on any one, informal systems of taxation (called "social pressure" and "philanthropy") would still operate powerfully to channel resources to the elderly. The resources would be expended anyhow, whether or not they passed through the Federal budget. Similarly, we could eliminate entirely Federal outlays on health or education, but probably expenditures nearly as large in size (although, to be sure, differently and perhaps more efficiently directed) would wind up being made by state and local governments and/or the private sector. That is why only the military budget decisions are of transcendent importance—what is not spent on the military at the Federal level, will not be spent at all.

The need to think of the Federal budget as an integral rather than somehow isolated aspect of a complex social process is even clearer as respects taxation. In taxation, the critical issue is *who* pays, rather than what is being paid for, or how much. When taxes are lowered, businesses and households go on with their normal lives and do not substantially elevate their scale of life unless and until the general economic climate changes in such a way as to indicate that more spending is sensible. For the most part, lowering of taxes merely means that government has to borrow more, but that the public has the added wherewithal needed to lend more to the government. Short-term economic consequences are minimal. Long-term consequences depend mainly on the incentive effects, not on the change in the aggregate level of taxes.

Conversely, when taxes are raised, absent a change in the economic climate, businesses and households simply persist in their previous habits and plans, spending the same but saving less and borrowing more. The deficit financing is simply shifted from the government to the public, without particular economic consequence. Since tax increases are likely to be accompanied by looser money and lower interest rates, as well as by much hoopla as to how all economic problems have been solved, the borrowing is easy and the economic effect normally expansionary (as in the 1969 example cited earlier).

The major budgetary reform that is needed is a tightening of spending discipline. Because advocates of Federal spending programs believe they can make others share the bill, such programs are too many and too large. Adoption of Dr. Santow's Congressional 60% vote requirement for new spending programs would be a most constructive step. (I am less enthusiastic about his proposal to make Presidential vetoes harder to override; as his work shows, Congress commits many budgetary sins, but the blockbusters are Presidential.)

If only we could find a rule analogous to the 55 miles-per-hour speed limit—the kind of limit that continues to restrain despite being frequently violated. But it is no use decreeing by law that people be saints rather than sinners, superhuman rather than human. It would be worse than futile to promulgate a 40-mile speed limit, even though many lives might, in theory, be saved. That is because such a rule would make almost everyone a determined lawbreaker and police hater. The Gramm-Rudman-Hollings law (and the balanced-budget amendment) has this insidious character. To meet their stipulations, accounts and estimates have to be distorted if not falsified, and palpable rule violations somehow legitimated. Lawmakers are forced into self- as well as public contempt. The need to fit the Procrustean stipulations of Gramm-Rudman-Hollings guarantees that Presidential budgets are and will remain "dead on arrival." The result is that the budgetary coin Dr. Santow has polished for us in this volume is rapidly being debased beyond usefulness.

Acknowledgments

Irving Auerbach, Joan Byrne, Arthur Samansky, and Claude Tygier have all made major contributions to this book. They contributed their thoughts, ideas, and a considerable amount of precious time. They took a roughly worded commentary, with many incomplete and not fully thought-through ideas, and helped to transform it into a relatively coherent text. Their varied backgrounds brought different insights to bear on the topics discussed, initiating some substantial rethinking and rewriting. Whether a book makes a major contribution in its field is always difficult for an author to judge. Yet, it is surely a far better work because of these people and their efforts.

Introduction

The federal budget, its deficit and its financing, has been a major topic of discussion in recent years. It is an area of great importance for the U.S. economy, as well as for the domestic and international financial markets. It has a direct impact on virtually every individual, corporation, and governing body in the nation, and many persons and institutions abroad. Yet, there are few books on the subject, and those which have been published are either conceptual in nature or politically oriented.

The reasons for the lack of such literature are not hard to find. The budget and fiscal policy have so many facets and aspects, it is difficult to bring them together in a readable and coherent manner. There is a general lack of expertise in this area as can be seen by arguments which continually rage as to who is to blame for the deficit problems. Some analysts are quite knowledgeable about the budget process, but do not have a good "feel" for what is happening to the budget numbers. Other analysts concentrate on the expenditure items and their trends, but show little interest in the receipts components. Then there are individuals who are quite knowledgeable with respect to Treasury financing and the government securities market, but have little understanding of the conceptual side, or the likely course of receipts and outlays.

Another reason for a lack of broadly based and practical books written about fiscal policy and the budget is that the data have to be gathered from numerous sources. Much of the data are old, and often difficult to obtain. There are often breaks in the data, and the way the numbers are categorized has been frequently changed. Coping with these problems requires fortitude and patience; it requires a knowledge of what is available and pertinent, and where it can be found.

Then too, in recent years, financial economists have seemed to concentrate on monetary rather than fiscal policy. Part of the reason is that Federal Reserve policy unfolds on a daily basis, and its actions strongly influence the decisions of many investors. Equally important, the monetary authorities publish a wealth of daily, weekly, and monthly information. Under these circumstances, it is not surprising there has been a proliferation of ''Fed watchers'' who have produced many books on the subject.

By contrast, there is no institution controlling the budget throttle on a daily basis. There seems to be little relationship between short-term budget results and investment opportunities, and while there are daily figures published, they are not presented in a manner which enables the easy monitoring of the deficit. The most useful information is published monthly with an approximate four-week time lag. If there is to be an increase in the ranks of budget watchers, officials need to make the Daily Treasury Statement similar to the Monthly Statement of Receipts and Outlays. (The accounts in the Daily Treasury Statement do not correspond with the receipts and expenditure categories in either the monthly statement or the budget.)

Finally, there is the problem of how to write a readable book on the budget, where little is understood and much is misunderstood, where many of the problems seem esoteric and obtuse, and where numbers proliferate and dominate the analyses; all of which make it difficult to hold the reader's attention for hundreds of pages. Nonexperts are at a special disadvantage, yet it is the nonexperts who make up the over-whelming majority of potential readers.

These problems in no way minimize the importance of the topic or the need for a comprehensive analysis. Rather, they add to the challenge and excitement of writing such a book.

To add to the book's readability, a Socratic approach is used. Fifty questions pertaining to fiscal policy and the budget are presented. Some questions are clearly more important than others, but all are included to paint a broad and well-rounded picture.

The questions are grouped into five basic areas. Part I addresses when the budget deficit problems began, who or what caused them, and when the problems should have been discovered. The section also looks at costs and the future.

Part II is devoted to the topics of tax reform and budget receipts. Special attention is given to increasing receipts to reduce the deficit. Some of the suggestions are quite technical and detailed, but if adopted, their impact would be broadly based and substantial. The discussion of what could be done should help explain the shortcomings of the current system.

Part III is devoted to Treasury financings and cash management, how they are currently being implemented, and how they can be improved. While these areas do not get to the heart of the basic budget problems, the improvements suggested could reduce the cost or limit the pain of budget deficits. As in Part II, many of the suggestions are detailed and technical in nature. However, this provides the reader with a better understanding of Treasury operations.

Part IV briefly discusses some recommendations to improve the budget document, process and presentation. It also touches upon several controversial issues. Many of the existing budget procedures are evolutionary, with the result that insufficient attention has been paid to their underlying appropriateness.

Part V is the most conceptual. It includes a series of topics which tend to be broadly based, where processes and relationships are analyzed. The recommendations are much broader in scope than in the other parts, and probably will create the most controversy. For the more academically inclined, this is probably the most worthwhile section of the book.

The use of a question-and-answer approach keeps the book modest in length. Readers can start almost anywhere without feeling they are coming in at the middle of the story. The book is replete with detailed tables and charts, but the most important points are addressed in the text. Thus, it is not necessary to concentrate on the wealth of statistical information presented to understand the major points of the book.

Finally, considerable thought has been given to the timing of this book. Interest in the budget usually intensifies before national elections, especially a presidential election. The 1988 presidential election campaign will no doubt have as its key economic topics, the twin deficits—budget and trade. During such a period, facts and substance are likely to be hard to come by. If this book can add to the American voter's understanding of the budget, and at the same time contribute to an increased dialogue by government officials as to how fiscal policy and the budget can be improved, it will have been worth the author's effort.

In a Nutshell

The primary objective of this book is to educate the reader on budget realities. The key areas discussed are when the deficit problem began, how it evolved, who is to blame, how the deficit was financed, where its impact was most keenly felt, and how the resulting fiscal and economic burdens can be lessened and the deficit itself reduced. The following are some of the most important thoughts presented.

- The deterioration in the U.S. budget picture was not spread over many decades. It took place from FY-74 through FY-86, and accelerated primarily during two periods, FY-75/FY-76 and FY-82/FY-83. The sharp deficit increase in the first period was due primarily to a large advance in government expenditures, while in the second period it was the result of both a rise in outlays and a receipts shortfall. The latter occurred in good part because of the Tax Reform Act of 1981 and to overly optimistic receipts estimates by supply-side economists associated with the Reagan administration.
- The sharp deterioration in the budget picture from FY-74 through FY-86 was not primarily due to the general economic or financial climate, but rather to budgetary policies and estimates. For example, if the weak receipts of FY-82/FY-83 had been accurately projected by the administration, Congress would no doubt have pared future government outlays.
- In the dozen years of deficit deterioration, no one political party can be held totally responsible, although there were years when a particular party or administration deserves most of the blame. In FY-82/FY-83—the period of greatest budget adversity—the Reagan administration must bear primary responsibility.
- From FY-74 through FY-86, tax receipts grew at a disappointing pace. The one area which experienced a major advance was trust accounts, and that was due to increases in both tax rates and earnings ceilings. The

amount of income taxes paid, compared with personal income and corporate profits, was very small, indicating a substantial number of individuals and institutions were not paying their fair share.

- The two largest spending categories from FY-74 through FY-86 were health and human services (HHS) and defense. Surprisingly, official estimates in these two areas were generally not that wide of the mark. Moreover, in the case of military outlays, in recent years the estimates have proven too high. Two other spending areas, however, had considerable estimating errors—interest payments and agricultural outlays. Both areas were substantially underestimated during most of the years studied, and although much smaller in total than either HHS or defense, they were primarily responsible for the underestimation of outlays.

- The Reagan administration has been credited (or blamed) for the sharp rise in military outlays. But it was during the Carter administration that the acceleration in defense spending began, and the percentage increase during the Carter years was larger than during the Reagan era. The Reagan administration, however, did show larger dollar increases, especially when adjusted for inflation. Even if the Reagan administration should get top billing in this regard, the Carter administration is much more responsible for increased military expenditures than the public seems to realize.

- The large amount spent on defense does not mean funds have been spent in an optimum manner. There is a need to improve the choice of weapons systems, and a reduction in interservice rivalry would be a step in the right direction. It would allow the United States to be either better prepared using the same dollar outlays, or able to reduce spending without damaging preparedness.

- The growth in government spending slowed substantially from FY-82 through FY-87, the main reasons being the sharp reduction in the rate of inflation and lower interest rates. Therefore, the slowing in outlays was not primarily due to paring of expenditures by the executive branch or Congress. With inflation and interest rates having increased during FY-87, the rate of growth in government spending is likely to pick up in FY-88 and FY-89. Thus, if the deficit is to be significantly reduced, a large growth in receipts must be a key ingredient.

- The budget deficit in FY-87 was $150 billion. However, as a result of the 1986 Tax Reform Act, there was a one-time receipts increase which amounted to between $30 billion and $40 billion. Looking ahead, this legislation is not likely to raise any new money in upcoming years and a recession is a reasonable possibility sometime in the next few years as there has not been one since 1982. Thus, to have a substantial increase in receipts, new money-raising measures need to be adopted.

- In FY-75/FY-76 and in FY-82/FY-83, the official budget estimates were wide of the mark. These errors were due in part to politicized estimates and also because of inaccurate assumptions. In both periods, not only should the errors have been smaller, but the forecasts should have been revised much sooner. It is circumstances such as these which suggest the need for an independent and private body strictly in the business of making budget forecasts.

- The budget results for President Reagan's two terms in office will be adverse and disappointing. On the positive side, considerable improvements will have been made in tax equity, as well as a major slowing in the growth of total government spending. Yet, these pluses will be more than offset by very large increases in both the deficit and public debt outstanding.

- The United States is paying a considerable price for its huge budget deficit. It includes limiting the ability of the government to stimulate the economy and to resolve domestic and international problems. It also induces the Federal Reserve to follow a firmer monetary policy than otherwise would be necessary, creates inflation fears in the minds of investors, and results in large interest payments, especially abroad. Moreover, it saps the people's confidence in their government and encroaches on the time public officials should be devoting to other more pressing problems. Finally, it hinders federal assistance to state and local governments and federal agencies.

- Gramm-Rudman-Hollings (GRH) legislation is badly flawed. One improvement for GRH would be to use the Congressional Budget Office's (CBO) GNP forecast for the new fiscal year as a basis for the deficit reduction target. The target could then be adjusted during the fiscal year as the CBO's real GNP forecast changes. Once the deficit declines to a point where it is at a moderate percentage of nominal GNP—1 percent or less—the formula would no longer be operative. Another improvement would be to allow the administration and Congress each to protect 25 percent of total spending from across-the-board reductions (excluding interest). The protection would not be complete, however, since there would be cost-of-living ceilings.

- A constitutional amendment that brings the budget deficit under control can be justified. Unfortunately, the current proposal is badly flawed. A far more practical amendment would be "if the unified budget in the previous fiscal year was in deficit, then passage by Congress of spending bills would require a 60 percent approval by each house and a 70 percent approval to override a presidential veto."

- The Tax Reform Act of 1986 should have had three prerequisites: (1) an increase in savings; (2) a stimulation of exports; (3) raising budget receipts and reducing the deficit. To increase savings, there should have been full IRA tax deductibility (it should have been placed on a sliding scale based on age), and capital gains tax benefits should have been retained. Corporations should have been induced to raise more equity funds and to reduce their amount of debt outstanding.

  To encourage exports, more-generous depreciation rules for exporters should have been instituted, with investment tax credits reintroduced for these firms. To help reduce the budget deficit, tax receipts could have been increased by making the minimum tax laws more stringent, limiting exemptions and deductions, and further minimizing interest deductibility for tax purposes. Special tax breaks could have been reduced or eliminated, and a temporary income tax surcharge considered.

- An income tax surcharge could be instituted for a calendar year when three factors are present: the deficit in the previous year has shown an increase, the deficit was over 2 percent of nominal GNP, and the economy had exhibited positive real growth. The amount raised would be equal to the increase in the deficit of the previous year. If Congress and the administration were to work steadily to lower the deficit, the surcharge would not be necessary, making it a much more attractive alternative than a continuing tax. The system could also be thought of as an alternative, rather than a supplement, to GRH or balanced-budget legislation.

- The government could raise a considerable amount of money through a tax amnesty system. One possible approach is when individuals voluntarily report previously undisclosed income, only interest would be assessed. There would be no penalties. Individuals could be placed on a three-year repayment program. The program would result in an inducement to pay, with no inducement to cheat.

- The Treasury relied heavily on three techniques to finance the expanded deficit from FY-74 through FY-87. It added to the list of maturities and the frequency with which they were issued, it put financings on a more routine basis, and it placed greater emphasis on issuing intermediate- and longer-term maturities. These techniques made a great deal of sense, and in combination, worked very well.

- The Treasury survey of ownership is not accurate. The "other" category is the largest and fastest growing, and a substantial part of its advance should be classified as "foreign holders" and "domestic individual holders." These latter two categories, as officially reported, are significantly understated.

- Foreign holdings did not increase substantially until 1983. Since then, they gave grown rapidly, and in 1986 and 1987, foreigners may have been responsible for about one-half of the net increase in marketable Treasury debt outstanding. The Japanese and Germans accounted for a very large portion of the 1986 and 1987 investments.

  Foreign official holders have become more aggressive in terms of the length of maturities they have purchased and the amount of trading done. In 1986, foreign private purchasers helped suppress U.S. interest rates, especially in longer maturities where the reduction may have been over 1 percent. In 1987, these investors were less of a positive force.

- Foreigners increased their holdings of Treasury issues between $100 and $200 billion in the three years ended in 1987. It is unlikely such a pace can be maintained in coming years. Fortunately, the budget deficit for FY-88 through FY-90 is likely to be less than in the three previous years, and interest rates are likely to have a lower average level.

- The Japanese government has invested a large portion of its foreign exchange reserves in U.S. Treasury bills, with the amount involved depending largely on the Japanese trade surplus. Recently, purchases in the intermediate market have picked up. A good case can be made that the Japanese government should own no bills and invest its reserves in 2-, 3-, 4-, and 5-year notes.

- Private Japanese investors tend to buy intermediate- and longer-term U.S. Treasury notes and bonds. Their future acquisitions will depend largely upon four factors: (1) long-term Japanese investors continuing to acquire sizable amounts of domestic funds, (2) U.S. investments appearing comparatively attractive, (3) the Japanese government encouraging an outflow of funds into U.S. notes and bonds, and (4) Japanese investors finding an acceptable degree of foreign exchange risk. When the United States reduces its trade deficit, it will have a much smaller impact on private Japanese purchases of U.S. government notes and bonds than many analysts think, and may even encourage purchases.

- The West German government—in contrast to the Japanese—has been more aggressive in investing official reserves and has shown considerable interest in buying U.S. Treasury notes and bonds. As long as West Germany continues to run large trade surpluses with its trading partners, private investors want to move capital out of Germany, and U.S. interest rates are viewed as relatively attractive, West German investors—both official and private—will place funds in U.S. Treasury notes and bonds.

- There is no direct cause-and-effect relationship between the United States' budget and trade deficits. All that can be proven is that both have grown substantially from the mid-1970s through the mid-1980s; some of the factors causing increased budget deficits have also had an adverse impact on the trade deficit; and, the more funds foreigners accumulate from trade surpluses, the more they have available to buy U.S. government securities.

- Fears that Treasury borrowing in recent years would crowd-out private issuers in the United States never materialized. The private sector of the economy was far from robust, a substantial portion of the U.S. budget deficit was financed from abroad, monetary policy was generally accommodative, and there were further moves toward deregulation. In addition, crowding-out does not appear likely in the foreseeable future.

- The Treasury should consider offering on a regular basis a new 18-month note, as well as reinstating the 20-year bond. That would give investors two important maturities and raise a large amount of money for the Treasury in a relatively short time.

- The Treasury can improve its cash management by limiting the large fluctuations in its cash balance. That can be accomplished through a better distribution of tax inflows during the year, and by having more of the taxes due at the beginning of the month rather than at mid-month. It could also auction 6-week bills early each month, and move ahead, by about two weeks, the timing of the 30-year bond auctions (reducing coupon offering congestion). Reduced liquidity fluctuations will save the Treasury interest costs and limit both reserve-adding and draining problems for the Federal Reserve.

- The increase in trading activity in government securities from 1974 through 1987 substantially outpaced the growth in government debt. The Treasury offered a broader group of maturities, and the growth of the mortgage-backed and futures markets facilitated a substantial amount of hedging operations using notes and bonds. There were technological improvements such as book-entry recordkeeping and dealer innovations such as stripping of coupon issues. There was a worldwide expansion of the government market with active trading in Tokyo and London. Moreover, there were more dealers which were better capitalized.

- The dealer community is likely to continue to expand, and the few remaining independent dealers will probably be purchased by large business and financial institutions. The dozen or so firms waiting in the wings will continue to press for reporting dealer status. In the 1990s, there will be no shortage of securities for dealers to trade. In this period and beyond, the refunding of Treasury issues will be enormous, and the gross amount of offerings will continue to expand.

- There are many reasons why there is a debt ceiling, virtually none of which have anything to do with containing the deficit. From FY-74 through FY-87, there were 35 increases and yet the deficit exploded to over $200 billion at one point. As illogical as a ceiling may be, the chances of its being abolished are remote. Therefore, to make it more meaningful, it should be revised annually with the amount based on the size of a reasonably targeted deficit.

- There are several budget recommendations which on the surface seem attractive, but if adopted, are likely to prove disappointing: dividing the budget into two components (capital and operations), having the budget period cover two years rather than one, and giving the president the power of a line-item veto. Yet there are several changes which should be seriously considered. These include the presentation of the new budget on or about June 1, rather than four months earlier, keeping virtually all items ''on budget,'' and giving a more prominent place in budget presentations to loan guarantees.

- The word ''policy'' in the term ''fiscal policy'' is a misnomer. There is no highly orchestrated simple policy, but rather a broad array of fiscal forces, often moving in different directions, where the results and their timing are unknown. Fiscal policy deficiencies are why the Federal Reserve should have much greater authority and responsibility for the shorter-term performance of the economy. Fiscal policy should concentrate on longer-term economic growth, budget performance, and the equitability of the fiscal system.

- Large budget deficits push interest rates higher as evidenced from FY-74 through FY-87. During this period, there appears to be a direct correlation between the deficit as a percentage of GNP and real interest rates—both rose substantially. If the United States wants to achieve substantially lower real interest rates, it should lower the deficit as a percentage of GNP.

- Objectives should be established to reduce the deficit. First, the economy must grow more rapidly than it did from 1974 through 1987. Second, the savings rate for individuals must increase to facilitate domestic financing of the deficit. Third, the growth in government spending must be held to less than the rate of advance in nominal GNP. Finally, the tax-take as a percentage of GNP must improve.

PART ONE

THE DEFICIT EXPLOSION— ITS TIMING, CAUSES, BLAME, COSTS, AND OUTLOOK

1. When did the budget deficit problem begin?

In fiscal year 1974 (FY-74), the Vietnam War was history and the Great Society social programs of the Kennedy and Johnson era had been in place for the better part of a decade. There was nothing to indicate the budget would deteriorate in any major way.

Government revenues (or receipts) in FY-74 stood at $263 billion and spending at $269 billion, for a deficit of a mere $6 billion, about half the amount officially estimated for that year. The deficit was less than 0.5 percent of gross national product (GNP) and government outlays were less than 20 percent of GNP. The debt ceiling at the end of FY-74 was only $476 billion and foreign holdings of U.S. government securities were about $68 billion. Interest payments amounted to less than $30 billion.

Republicans had control of the White House, a supposedly advantageous situation for those who favor budget frugality. On the domestic economic scene, a few items were of concern: the slumping economy, considerable inflation, and high interest rates. Problems with the Organization of Petroleum Exporting Countries (OPEC) were in their embryonic stage.

Twelve years later, in FY-86, revenues were $769 billion, expenditures were $990 billion, and the budget deficit was $221 billion—36 times the $6 billion deficit of FY-74. (Figure I-1.1 shows the deficit explosion.) The shortfall was more than 5 percent of GNP, or more than 10 times the amount in FY-74; expenditures were close to 24 percent of GNP, or about 5 percent above the earlier level. The debt ceiling exceeded $2.1 trillion and would soon be raised to $2.3 trillion, roughly 5 times the FY-74 level.

Foreign holdings of government securities reportedly amounted to about $250 billion, almost 4 times the level of 12 years earlier. Moreover, the reported foreign holdings appear to be grossly understated as the Treasury ownership survey apparently places many foreign holders in the "all other" category. Interest payments were running at about $200 billion per year, which was about 7 times the FY-74 figure.

How could such radical and unexpected changes take place in such a relatively short period?

The overall state of the economy certainly does not provide the answer. In this 12-year period, only about four years could be classified as recessionary, and the last four years (1983 through 1986) were not recessionary at all. GNP had moved to about $4.2 trillion in 1986, from

FIGURE I-1.1 Officially Estimated Versus Actual Budget Figures* (Billions of Dollars)

Fiscal Year	Receipts			Expenditures			Deficit			Fiscal Year
	Actual	Estimated	Difference	Actual	Estimated	Difference	Actual	Estimated	Difference	
1974	263.2	256.0	+ 7.2	269.4	268.7	+ .7	− 6.1	− 12.7	+ 6.6	1974
1975	279.1	295.0	− 15.9	332.3	304.4	+ 27.9	− 53.2	− 9.4	− 43.8	1975
1976	298.1	297.5	+ .6	371.8	349.4	+ 22.4	− 73.7	− 51.9	− 21.8	1976
1977	355.6	351.3	+ 4.3	409.2	394.2	+ 15.0	− 53.6	− 43.0	− 10.6	1977
1978	399.6	393.0	+ 6.6	458.7	449.1	+ 9.6	− 59.2	− 56.1	− 3.1	1978
1979	463.3	439.6	+ 23.7	503.5	512.7	− 9.2	− 40.2	− 73.1	+ 32.9	1979
1980	517.1	502.6	+ 14.5	590.9	543.5	+ 47.4	− 73.8	− 41.0	− 32.8	1980
1981	599.3	600.0	− .7	678.2	633.9	+ 44.3	− 78.9	− 33.9	− 45.0	1981
1982	617.8	711.8	− 94.0	745.7	757.6	− 11.9	− 127.9	− 45.8	− 82.1	1982
1983	600.6	666.1	− 65.6	808.3	773.3	+ 35.0	− 207.8	− 107.2	− 100.6	1983
1984	666.5	659.4	+ 7.1	851.8	862.5	− 10.7	− 185.3	− 202.8	+ 17.5	1984
1985	734.1	745.1	− 11.0	946.3	940.3	+ 6.0	− 212.3	− 195.2	− 17.1	1985
1986	769.1	793.7	− 24.6	990.3	972.2	+ 18.1	− 221.2	− 178.5	− 42.7	1986
1987	854.1	850.4	+ 3.7	1004.6	994.0	+ 10.6	− 150.4	− 143.6	− 6.8	1987
1988		916.6			1024.3			− 107.8		1988

*Estimates are figures presented in budget book for upcoming fiscal year.

Official receipts estimates were reasonably good except for FY-82 and FY-83, when they were grossly overestimated. Official spending estimates have typically been underestimated, although since FY-84 they have been fairly accurate. The budget deficit has been understated in 11 out of 14 years.

Source: Budget of the U.S. Government

3

about $1.5 trillion in 1974—a threefold increase. By the end of 1986, inflation and interest rates were at levels much below those in 1974.

At that earlier date, inflation was at more than 9 percent and yields on three-month Treasury bills were close to 8 percent. In 1986, inflation was between 2 percent and 3 percent and yields on bills averaged less than 6 percent.

In 1986, the United States was not involved in any major military conflict and had not been for some time, and parts of the Great Society program had been dismantled. Through much of this 12-year period, the White House was occupied by Republicans, none of whom were considered liberal. Finally, most of OPEC's power had dissipated and oil prices (as well as many other commodity prices) had dropped substantially.

Thus, the reasons for the sharp deterioration in the budget were in its specific components, as well as the policies which brought about the weak performance of receipts and the strong increase in spending.

2. What caused the massive increase in the budget deficit from FY-74 to FY-86?

The 12-year deterioration did not occur gradually. Rather, it took place in two periods, each of two years (FY-75/FY-76 and FY-82/FY-83). The remaining eight years showed no discernible trends in the deficit numbers. In FY-75/FY-76, the deficit widened by $68 billion, and in FY-82/FY-83 it increased by $129 billion.

Clearly, the latter deterioration was by far the more serious of the two, yet the importance of FY-75/FY-76 should not be minimized. There was considerable shock in moving from an almost-balanced budget to a large deficit. In the second period, the shock was in moving from a relatively large deficit to a massive one.

Figure I-1.1 shows how these four adverse years stand out in the overall FY-74/FY-86 period, and vividly demonstrates the size of the official estimating errors. Figure I-2.1 graphically displays these errors. Figure I-2.2 shows which receipts and expenditures categories had the largest advances.

INCREASE IN EXPENDITURES. Starting with the FY-75/FY-76 period, the main reason for the deterioration in the deficit was a sharp advance in expenditures. FY-75 expenditures rose $63 billion, to $332 billion, and in FY-76 increased almost $40 billion, to $372 billion. Thus, in two years the spending advance was more than $100 billion or nearly 40 percent. Not only was this a large increase, it was about $50 billion more than the original official estimate, or roughly double expectations.

The largest increase in spending came in the area now classified as health and human services (HHS).[1] In FY-75/FY-76, HHS grew to $122 billion, from $88 billion, a $34 billion increase, or about one-third of the total spending advance during the two years. In FY-75, the government underestimated these outlays by only about $2 billion, but in FY-76 the underestimation was roughly $10 billion.

The next biggest area of spending increase occurred in the unemployment trust accounts, which grew about $12 billion. The recession in late 1974 and 1975 contributed significantly to this sharp advance. Under such circumstances, it is not surprising unemployment outlays were underestimated by about $6 billion in FY-75. In FY-76, however, the official estimate was reasonably accurate.

---

[1] In FY-75/FY-76, HHS was called health, education, and welfare (HEW). Currently, HHS does not include education.

FIGURE I-2.1 Deficits—Actuals Versus Estimates (Billions of Dollars)

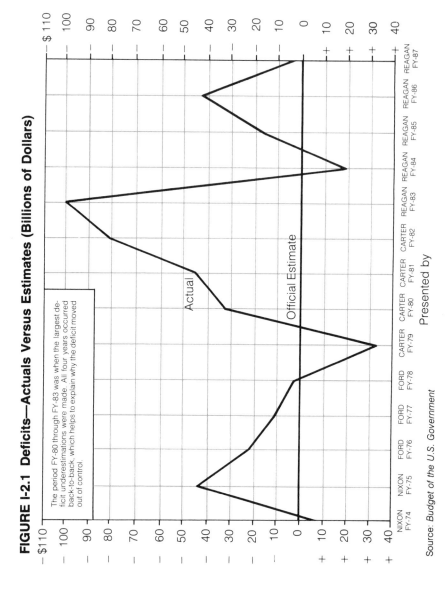

The period FY-80 through FY-83 was when the largest deficit underestimations were made. All four years occurred back-to-back, which helps to explain why the deficit moved out of control.

Actual

Official Estimate

NIXON FY-74 | NIXON FY-75 | FORD FY-76 | FORD FY-77 | FORD FY-78 | CARTER FY-79 | CARTER FY-80 | CARTER FY-81 | CARTER FY-82 | REAGAN FY-83 | REAGAN FY-84 | REAGAN FY-85 | REAGAN FY-86 | REAGAN FY-87

Presented by

Source: *Budget of the U.S. Government*

(Billions of Dollars)

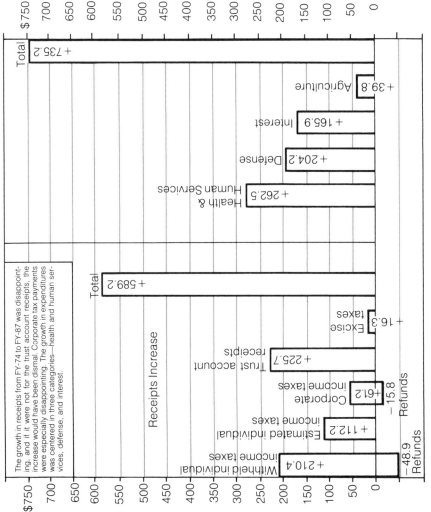

The growth in receipts from FY-74 to FY-87 was disappointing, and if it were not for the trust account receipts, the increase would have been dismal. Corporate tax payments were especially disappointing. The growth in expenditures was centered in three categories—health and human services, defense, and interest.

Receipts Increase

Withheld individual income taxes	+210.4
	−48.9 Refunds
Estimated individual income taxes	+112.2
Corporate income taxes	+61.2
	−15.8 Refunds
Trust account receipts	+225.7
Excise taxes	+16.3
Total	**+589.2**

Health & Human Services	+262.5
Defense	+204.2
Interest	+165.9
Agriculture	+39.8
Total	**+735.2**

$750 700 650 600 550 500 450 400 350 300 250 200 150 100 50 0

Source: *Budget of the U.S. Government*

7

Third in importance were military outlays, although the advance was barely more than $12 billion. The post-Vietnam period was not a popular time to request large increases in military spending. Thus, for both years, military outlay estimates were reasonably accurate.

In fourth place in terms of growth was interest cost, which increased $8 billion. In each year these costs were underestimated by over $2 billion. The growing budget deficits and high interest rates had much to do with this relatively large advance.

These four areas accounted for over half of the spending advance. The rest was distributed among different categories, such as agriculture. In FY-75, the official estimate for agriculture was quite close to actuality, but in FY-76, outlays were about $3 billion above estimate.

These spending data, and where the estimating errors occurred, indicate it was not a "butter-and-guns" problem in FY-75/FY-76, but rather a sharp rise in a handful of nondefense areas.

In general terms, the recession, high interest rates, and substantial inflation were the primary factors contributing to the large spending advance.

POLITICAL ENVIRONMENT. The political aspects of this period represent another factor in the spending surge. President Gerald Ford had taken over at a time when there was a leadership void and the Democrats dominated both houses of Congress. This was not a situation which led to frugality, especially with a relatively soft economy and at a time not far from both presidential and congressional elections. These circumstances suggest it would be difficult to blame one individual, one party, or one area of government for the large deficit increase in FY-75/FY-76.

THE RECEIPTS SHORTFALL. The second deficit explosion period (FY-82/ FY-83) differed from the first, not only in magnitude, but in causes. Of the areas responsible for the $129 billion deficit deterioration, one stands out: the receipts shortfall. In these two fiscal years, receipts were virtually unchanged. Had they grown as rapidly as nominal GNP during the period, they would have been close to $70 billion higher. Thus, the 1982 recession cannot be blamed for the receipts shortfall. It is clear that disappointing tax revenues stemming from the tax law changes of 1981 were a major contributing factor.[2]

---

[2]The Economic Recovery Tax Act of 1981 included (1) across-the-board reductions of individual income tax rates; (2) other individual income tax reductions; (3) annual adjustment for inflation of the zero-bracket amount, personal exemption, and individual income tax brackets; and (4) accelerated cost recovery system for depreciation of capital expenditures.

Simply put, not only did supply-side economics[3] fail to generate the tax receipts the Reagan administration had hoped for, it caused a very large shortfall as well. Moreover, since receipts did not achieve any meaningful growth for a number of years thereafter, it is not a matter of misjudging time lags.

A look at the official receipts projections for FY-82 and FY-83 illustrates the magnitude of the budget estimating errors. (See Figure I-2.3.)

About eight months prior to the start of FY-82, the official receipts estimate was $712 billion. The actual number turned out to be $618 billion. Individual taxes were overestimated by about $33 billion; corporate income taxes, $15 billion; and excise taxes (because of a decline in the windfall profits tax on oil), $33 billion. Excise taxes were slightly over half of what had been projected.

Eight months prior to the start of FY-83, receipts were officially estimated at $666 billion. The actual number turned out to be $601 billion. The shortfall was about $15 billion for individual taxes and $28 billion for corporate income taxes. (The excise tax shortfall this time was a mere $6 billion.) The biggest error in the corporate category occurred in refunds, where the official estimate was $9 billion and the actual figure was almost $25 billion. The tax act of 1981 was largely responsible for these huge refunds, as well as the disappointing gross receipts.

While now history, these misjudgments have important implications. It is questionable whether the Reagan administration significantly improved the quality of its receipts estimates regarding tax reform. In FY-87, the Tax Reform Act of 1986 brought in $30 billion to $40 billion of one-time tax receipts, some of which will take away from future payments. The administration had expected less than half that increase. There is a risk that future receipts will be overstated because of this one-time bulge.

Finally, when the official receipts estimates for FY-82 and FY-83 were released, it was pointed out by many private analysts that, from the administration's viewpoint, they were a combination of projection and prayer—light on the projection and heavy on the prayer.

The approach has proved quite costly. The receipts shortfall in the combined FY-82/FY-83 period was $160 billion. If the administration

---

[3]A supply-side proponent believes the best way to stimulate the economy is to induce individuals, and not the government, to create goods and services. Pertaining to the budget, the reasoning is that if tax rates are low enough, they will stimulate economic activity to a degree that overall tax revenues will rise.

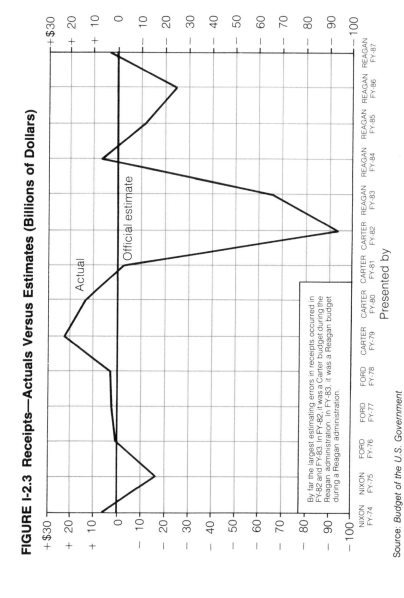

FIGURE I-2.3 Receipts—Actuals Versus Estimates (Billions of Dollars)

By far the largest estimating errors in receipts occurred in FY-82 and FY-83. In FY-82, it was a Carter budget during the Reagan administration. In FY-83, it was a Reagan budget during a Reagan administration.

Actual

Official estimate

Presented by

Source: *Budget of the U.S. Government*

NIXON FY-74 NIXON FY-75 FORD FY-76 FORD FY-77 FORD FY-78 CARTER FY-79 CARTER FY-80 CARTER FY-81 CARTER FY-82 REAGAN FY-83 REAGAN FY-84 REAGAN FY-85 REAGAN FY-86 REAGAN FY-87

10

had used much smaller, more realistic receipts estimates, Congress, based on its spending concerns about three years later, might have seriously considered paring some items. Thus, the estimates helped to inflate the deficit. Clearly the message here is for administrations to err on the conservative side when making receipts estimates, and to avoid encouraging Congress to believe it has any leeway to spend.

THE EXPENDITURE EXPLOSION. Turning to expenditures, in FY-82/FY-83, the outlay estimates were not exemplary, but they were better than the receipts projections. (See Figure I-2.4.)

In the two areas where expenditure increases were the largest—defense and HHS—the official estimates proved quite accurate. Each showed an advance of about $50 billion during the two-year period. Since the Reagan administration's philosophy was to rebuild the military, the large defense outlays were to be expected, and the spending figure actually came in at about $10 billion less than the two-year estimate. It appears it took longer to spend the money because of delays in defense projects. Also there was an overestimation of inflation and a larger-than-expected decline in oil prices. It can be argued that the administration asked for a larger amount of defense outlays than it wanted, knowing Congress would reduce them.

In the case of HHS, outlays were actually $4 billion less than officially estimated for the two years. An overestimation of inflation was no doubt partially responsible when price increases, as measured by the GNP deflator, dropped to 3.9 percent in calendar 1983, down from 9.7 percent in calendar 1981.

In other areas—agriculture, unemployment, and interest costs—the administration's spending estimates were appalling.

In agriculture, expenditures rose about $20 billion, while the administration had expected a two-year advance of a mere $3 billion. The entire error was made in FY-83.

In unemployment payments, the increase was $14 billion, while the two-year estimate showed a decline of $7 billion. The problem was due to a substantial overestimation of economic strength which meant the unemployment rate was well above expectations. In January 1981, the administration had estimated an unemployment rate for calendar year (CY)-82 of 7.5 percent; it turned out to be 9.5 percent. In January 1982, the estimated unemployment rate for CY-83 was 7.9 percent; the actual rate was 9.5 percent.

FIGURE I-2.4 Expenditures—Actuals Versus Estimates (Billions of Dollars)

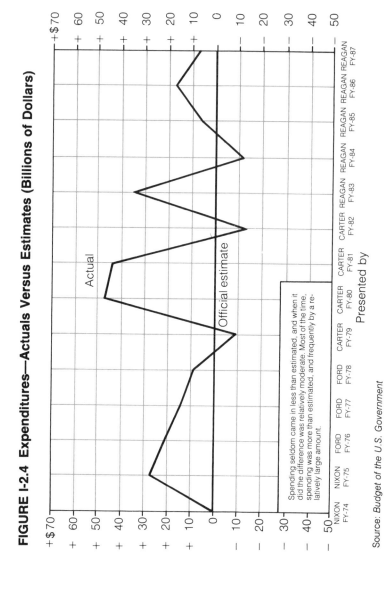

Spending seldom came in less than estimated, and when it did the difference was relatively moderate. Most of the time, spending was more than estimated, and frequently by a relatively large amount.

Source: *Budget of the U.S. Government*

12

The increase in interest payments for the two years was about $33 billion (an $11 billion FY-82 underestimate and a $4 billion FY-83 overestimate). Surprisingly, the estimating error was not due to the interest rate forecast because, for FY-82, the administration's forecast for the three-month bill rate was quite close to the mark. Moreover, in FY-83, the average bill rate actually came in at close to 2 percent under the estimate. The problem was in the extra financing costs associated with a much larger budget deficit than had been expected.

Finally, in looking separately at the two years, in FY-82 the total estimating error was $82 billion, somewhat smaller than the total FY-83 error of $101 billion.

The reasons for these miscalculations were totally different. In FY-82, receipts were overestimated $94 billion, partially offset by a $12 billion overestimation of expenditures. In FY-83, however, there were no offsetting errors. The receipts shortfall was $66 billion, while spending was underestimated by $35 billion. (The data are presented in Figure I-1.1.)

These numbers lead to an interesting question. If receipts had not been overestimated by a combined $161 billion in FY-82 and FY-83, would spending in FY-83 have come in at $35 billion over target?

Probably not. Spending would still have to come in over target, but not by as much. Cutbacks would have been fairly modest, since the three categories causing the error—agriculture, unemployment, and interest—would have been difficult to contain, especially unemployment payments and interest costs. However, if receipts had been accurately projected, and if the more controllable outlays had been pared in FY-82 and FY-83, lower levels of spending would have occurred in FY-84 and beyond.

Thus, while the rate of spending growth dropped from 14.8 percent in FY-81 to 10 percent in FY-82, to 8.4 percent in FY-83, and to 5.4 percent in FY-84, it might have dropped even more rapidly if there had been proper receipts estimates in FY-82 and FY-83.

Much of the slowing in spending from FY-81 to FY-84 was due to lower inflation and interest rates. Thus, there was more room for budget frugality.

3. What has happened to tax receipts since FY-74?

From FY-74 to FY-86, tax receipts were dominated by six components, the largest being withheld individual income taxes, followed by trust account receipts, nonwithheld individual income taxes, corporate income taxes, excise taxes, and tax refunds.[1]

At first glance, from FY-74 to FY-86, receipts looked quite respectable, having increased by more than 9 percent annually during the period. Figure I-3.1 details this performance. However, the increase is somewhat misleading since the growth was far from steady.

From FY-74 through FY-81, receipts performed brilliantly. There were double-digit rates of advance for five straight years. The rapid rate of growth was fortunate, because the spending increases were even larger.

Beginning with FY-82, however, the growth in receipts softened noticeably, and while expenditure growth also slowed, the moderation in receipts was far greater. As would be expected, the budget deficit moved sharply higher—to $221 billion in FY-86, from $74 billion in FY-81. FY-87 is excluded from this analysis since there was a one-time increase in tax receipts of $30 billion to $40 billion, much of which is borrowed from future receipts.

To gain a better understanding of the difference in receipts performance during these two periods (FY-74 through FY-82, and FY-82 through FY-86), it is necessary to look at each of the six components in detail.

WITHHELD INDIVIDUAL INCOME TAXES. Gross withheld individual taxes in FY-86 amounted to about 40 percent of total net tax receipts, which makes it the largest tax receipts category. (The main receipts categories are detailed in Figure I-3.2.) The information also is presented in chart form in Figure I-3.3.) The growth rate for withheld taxes during the total period was about 9 percent per year, which was almost the same as the rate of advance for net receipts as a whole.

The two most surprising aspects of the withheld taxes are the relatively large swings between years, and that it averaged only about 15 percent of wages and salaries income. The percentage seems unusually small. During much of the period, there was a sharply graduated tax

---

[1]The excise tax category is included only because it contains the windfall profit tax on oil, which accounted for a significant inflow of funds during several years. Tax refunds are included as the sixth component, because they had a strong influence on net receipts for a number of years.

FIGURE I-3.1 Budget Receipts (Billions of Dollars)

End of FY	Total	Individual Income Taxes (Net)	Corporate Income Taxes (Net)	Trust Account Receipts	Excise Taxes	Estate and Gift Taxes	Customs Taxes	End of FY
June 1974	263.2	118.9	38.6	77.3	17.1	5.1	3.4	June 1974
June 1975	279.1	122.4	40.6	86.8	16.8	4.7	3.8	June 1975
June 1976	298.1	131.6	41.4	93.2	17.3	5.3	4.2	June 1976
Sept. 1977	355.6	157.6	55.0	109.1	17.8	7.4	5.3	Sept. 1977
Sept. 1978	399.6	181.0	60.0	124.0	18.7	5.4	6.7	Sept. 1978
Sept. 1979	463.3	217.8	65.7	138.9	18.7	5.4	7.4	Sept. 1979
Sept. 1980	517.1	244.1	64.6	157.8	24.3	6.4	7.2	Sept. 1980
Sept. 1981	599.3	285.9	61.1	182.7	40.8	6.8	8.1	Sept. 1981
Sept. 1982	617.8	297.7	49.2	201.5	36.3	8.0	8.9	Sept. 1982
Sept. 1983	600.6	288.9	37.0	209.0	35.3	6.1	8.7	Sept. 1983
Sept. 1984	666.5	298.4	56.9	239.4	37.4	6.0	11.4	Sept. 1984
Sept. 1985	734.1	334.5	61.3	265.2	36.0	6.4	12.1	Sept. 1985
Sept. 1986	769.1	349.0	63.1	283.9	32.9	7.0	13.3	Sept. 1986
Sept. 1987	854.1	392.6	83.9	303.3	32.5	7.5	15.1	Sept. 1987
1974–87	+225%	+230%	+117%	+292%	+90%	+47%	+344%	1974–87

The growth in receipts was moderate from FY-74 to FY-86 and especially from FY-82 through FY-86. There was no major category that did well. In FY-87, receipts grew substantially ($85 billion), but almost half was due to one-time benefits from the 1986 Tax Reform Act.

Sources: Budget of the U.S Government, Monthly Treasury Statement of Receipts and Outlays of the U.S. Government

FIGURE I-3.2 Selected Receipts Categories—Actuals Versus Estimates—FY-74 Through FY-87 (Billions of Dollars)

End of FY	Withheld Individual Taxes			Nonwithheld Individual Taxes			Corporate Income Taxes			Excise Taxes			Refunds Individuals			Refunds Corporations			End of FY
	Est.	Act.	Diff.	Est.	Act.	Diff.	Est.	Act.	Diff.	Est.	Act.	Diff.	Est.	Act.	Diff.	Est.	Act.	Diff.	
June 1974	108.4	112.1	+ 3.7	26.2	30.8	+ 4.6	39.5	41.7	+ 2.2	16.8	17.1	+ .3	−23.0	−24.0	− 1.0	− 2.5	− 3.1	− .6	June 1974
June 1975	128.5	122.1	− 6.4	28.0	34.3	+ 6.3	51.0	45.7	− 5.3	17.4	16.8	− .6	−27.5	−34.0	− 6.5	− 3.1	− 5.1	− 2.0	June 1975
June 1976	111.3	123.4	+12.1	29.6	35.5	+ 5.9	51.4	46.8	− 4.6	32.1	17.3	−14.8	−34.6	−27.4	+ 7.2	− 3.7	− 5.4	− 1.7	June 1976
Sept. 1977	146.3	144.8	− 1.5	42.1	42.1	—	55.3	60.1	+ 4.8	17.8	17.8	—	−34.7	−29.3	+ 5.4	− 5.8	− 5.1	+ .7	Sept. 1977
Sept. 1978	166.8	165.2	− 1.6	46.5	47.8	+ 1.3	65.1	65.4	+ .3	18.5	18.7	+ .2	−41.7	−32.1	+ 9.6	− 6.2	− 5.4	+ .8	Sept. 1978
Sept. 1979	173.6	195.3	+21.7	57.7	56.2	− 1.5	68.0	71.4	+ 3.4	25.5	18.8	− 6.7	−38.1	−33.7	+ 4.4	− 5.6	− 5.8	− .2	Sept. 1979
Sept. 1980	202.7	223.8	+21.1	65.6	63.7	− 1.9	76.9	72.4	− 4.5	18.5	24.6	+ 6.1	−40.9	−43.5	− 2.6	− 5.9	− 7.8	− 1.9	Sept. 1980
Sept. 1981	257.5	256.0	− 1.5	69.3	76.8	+ 7.5	77.7	73.7	− 4.0	40.2	41.2	+ 1.0	−52.4	−47.3	+ 5.1	− 6.1	−12.6	− 6.5	Sept. 1981
Sept. 1982	307.3	267.5	−39.8	78.7	85.1	+ 6.4	73.4	66.0	− 7.4	69.6	36.7	−32.9	−54.4	−54.5	− .1	− 8.7	−16.8	− 8.1	Sept. 1982
Sept. 1983	278.7	266.0	−12.7	82.1	83.6	+ 1.5	74.3	61.8	−12.5	41.7	35.7	− 6.0	−56.3	−60.7	− 4.4	− 9.1	−24.8	−15.7	Sept. 1983
Sept. 1984	280.8	279.3	− 1.5	74.1	81.3	+ 7.2	63.5	74.2	+10.7	40.4	37.9	− 2.5	−58.1	−64.8	− 6.7	−11.7	−17.3	− 5.6	Sept. 1984
Sept. 1985	300.8	298.9	− 1.9	88.0	101.3	+13.3	89.2	77.4	−11.8	38.4	36.7	− 1.7	−60.4	−65.7	− 5.3	−12.6	−16.1	− 3.5	Sept. 1985
Sept. 1986	331.7	314.8	−16.9	100.0	106.0	+ 6.0	87.7	80.4	− 7.3	35.0	33.7	− 1.3	−72.9	−71.9	+ 1.0	−13.6	−17.3	− 3.7	Sept. 1986
Sept. 1987	358.3	322.5	−35.8	109.6	143.0	+33.4	101.1	102.7	+ 1.6	35.2	32.4	− 2.8	−80.8	−72.9	+ 7.9	−14.4	−18.9	− 4.5	Sept. 1987

There were several unusual estimating errors. Withheld taxes were substantially underestimated in FY-79 and FY-80 because tax proposals did not materialize. In FY-82 there was a huge shortfall in excise taxes as oil prices dropped sharply and so did windfall profits taxes. In FY-87, total individual taxes were close to estimate, but there were large forecasting errors between its two components, due to misestimating the effect of the 1986 Tax Reform Act.

Sources: *Budget of the U.S Government, Monthly Treasury Statement of Receipts and Outlays of the U.S. Government*

16

FIGURE I-3.3 Selected Receipts Categories—Actuals Versus Estimates—FY-74 Through FY-87 (Billions of Dollars) (Actuals More Than Estimates Plotted As a Plus)

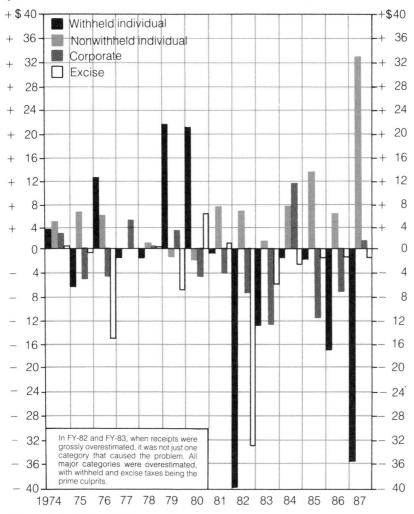

Source: *Budget of the U.S. Government*

system, and an attempt by officials to increase withheld, as opposed to nonwithheld, tax payments.

The sharp rise in marginal tax rates may explain why the growth in withheld taxes was far less stable than the growth in wage and salary income. Especially noteworthy is that in FY-80 and FY-81, the growth in withheld taxes was considerably larger than the increase in wages and salaries. However, in FY-82 the situation began to change, and by FY-84 it had reversed substantially. In FY-85 and FY-86, both categories ran at about the same rate of growth. The analysis suggests the tax reduction in CY-81 had a very adverse impact on withheld tax receipts for the following three years with no perceptible benefit thereafter. So much for the supply-side notion that substantial individual tax rate reductions can stimulate the economy to such a degree that the reductions ultimately will add to total tax receipts.

Official estimates of withheld taxes were reasonably accurate in only seven of the thirteen fiscal years studied.

Of the remaining six years, taxes were considerably less than expected in FY-82, FY-83, and FY-86. In FY-76, FY-79, and FY-80, while withheld receipts were substantially more than estimated, only in FY-76 was this due to a much better economy than anticipated. In FY-79 and FY-80, tax-rate reductions had been built into the estimates, but they did not materialize.

Withheld tax receipts estimates should not be missed by as much as they were in the period. They comprise such a small proportion of personal income that to err in the latter by as much as $20 billion or $30 billion should result in a corresponding error in withheld taxes of only about $3 billion or $4 billion. Even if the tax take per dollar of income is badly estimated, the result should be no more than another $3 billion or $4 billion. Yet, in the six years of major errors, the misestimates ranged from $12.1 billion to $39.8 billion, suggesting political considerations often dominated these projections.

TRUST ACCOUNT RECEIPTS. Trust account receipts were the largest positive receipts segment for the FY-74 to FY-86 period. The category grew more in dollar terms than any other, besting withheld individual tax receipts $207 billion to $203 billion. Its overall growth during the entire period was close to 12 percent on an annual basis, the largest of all the major categories. Without this significant increase in trust receipts, the tax receipts performance for the FY-74/FY-86 period would have been dismal. Excluding the trust account category, receipts in FY-86 would have been only $484.1 billion versus $187.6 billion in FY-84, an annual rate of advance of only about 8 percent.

However, the positive performance of the trust account receipts was not due to a major underlying improvement in the economy (although the increases in the number of people working did help). Rather, it was due to changes in the contribution laws for employees and employers, particularly in social security. The tax rates paid and the maximum level of wages to be assessed moved up sharply through this FY-74/FY-86 period as vividly demonstrated in Figure I-3.4.

For those paying at the ceiling, the increase from January 1, 1974 to January 1, 1988 was well over 300 percent. Thus, the main factor contributing to the respectable receipts performance was a tax increase, albeit in a somewhat disguised form.

The analysis is important because as Figure I-3.4 shows, social security tax increases are not over. Both the employee and the employer have more to pay.

Many individuals do not complain about these large increases because the funds are viewed as money they ultimately will see in the form of retirement benefits. Income tax payments are viewed as gone forever. Also, the funds are "quietly" deducted from individuals and many are not fully aware of what they are paying. With income tax rates, individuals are very much involved with what is being withheld.

Probably those most aware, and most disadvantaged by these tax increases, are small businesses with heavy labor costs. These taxes can put quite a dent in profit margins.

NONWITHHELD INDIVIDUAL INCOME TAXES. The category performed substantially better than withheld receipts.

Nonwithheld taxes grew at a respectable rate during the FY-74/FY-86 period—an annual increase of about 11 percent versus about 9 percent for withheld taxes. That was to be expected, since high-income individuals usually pay estimated taxes and their marginal tax rates move up as their income rises.

As might also be expected, the annual variability of nonwithheld taxes was considerably greater than withheld taxes because of greater fluctuations in their incomes. Capital gains taxes are included in this category, and the year-to-year fluctuations in capital gains are substantial. Thus, in a "good" year, the percentage growth in nonwithheld taxes can be quite a bit larger than the advance in withheld taxes. In a "bad" year, however, the percentage growth is usually not that different.

Looking back during the period, in only one case (FY-84) was the growth in the nonwithheld category substantially less than in withheld taxes.

Despite the sizable percentage increase in nonwithheld taxes in the FY-74/FY-86 period, the dollar amount was not that large. In FY-86,

FIGURE I-3.4 Social Security Taxes—Payments and Ceilings

Date	Percentage of Earnings Paid in by Employers and Employees	Taxable Earnings Ceiling	Amount Paid in at Ceiling	Percentage Change in Amount Paid at Ceiling
1/1/74	11.70%	$13,200	$1,544	100.0%
1/1/75	11.70	14,100	1,650	106.9
1/1/76	11.70	15,300	1,790	115.9
1/1/77	11.70	16,500	1,931	125.1
1/1/78	12.10	17,700	2,142	138.7
1/1/79	12.26	22,900	2,800	181.9
1/1/80	12.26	25,900	3,175	205.6
1/1/81	13.30	29,700	3,950	255.8
1/1/82	13.40	32,400	4,342	281.2
1/1/83	13.40	35,700	4,784	309.8
1/1/84	14.00	37,800	5,292	342.7
1/1/85	14.10	39,600	5,584	361.7
1/1/86	14.30	42,000	6,006	389.0
1/1/87	14.30	43,800	6,261	405.5
1/1/88	15.02	45,000	6,759	437.8
1/1/89	15.02p*	46,500	6,984	452.3
1/1/90	15.30p	48,900	7,482	484.6
1/1/91	15.30p	51,600	7,895	511.3

*p = preliminary

Source: Budget of the U.S. Government

this category was barely over $100 billion. Considering that in CY-86, personal income was close to $3.5 trillion, and that a segment consisting of proprietor, rental, dividend, and interest income totaled between $800 billion and $900 billion, the nonwithheld tax-take seemed unduly small.

Moreover, the tax receipts figures are actual numbers, while the income figures are substantially understated because of unreported sources. Even if nonwithheld taxes are combined with withheld taxes, they amounted to only $421 billion in FY-86, compared with an understated total personal income of $3.5 trillion.

The small percentage tax-take, despite the high marginal tax rates which existed, strongly suggests many individuals have not been paying their fair share of taxes.

Given the considerable underlying variability of nonwithheld taxes, official estimates of these figures were not that bad. No major estimating error occurred between FY-74 and FY-86. Only in FY-87 was there a major error and that was due to tax reform misestimation and bad judgment in forecasting the split between withheld and nonwithheld categories.

Moreover, in the period studied (FY-74 through FY-86 inclusive), there were underestimations in ten of those years, including the last six. That was quite a different performance from most of the other major receipts categories. Perhaps the most telling point is that when total receipts estimates were wildly overstated in FY-82 and FY-83, nonwithheld taxes were understated. It appears the estimates in this category are much less politicized, and therefore more accurate than for most other categories. Figure I-3.3 shows the size of the annual errors.

CORPORATE INCOME TAXES. Corporate income taxes did not make a meaningful contribution to the total tax-take from FY-74 through FY-86. In FY-87 this category amounted to $103 billion on a gross basis (or less than 12 percent of total tax receipts), and when refunds were subtracted, the net result was only $84 billion. Moreover, the annual corporate tax payment figures were highly erratic, and in adverse years they were rather dismal.

There were two primary reasons for the disappointing FY-74/ FY-86 showing: a growth rate of only about 170 percent in corporate profits during the period (about 5 percent annually) and legislative changes which reduced tax rates and gave corporations considerable tax writeoff benefits. The 1981 tax reforms were notable in this regard.

It was thought by giving corporations the benefit of reduced taxes, they would expand, profits would rise, and tax receipts would increase. The supply-side approach of inducing plant and equipment outlays did have a positive impact. However, when it came to corporate taxes, the higher outlays never translated into tax receipts.

Official estimates of corporate tax receipts were not especially accurate. In 8 of the 13 years, the estimates were too high. And, from FY-82 through FY-86, there was not one good estimate, especially when the rather modest size of the corporate tax receipts category is considered. Accurately estimating corporate profits on an annual basis is not easy, but the government's estimating errors were unduly large.

EXCISE TAXES. Excise taxes in FY-87 amounted to only $32 billion, or about 4 percent of receipts. They are included in this analysis because windfall profits taxes on oil are part of the excise tax category, and there were several years when this tax had quite a noticeable impact on receipts. In FY-79, excise taxes amounted to only $19 billion, but in the next two years rose to almost $25 billion, and then ballooned to a peak $41 billion. They have since moved lower. In the two-year period when excise taxes rose $22 billion, the growth in total tax receipts was about $136 billion. Thus, the excise tax component accounted for about one-sixth of the total tax increase.

Yet, from an official estimating viewpoint the period when excise taxes in general (and the windfall profits tax in particular) played such a meaningful role occurred in FY-82 and FY-83, when total tax receipts collapsed. That was especially true in FY-82 when the estimating error for excise taxes was $32.9 billion. Their role in the total shortfall picture is displayed in Figure I-3.3.

The error in estimating the windfall profits tax on oil in FY-82 and FY-83 is somewhat more understandable than other misforecasts. In late CY-80 and early CY-81, there was great uncertainty as to where oil prices were heading; the administration's estimates, while optimistic, had some support among private sector economists. The situation is completely different from withheld individual tax receipts where the official estimates had virtually no support from private-sector forecasters.

Another reason for paying special attention to excise taxes is that it shows how a nonincome tax area can make a meaningful contribution to receipts without receiving much publicity. These not-very-obvious taxes which can raise substantial amounts of money can have strong political appeal. When it is realized the spending reductions will not lower the deficit as much as hoped for under Gramm-Rudman-Hollings, politicians can turn to nonincome taxes. Excise taxes would be more politically and philosophically palatable to most administrations than an income tax increase, and especially to one such as the Reagan administration, which took primary credit for the income tax reductions passed in October 1986.

TAX REFUNDS. Special attention is given to tax refunds for one primary reason: the total amounted to $94 billion in FY-87—a not inconsequential figure.

From FY-74 through FY-86, the growth in refunds averaged about 7 percent annually. Individual refunds increased steadily throughout the period, while corporate refunds advanced sharply after the 1981 tax law changes. In FY-81, refunds were $61 billion, and by FY-83 they were $87 billion.

The timing of this lost revenue, due in good part to overly generous provisions of the 1981 tax act, could not have been worse because it occurred when all major areas of tax receipts were performing badly. This refund performance, shown in Figure I-3.5, played an important role in the gross misestimate of budget receipts in FY-82 and FY-83.

Looking ahead, from the Treasury's perspective, things seem somewhat brighter with regard to limiting refunds. Corporate refunds have held steady since FY-83, and with the passage of the Tax Reform Act of 1986, should show no major advances. Increases in individual refunds also seem to have moderated. The lower and less progressive marginal tax rates should limit the degree of overwithholding, especially in years when the economy performs in a disappointing manner. Therefore, the very large percentage growth in tax refunds over the FY-74/FY-86 period—and the FY-80/FY-83 period in particular—should not be repeated in the foreseeable future.

FIGURE I-3.5 Major Tax Refunds—Actuals Versus Estimates—FY-74 Through FY-87 (Billions of Dollars) (Actuals More Than Estimates Plotted As a Minus)

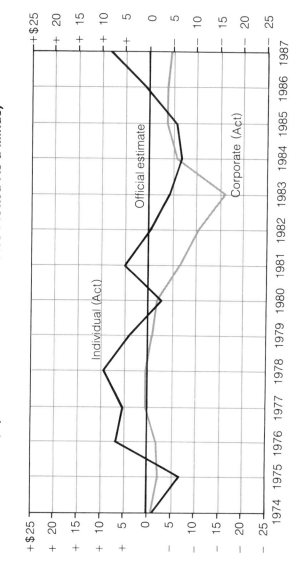

Source: *Budget of the U.S. Government*

24

4. What expenditure areas deserve primary attention from FY-74 to FY-87?

There are four categories of outlays which should receive primary attention—health and human services (HHS), defense, interest on the public debt, and agriculture.

Together they accounted for 88 percent of total spending in FY-87. HHS was the largest at 35 percent, followed by defense at almost 28 percent. Interest was next at 19 percent, with agriculture at 5 percent. Thus, HHS and defense accounted for almost two-thirds of the spending in FY-87. These two areas also accounted for close to two-thirds of expenditure growth from FY-74 to FY-87—$467 billion of a total increase of $735 billion. The changes in the major categories are presented in Figure I-4.1.

Despite the large advances from FY-74 through FY-87 in HHS and defense, official estimates for those two categories were not as bad as might have been expected. In the case of HHS, there were only three years when the increases were substantially larger than estimated. Even more surprisingly, in each year since FY-83, military outlays have been less than officially estimated. These estimating errors are presented in some detail in Figures I-4.2 and I-4.3.

Despite this performance, expenditures as a whole were considerably underestimated from FY-74 through FY-87 despite the relatively respectable estimates for the two largest categories.

The basic problem was in interest payments and agricultural outlays. They have similarities, although in absolute terms interest costs were by far greater. Both grew at a considerably faster rate during this period than did the average increase in spending, and in almost every year both were understated, often by surprisingly large amounts.

In the case of interest costs, rate levels and the size of the deficit (and therefore financing) were typically underestimated. And, when the official agricultural outlay estimates were made, the government's attitude seemed to be that the sector could be successful without any special assistance, and farm prices would remain high enough to preclude large subsidy payments. Nevertheless, unexpectedly large amounts for agricultural assistance could not be avoided.

From FY-74 through FY-87, there were only two years when all four major spending categories were officially underestimated—FY-80 and FY-81—both budgets submitted by the Carter administration.

FIGURE I-4.1 Budget Expenditure Components (Billions of Dolla

End of FY	Total	Health and Human Services	Defense	Interest	Agriculture	Veterans Administration
June 1974	269.4	88.8	77.8	29.3	9.8	13.3
June 1975	332.3	106.0	85.6	32.7	9.7	16.6
June 1976	371.8	122.0	89.4	37.1	12.8	18.4
Sept. 1977	409.2	139.8	97.2	41.9	16.7	18.0
Sept. 1978	458.7	154.1	104.5	48.7	20.4	19.0
Sept. 1979	503.5	170.5	116.3	59.8	20.6	19.9
Sept. 1980	590.9	194.7	134.0	74.8	24.6	21.2
Sept. 1981	678.2	227.0	157.5	95.5	26.0	23.0
Sept. 1982	745.7	251.3	185.3	117.2	36.2	24.0
Sept. 1983	808.3	276.5	209.9	128.6	46.4	24.8
Sept. 1984	851.8	292.2	227.4	153.8	37.4	25.6
Sept. 1985	946.3	315.6	252.7	178.8	49.6	26.3
Sept. 1986	990.3	333.9	273.4	190.2	58.7	26.4
Sept. 1987	1004.6	351.3	282.0	195.3	50.4	26.8
1974-87	+273%	+296%	+262%	+567%	+414%	+102%

The largest outlay categories are health and human services and defense. Yet, the largest percentage increase in major categories took place in interest and agriculture. The total Increase in spending from FY-74 to FY-87 was about $735 billion. This amounted to a 273% increase, or close to 11% on an annual basis.

Sources: *Budget of the U.S. Government, Monthly Treasury Statement of Receipts and Outlays (the U.S. Government*

In FY-80, receipts, fortunately, were underestimated and in the previous year (FY-79), the deficit dropped noticeably; therefore, the two-year deficit increase was not massive.

In FY-81, there were circumstances which cushioned the expenditure error. Official estimates indicated a very large decline in the deficit was likely, with help coming from both receipts and spending. Receipts managed to come in at about the anticipated level, while outlays were noticeably higher. The expenditure underestimation meant that instead of the deficit dropping almost $40 billion, it rose $5 billion.

But neither FY-80 nor FY-81 were major contributors to the budget disaster which occurred in FY-82 and FY-83.

It took more than an underestimation of expenditures to create the budget debacle—it took a virtual collapse of tax receipts.

Employment Trust	Education	Housing and Urban Development	Federal Highway Trust	Energy	International Security Assistance	NASD	Revenue Sharing
6.1	4.9	4.7	4.5	2.3	3.3	3.2	6.1
13.2	6.4	7.5	4.7	3.2	1.4	3.3	6.1
17.9	6.8	7.1	6.4	3.8	1.1	3.7	6.2
14.1	7.7	5.8	6.0	5.0	.3	3.9	6.8
11.2	8.8	7.6	6.9	6.3	2.0	4.0	6.8
11.2	10.7	9.2	6.9	7.9	.8	4.2	6.8
16.4	13.1	12.6	9.0	6.4	3.9	4.8	6.8
18.7	15.1	14.0	9.0	11.6	3.5	5.4	5.1
24.3	14.1	14.5	7.8	7.6	3.1	6.0	4.6
32.7	14.6	15.3	8.7	8.3	3.7	6.7	4.6
26.1	15.1	16.5	10.4	8.3	5.0	7.0	4.6
23.8	16.7	28.7	12.6	10.2	8.3	7.3	4.6
21.8	17.7	14.1	14.2	11.0	10.4	7.4	5.1
20.5	16.8	15.5	12.6	10.7	6.8	7.6	.1
+236%	+243%	+230%	+180%	+365%	+106%	+138%	−99%

FIGURE I-4.2 Major Expenditure Categories—Actuals Versus Estimates—FY-74 Through FY-87 (Billions of Dollars)

End of FY	Health and Human Services			National Defense			Interest			Agriculture			Total Diff.	End of FY
	Est.	Act.	Diff.	Est.	Act.	Diff.	Est.	Act.	Diff.	Est.	Act.	Diff.		
June 1974	88.8	88.0	− .8	81.1	77.8	− 3.3	26.1	29.3	+ 3.2	9.6	9.8	+ .2	− .7	June 1974
June 1975	104.6	106.0	+ 1.4	87.7	86.5	− 1.2	30.5	32.7	+ 2.2	9.2	9.7	+ .5	− 2.9	June 1975
June 1976	112.2	122.0	+ 9.8	94.0	89.6	− 4.4	36.0	37.1	+ 1.1	9.7	12.8	+ 3.1	+ 9.6	June 1976
Sept. 1977	133.8	139.8	+ 6.0	101.0	97.2	− 3.8	45.0	41.9	− 3.1	10.8	16.7	+ 5.9	+ 5.0	Sept. 1977
Sept. 1978	151.4	154.1	+ 2.7	112.3	104.5	− 7.8	44.6	48.7	+ 4.1	12.8	20.4	+ 7.6	+ 6.6	Sept. 1978
Sept. 1979	171.0	170.5	− .5	117.8	116.3	− 1.5	55.4	59.8	+ 4.4	17.7	20.6	+ 2.9	+ 5.3	Sept. 1979
Sept. 1980	188.2	194.7	+ 6.5	125.8	134.0	+ 8.2	65.7	74.8	+ 9.1	18.4	24.6	+ 6.2	+30.0	Sept. 1980
Sept. 1981	219.3	227.0	+ 7.7	146.2	157.5	+11.3	79.4	95.5	+16.1	20.1	26.0	+ 5.9	+41.0	Sept. 1981
Sept. 1982	258.2	251.3	− 6.9	184.4	185.3	+ .9	106.5	117.2	+10.7	28.0	36.2	+ 8.2	+12.9	Sept. 1982
Sept. 1983	274.2	276.5	+ 2.3	221.1	209.9	−11.2	132.9	128.6	− 4.3	23.5	46.4	+22.9	+ 9.7	Sept. 1983
Sept. 1984	288.8	292.2	+ 3.4	245.3	227.4	−17.9	144.5	153.8	+ 9.3	35.0	37.4	+ 2.4	− 2.8	Sept. 1984
Sept. 1985	318.1	315.6	− 2.5	272.0	252.7	−19.3	164.7	178.9	+14.2	37.7	49.6	+11.9	+ 4.3	Sept. 1985
Sept. 1986	330.3	333.9	+ 3.6	285.7	273.4	−12.3	198.8	187.1	−11.7	38.5	57.1	+18.6	− 1.8	Sept. 1986
Sept. 1987	345.6	351.3	+ 5.7	282.0	281.7	− .3	206.9	195.3	−11.6	44.6	50.4	+ 5.8	− .4	Sept. 1987

Expenditures in the four largest categories combined ran close to estimate for the last 4 years (FY-84 through FY-87). In the previous 4 years there were large cost overruns. Agricultural outlays were underestimated in all 13 years presented while surprisingly defense was overestimated in 10 out of 13 years.

Sources: *Budget of the U.S. Government, Monthly Treasury Statement of Receipts and Outlays of the U.S. Government*

FIGURE I-4.3 Major Expenditure Categories—Actuals Versus Estimates—FY-74 Through FY-87 (Billions of Dollars) (Actuals More Than Estimates Plotted as a Plus)

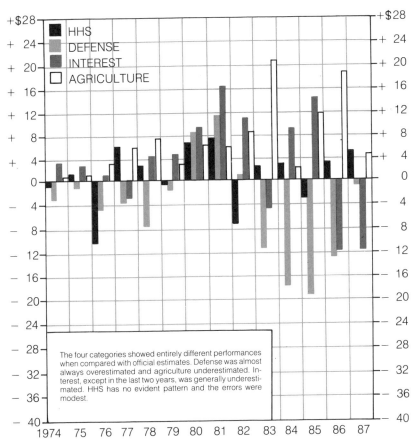

The four categories showed entirely different performances when compared with official estimates. Defense was almost always overestimated and agriculture underestimated. Interest, except in the last two years, was generally underestimated. HHS has no evident pattern and the errors were modest.

Source: *Budget of the U.S. Government*

5. *Is there a story to tell about each of the four major spending categories?*

To understand the reasons behind the large growth in spending, and allow some judgments about the future course of government outlays, each of the four categories must be studied.

HEALTH AND HUMAN SERVICES.   HHS is an area of great political sensitivity because so many people are directly affected by its various components and because it is the largest spending category.

Changes in the major components of HHS (Old Age Survivors Insurance [OASI], Federal Hospital Insurance [FHI], Grants to States, and Federal Disability Insurance [FDI]) and how close they came to official estimates are presented in Figure I-5.1. Given its size and importance, it should come as no surprise that all of its major components grew every year from FY-74 through FY-87. Since most of the factors which influence HHS spending are fairly well known before the year begins, it is not that difficult to make relatively accurate projections. In the period studied, there were eight years of fairly accurate official estimates and six years which were not on target. Of the latter group, in only one year was there an embarrassingly large error—more than $10 billion in FY-76—and that was an overestimation.

In FY-87, HHS amounted to slightly more than one-third of total government outlays. From FY-74 to FY-87 it grew about 11 percent annually. This was just slightly above the percentage growth for federal spending as a whole. Old Age Survivors Insurance (OASI), typically referred to as social security, accounted for more than half of HHS's outlays.

The most interesting aspects of HHS growth was how well the annual increases correlated with inflation. Since cost-of-living adjustments in this area are made on the basis of the previous year's CPI figures, the inflation impact on HHS occurs with a time lag. Figure I-5.2 points out this relationship.

Another factor which has played a smaller, but nevertheless important role in HHS costs, involved the programs providing for the growing number of elderly. In CY-87, for example, Medicare provided health insurance for an estimated 31 million people; its two key programs being hospital insurance and supplemental medical insurance. In addition to the growth in these programs, there has been a steady annual

FIGURE I-5.1 Health and Human Services—Actuals Versus Estimates (Billions of Dollars)

End of FY	OASI*			FHI†			Grants to States			FDI‡			End of FY
	Est.	Act.	Diff.	Est.	Act.	Diff.	Est.	Act.	Diff.	Est.	Act.	Diff.	
June 1974	49.1	49.5	+.4	9.2	8.1	−1.1		N.A.		6.5	6.4	−.1	June 1974
June 1975	57.6	56.7	−.9	10.2	10.6	+.4		N.A.		7.8	8.0	+.2	June 1975
June 1976	62.5	64.3	+1.8	11.7	12.6	+.9		N.A.		9.5	9.6	+.1	June 1976
Sept. 1977	72.8	73.5	+.7	13.3	15.2	+1.9	10.7	N.A.		11.2	11.6	+.4	Sept. 1977
Sept. 1978	79.6	81.2	+1.6	16.4	17.9	+1.5	12.0	10.7	—	12.8	12.7	−.1	Sept. 1978
Sept. 1979	89.6	90.2	+.5	20.3	20.3	—	12.4	12.4	+.4	14.9	13.9	−1.0	Sept. 1979
Sept. 1980	101.0	103.2	+2.2	22.0	24.3	+2.3	12.4	14.0	+1.6	15.6	15.3	−.3	Sept. 1980
Sept. 1981	121.2	123.2	+2.1	25.5	29.2	+3.7	15.8	16.8	+1.0	17.3	17.3	—	Sept. 1981
Sept. 1982	142.2	137.9	−4.3	31.6	34.9	+3.3	18.1	17.4	−.7	19.4	18.0	−1.4	Sept. 1982
Sept. 1983	154.4	154.0	−.4	38.1	38.6	+.5	17.0	19.0	+2.0	19.2	18.3	−.9	Sept. 1983
Sept. 1984	162.8	162.4	−.4	44.3	42.3	−2.0	20.8	20.1	−.7	17.9	18.5	+.6	Sept. 1984
Sept. 1985	174.4	171.6	−2.8	51.9	48.7	−3.2	22.1	22.7	+.6	18.8	19.4	+.6	Sept. 1985
Sept. 1986	183.8	179.6	−4.2	48.0	49.7	+1.7	23.7	25.0	+1.3	20.4	20.2	−.2	Sept. 1986
Sept. 1987	191.8	186.8	−5.0	49.9	50.8	+.9	24.7	27.4	+2.7	21.1	21.3	+.2	Sept. 1987

*OASI = Old Age Survivors Insurance

†FHI = Federal Hospital Insurance

‡FDI = Federal Disability Insurance

OASI is by far the largest portion of HHS. After very rapid growth through FY-83, the increase in OASI has moderated. FHI has had a similar pattern, except that the rapid growth came to an end in FY-86. There were no major estimating errors in any category.

Sources: Budget of the U.S. Government, Monthly Treasury Statement of Receipts and Outlays of the U.S. Government

FIGURE I-5.2 Increases in HHS Spending Compared with Advances in the Consumer Price Index (CPI)

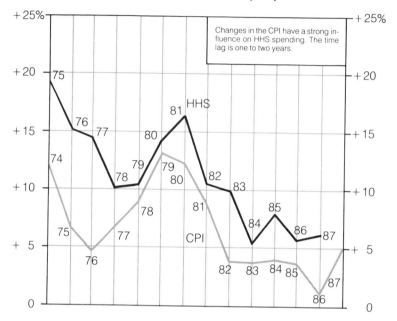

	HHS (FY)		CPI (Dec.–Dec.)
1975	+19.4%	1974	+12.2%
1976	+15.1	1975	+ 7.0
1977	+14.6	1976	+ 4.8
1978	+10.2	1977	+ 6.8
1979	+10.6	1978	+ 9.0
1980	+14.2	1979	+13.3
1981	+16.6	1980	+12.4
1982	+10.7	1981	+ 8.9
1983	+10.0	1982	+ 3.9
1984	+ 5.6	1983	+ 3.8
1985	+ 8.0	1984	+ 4.0
1986	+ 5.8	1985	+ 3.8
1987	+ 5.2	1986	+ 1.1
		1987	+ 4.4

Sources: *Budget of the U.S. Government, Economic Indicators, Economic Report of the President*

advance in the number of elderly individuals. Thus, the cost-of-living adjustments must cover an ever-expanding number of recipients.

It is not surprising HHS spending growth in FY-87 held up better than most other government outlays, given the political sensitivity to any cutbacks in this area, the use of a CPI formula where there is a time lag as inflation declines, and the steadily increasing number of recipients. HHS expenditures increased 5.2 percent in FY-87, while many other government outlays actually declined. Since the CPI advanced only slightly more than 1 percent in CY-86 and 4 percent in CY-87, HHS spending growth on a real basis was considerable.

DEFENSE. From FY-74 to FY-87, defense spending increased about 8 percent, roughly the same advance as for spending as a whole. Yet these numbers do not tell the entire story. From FY-74 to FY-78, the defense spending increase was quite modest. It amounted to only $27 billion, or about 34 percent.

However, in the next four years, the advance was much larger with the rate of growth increasing every year. The total advance between FY-78 and FY-82 was about $81 billion, three times the advance in the previous four years.

The most surprising aspect of the FY-78 to FY-82 advance was that over half of it occurred during the Carter administration. Carter took office in January 1977; the budget then being presented was that of the Ford administration. The first Carter budget was presented in January 1978 for FY-79, the year the sharp increases in defense spending began. Thus, it is fair to say that a considerable portion of the responsibility for the large increase in defense spending belongs to the Carter administration.

Supporting this view, in the next four years (FY-82 to FY-86) the Reagan administration showed an increase in defense spending of roughly $88 billion (and the advance in FY-87 was very modest). This was only $7 billion more than the preceding four-year period; on a percentage basis the 1978–82 growth was actually larger than the FY-82/FY-86 advance—77 versus 48 percent.

Looking closely at these two periods, from FY-78 to FY-82, the largest advance in military outlays occurred in procurement, primarily the purchase of weapons systems and related items. It moved to more than $43 billion from $20 billion—in excess of a 100 percent increase. In the next four years (the Reagan period), procurement grew to about $77 billion.

While the Reagan increase represented a larger dollar advance, the lead time from when plans and commitments are made to when the money is actually spent can be longer than for other types of spending. Thus, the Carter administration is in part responsible for the procurement dollars spent for several years after FY-82.

Finally, as early as FY-84, there were signs of a slowing in defense spending. The growth in operations and maintenance costs clearly moderated, and there was a slowing in procurement. The largest dollar advance in total defense outlays was $28 billion in FY-82. In FY-87, the increase was only $8 billion.

Thus, not only was the Carter administration in large part responsible for the big advance in defense spending that began in the late 1970s, but in the Reagan administration's second term, the growth in defense slackened noticeably. While Congress played a considerable role in this slowdown, the Reagan administration seemed more willing to compromise on defense spending during its last few years.

There are two other factors which should be considered when comparing these different periods. First, there was a much higher rate of inflation during the Carter administration. Relatedly, the Carter administration grossly underestimated defense spending.

In FY-80, the Carter administration estimated inflation at 6.8 percent (GNP deflator) and defense spending at $126 billion. The deflator turned out to be 9 percent and defense spending came in at $134 billion, or $8 billion above estimate. In FY-81, the original deflator estimate was 8.8 percent and defense spending was estimated to be $146 billion. In fact, the deflator increased 9.7 percent and defense outlays came in at $158 billion, or $12 billion above forecast. The inflation estimates and how the numbers turned out are presented in Figure I-9.2 on pages 50 and 51.

When FY-80 and FY-81 are combined, the total estimating error amounts to $20 billion. The actual defense spending increase for this two-year period turned out to be $41 billion. Thus almost half of the advance came as a surprise to the Carter administration, with higher-than-expected inflation part of the reason. Figure I-5.3 shows the misestimates for the major defense components.

The analysis highlights several important points.

While the Carter administration was responsible for the initial surge in defense spending in the late 1970s and early 1980s, the inflation rate during those years was considerably higher than during the Reagan administration. In the four years ended in CY-82, the years of Carter's

FIGURE I-5.3 National Defense (Billions of Dollars)

End of FY	Procurement			Operations and Maintenance			Personnel and Military Retirement			Research and Development			End of FY
	Est.	Act.	Diff.	Est.	Act.	Diff.	Est.	Act.	Diff.	Est.	Act.	Diff.	
June 1974	16.5	15.2	−1.3	21.7	22.4	+.7	27.2	28.9	+1.7	8.1	8.6	+.5	June 1974
June 1975	16.4	16.0	−.4	24.9	26.3	+1.4	30.1	31.2	+1.1	8.9	8.9	—	June 1975
June 1976	16.6	16.0	−.6	28.2	27.9	−.3	31.9	32.4	+.5	9.6	8.9	−.7	June 1976
Sept. 1977	20.4	18.2	−2.2	30.7	30.7	—	33.6	33.9	+.3	10.4	9.8	−.6	Sept. 1977
Sept. 1978	23.7	20.0	−3.7	33.5	33.6	+.1	35.0	36.2	+1.2	11.4	10.5	−.9	Sept. 1978
Sept. 1979	24.2	25.4	+1.2	36.5	36.4	−.1	37.0	38.7	+1.7	11.9	11.2	−.7	Sept. 1979
Sept. 1980	25.7	29.0	+3.3	38.7	44.8	+6.1	39.9	42.8	+2.9	13.0	13.1	+.1	Sept. 1980
Sept. 1981	30.5	35.2	+4.7	46.4	51.9	+5.5	45.4	50.1	+5.7	14.8	15.3	+.5	Sept. 1981
Sept. 1982	40.1	43.3	+3.2	59.7	59.7	—	54.3	57.3	+3.0	18.5	17.7	−.8	Sept. 1982
Sept. 1983	55.1	53.6	−1.5	67.3	64.7	−2.6	61.0	61.5	+.5	22.2	20.6	−1.6	Sept. 1983
Sept. 1984	68.2	61.9	−6.3	71.6	67.4	−4.2	64.4	64.2	+.2	26.3	23.1	−3.2	Sept. 1984
Sept. 1985	77.6	70.4	−7.2	76.9	72.3	−4.6	67.3	67.8	+.5	30.5	27.1	−3.4	Sept. 1985
Sept. 1986	83.0	76.5	−6.5	79.6	75.3	−4.3	72.8	71.5	−1.3	34.0	32.3	−1.7	Sept. 1986
Sept. 1987	76.7	80.7	+4.0	80.9	76.2	−4.7	73.6	72.0	−1.6	31.6	33.6	+2.0	Sept. 1987

From FY-80 through FY-82, all major defense components were underestimated. Beginning with FY-83, however, the situation reversed. Even with recent overestimations, the absolute increases, except for FY-87, were all relatively large.

Sources: Budget of the U.S. Government, Monthly Treasury Statement of Receipts and Outlays of the U.S. Government

prime budget-expenditure responsibility, the GNP deflator rose at an average annual rate of 8.5 percent. From CY-82 through CY-87—years of Reagan administration responsibility—the GNP deflator increased only 3.3 percent. Thus, from a purchasing power perspective, a much larger share of defense outlays went to pay for inflation during the Carter administration.

While the Reagan administration was not primarily responsible for lower inflation, it was the beneficiary. Much of the decline was due to a lackluster world economic growth, softening of world commodity prices, and the impact of a restrictive Federal Reserve policy in the early 1980s. Factors such as time lags, spending on a real basis, and who or what brought about lower inflation, make it difficult to determine exact spending responsibility.

Nevertheless, one thing is clear—the Carter administration played a much more important role in the large defense spending increase than is generally perceived by the public.

INTEREST EXPENSE.   Interest expense is different from other major spending areas. In the FY-74 through FY-87 period, these outlays grew at about double the rate of overall spending. The average annual increase was about 16 percent, although advances of about 20 percent or more were quite common. For example, in the four years ending with FY-82, all of the annual interest expense increases were over 20 percent and the total dollar growth was about $68 billion.

Two factors explain this $68 billion increase—a rise in interest rates and large deficits.

In attempting to determine exactly what brought about the interest cost increase, the advance in interest rates for the four years is the best place to start. The average cost on outstanding debt at the start of the period (the last month of FY-78) was 7.13 percent, and the interest-bearing debt outstanding was $767 billion. By FY-82, the average interest cost outstanding was 11.49 percent and the average debt outstanding was $1,060 billion. If the only change during the four years had been higher interest rates, the 4.36 percent increase on the $767 billion debt outstanding at the beginning of the period would have added more than $33 billion to interest costs for FY-82.

Yet, even this amount understates the impact of high interest rates. Part of the growth in outstanding debt from FY-78 to FY-82 was the result of higher interest rate levels. That factor appears to have added another $3 billion or so to interest costs. Therefore, the total cost due to higher rates was about $36 billion, or slightly more than half the $68 billion increase from FY-78 to FY-82.

The importance of rate levels in interest costs is even more evident in examining FY-85 and FY-86 results.

In FY-85, the increase in interest costs was $25 billion, up more than 16 percent from the previous year. In FY-86, however, the increase was only $8 billion, or less than a 5 percent advance. Yet the increase in public debt was greater in FY-86 than it was in FY-85. The reason for the slowing is the interest rate decline.

If interest rates were to stay close to FY-86 and FY-87 levels, the increase in interest costs would moderate in the years ahead because many securities which were sold at relatively high yields from FY-78 through FY-85 would be refunded at lower rate levels. The rise in rates in FY-87, however, indicates that future cost reductions will be less than hoped for.

AGRICULTURE. Government outlays in the agricultural sector have grown sharply. The rate of growth is strongly related to the lack of prosperity in the farming community. When commodity prices are soft and the plight of the farmer is considerable, government outlays increase substantially, because the agricultural community, and those who serve it, continue to have political clout beyond their numbers. Much of this power is a carryover from the days when the United States was mainly agrarian. Even today, the farm states can be a potent political force, especially in the Senate or in a close presidential race where the agricultural bloc can be a major factor.

Government also is sensitive to the needs of agriculture because of its role in foreign trade and its impact on the business and financial institutions which serve the farm community.

For example, when the United States was running an overall trade surplus in the 1970s, there was a large agricultural trade surplus, which peaked at almost $27 billion in CY-81. In CY-87, the U.S. trade deficit was $171 billion and the agricultural surplus had virtually disappeared. Many financial institutions which are closely tied to agriculture, such as the Federal Farm Credit System and many midwestern depository institutions, have suffered setbacks. It is little wonder, therefore, that the agricultural situation has had a strong adverse impact on the budget during the 1980s, or that the government, unwilling to admit the likelihood of additional deterioration, has continually underestimated both the degree of adversity and the size of expenditures on agriculture.

From FY-74 to FY-86, agricultural outlays grew close to 16 percent annually. A decline in FY-87 lowered the increase for the total period to about 13 percent. While the annual percentage increases throughout the period were large, it was not until FY-82 that the dollar amount became substantial. In FY-81, agricultural outlays were about $16 billion above the FY-74 level; in FY-86 they were $31 billion above the FY-81 level and the second increase was over a shorter time.

The key to the huge growth in agricultural expenditures and the large errors in official budget estimates was the Commodity Credit Corp. (CCC) and its price-support programs. In FY-74, CCC outlays were only about $1 billion, and even in FY-81 were still only about $4 billion. However, by FY-86 they were close to $26 billion before slipping in FY-87. Add to this situation a large and steady growth in food and nutrition services and the serious adverse impact of agriculture on the budget deficit becomes clear.

6. Are there nondefense areas where large cutbacks in outlays are possible?

Any major cutback must come in one of three areas: health and human services (HHS), interest costs, or agriculture. However, the potential for major reductions is different for each category. Further, there are considerable differences among various items comprising each category.

HEALTH AND HUMAN SERVICES. HHS is by far the largest area of non-defense spending, so it seems logical to assume the greatest potential for cutbacks is in that category. Yet, a look at its various components suggests the possibilities are not as great as expected. OASI, commonly referred to as social security, makes up the largest part of HHS, and except for a less-generous cost-of-living formula (which has already been implemented on one occasion, leaving little room for additional reductions), not much can be done. Putting social security on a voluntary basis is not a viable option because of the size of the program, its growth, and the number of individuals involved. Also, the social security program has been bringing in a surplus for the government and is likely to do so for many years to come. That limits the argument of a financial need for cutting back on social security outlays.

Almost all social security recipients believe they are entitled to the benefits because of their contributions and those of their employers. All social security recipients are eligible voters, and many reside in politically important states such as California and Florida. Thus, social security, which comprises more than half of the largest nondefense spending category in the budget, has limited potential for spending reductions.

The second largest area in HHS is federal hospital insurance (FHI). It is much smaller than social security and its growth seems to be slowing. Since it deals with the elderly, it is a politically sensitive area which limits the amount by which it can be cut. Yet there is greater potential for savings here than in the case of social security because much of the increase in recent years has been due to the very rapid acceleration in hospital charges. Further, this category is much different from social security since the cost to the government for FHI is payment for fees charged, rather than recipients receiving funds they believe they have earned. If "runaway" hospital charges can be substantially reduced, FHI expenditure growth can be limited.

Grants to states is the third largest HHS item, and because payments are not made directly to the public, there are opportunities for savings. The federal government being able to end revenue sharing supports this view.

Finally, there is federal disability insurance (FDI). The amount spent in this area is relatively small and has grown modestly in recent years. But by the very nature of its recipients, large reductions are both socially and politically difficult.

Thus of the four major HHS areas, two have a moderate potential for reductions and two have negligible potential. The two with moderate potential—FHI and grants to states—accounted for $78 billion in outlays in FY-87, or about 8 percent of total government spending.

INTEREST COSTS.   Interest costs represent the second largest nondefense category, but is considerably smaller than HHS. Interest costs are a function of the amount of debt outstanding, the level of past and current interest rates, and the size of the current budget deficit. Of the three, the amount of debt outstanding is by far the dominant factor since more than a $2.3 trillion debt existed by the end of FY-87. Next in importance is the past and current level of interest rates, especially since rates have been considerably higher throughout the 1980s. The current budget deficit is the least important component of interest costs since it has only a one-year impact.

One interesting aspect of this analysis is that, in looking ahead, the size of current and future deficits changes from being the least important factor in the trend of interest costs to being the most important.

The size of future budget deficits *is*, to a considerable degree, controllable *if* the executive and legislative branches can reduce their political partisanship with respect to taxes, defense, and nondefense spending. Yet, there is a considerable time lag before the benefits of a reduced federal budget can hold down interest costs. After a number of years, however, interest cost savings can be substantial.

AGRICULTURE.   The final nondefense category is the agricultural sector. The expenditures represent but a small portion of total government outlays and are typically a function of the health of U.S. agriculture. The outlays are related to the agricultural situation abroad and to the protectionist policies of foreign governments as well. It is difficult to reduce substantially federal agricultural programs since the farm belt is politically powerful. One bright spot is that at the end of FY-87, the agricultural sector began to show signs of improvement, and FY-87 spending was over $9 billion below the previous year's level.

The foregoing analysis suggests nondefense areas with the greatest potential for cutbacks in outlays are federal hospital insurance, government grants to states, and interest costs on the public debt. Yet the fact that there is potential does not necessarily mean that it will be acted upon, or that, in every instance, it should be.

In the case of grants to states, there is the question of the amount the federal government should share with state and local governments. There are also questions of how much of a burden the federal government should assume in hospital insurance versus the individual, and what can be done to limit the rapid rise in hospitalization costs. As for reduced interest costs (brought about by smaller deficits), progress will be difficult to achieve until there is a willingness to raise receipts and, at the same time, control defense and nondefense spending.

Thus, major nondefense savings are not right around the corner (irrespective of Gramm-Rudman-Hollings), inasmuch as the potential for such savings appears to be less than proponents are willing to admit, especially in view of the reductions in recent years. The potential which does exist is limited by political differences and the fact that the time necessary to institute such savings is longer than many politicians will tolerate.

One thing is certain, there are *not* tens of billions of dollars to be saved by mere belt tightening.

7. *Can major savings be made in the defense budget?*

Yes, but not in the way the general public thinks. Defense spending is the responsibility of the federal government; it is not possible to share either the tasks or the cost with state and local governments. It is not something which can be left in the hands of individuals and, therefore, is different from most nondefense spending. In a highly sophisticated world the cost of defense is tremendous. Moreover, the United States is a superpower and has responsibilities commensurate with that position. Surely, it is better to err on the side of overpreparedness rather than underpreparedness inasmuch as the results of the latter can be fatal.

Not only does defense for a superpower such as the United States involve many big-ticket items, but three of the four major expenditure categories—personnel, operations and maintenance, and research and development—have little leeway for significant cutbacks. There is minimum opportunity to cut personnel costs since individuals must be trained and paid, and military service must remain competitive with other professions as an attractive career choice. Otherwise, the result would be a shortfall of highly qualified individuals, as well as the reinstitution of the draft. Few would be willing to support the latter proposal, especially in peacetime. As for the numbers serving in the military, there have already been cutbacks during the 1980s, and few military experts believe that large reductions are warranted.

Operations and maintenance outlays are needed to run the military on a daily basis. Of course, there is always room for improvement when it comes to running any operation on a more efficient or economical basis (such as closing some unnecessary installations), but the degree of savings to be realized in this area is fairly limited. Moreover, the military in recent years *has* become more businesslike in the way it functions on a day-to-day basis.

Research and development is an area where large amounts of outlays can be postponed. However, the savings are often illusory because if there is a perception that the United States is falling behind in any particular area, expensive crash programs are instituted. The United States cannot maintain an adequate defense if it has an inadequate research and development program.

Yet, there is one area where a substantial amount of savings is possible—procurement. That observation probably would not come as any surprise to most Americans. After all, they have heard about hundreds of dollars being spent on items such as screwdrivers, hammers, and toilet seats. As dismaying as such revelations are, they represent an infinitesimally small part of the overall procurement budget. These disclosures also mislead the American people into believing that the way to reduce procurement by many billions of dollars is to crack down on defense contractors who rip off the government.

While no one denies that there are abuses in this area, the real problem occurs much earlier in the procurement process, namely in how decisions are reached as to what weapons systems are to be built, and how interservice rivalry influences such decisions.

The competition between services for the defense dollar is intense, leading to questionable weaponry being ordered, excessive duplication of weapons systems, involvement of excessive numbers of contractors and subcontractors, and, often, lack of coordination and exchange of information between contractors and the services. Military leaders typically have a strong commitment to their respective service members. No branch of the military wants to be limited, or closed out, of a major defense area. During the Reagan administration, there is little doubt that in this competition for dollars and weapons systems, the Navy is well ahead, and that the others would like to catch up.

There is little doubt that during the 1980s, there has been a major improvement in the United States' defense capability—despite a flawed decision-making procurement process. If the procurement system had been based strictly on military need, with no interservice rivalry, the price tag for our present defense preparedness would have been considerably less. Or, putting the analysis another way, the United States would have a stronger defense position if recent levels of expenditures were combined with a more efficient procurement system.

To change the present procurement process, it is necessary for the military to have less influence in determining priorities with regard to weapons systems. In addition, greater emphasis should be placed on how money is being spent in terms of types of missions, and how effectively they are being conducted. This point will also be discussed in Part IV under the topic of straightforward budget reporting. Ten mission categories could be used: strategic forces; general-purpose forces; intelligence and communications; sea- and airlift; guard and reserves; research and development; central supply and maintenance; training, medical, and other general personnel activities; administration and associated activities; and support of other nations.

While this approach may not inform analysts as to *how effectively* defense money is being spent, it will indicate the *purposes* for which it *is* being spent. That should make it easier to detect spending imbalances among the various mission categories. The current system using only four rather broadly based categories—personnel, operations and maintenance, procurement, and research and development—is not designed to detect such imbalances.

8. Should the Reagan administration receive most of the credit for substantially slowing the growth of government outlays?

The Reagan administration has been responsible for part of the slowing in spending, but not the *major* part. There have been a number of important contributing factors limiting spending, only one of which is the result of Reagan administration policies.

As for the degree of the slowing, federal government outlays rose at a 14.8 percent annual rate in FY-81, 4.6 percent in FY-86, and only 1.4 percent in FY-87.

To determine *why* the slowing in government spending occurred, it is necessary to examine *where* it occurred. Two main areas were health and human services (HHS) and interest costs. The FY-81 increase in HHS was $32 billion and in FY-87 was $17 billion. Interest costs advanced $21 billion in FY-81, but only $8 billion in FY-87. Since the increase in total government outlays for FY-87 was $73 billion less than in FY-81, these two major categories accounted for $28 billion, or about 38 percent of the slowdown. Most of the credit for this must go to the Federal Reserve and its policies; in the case of HHS, inflation containment was the key factor, and in the case of interest costs, interest rates were the dominant consideration. Figure I-8.1 documents these relationships.

In CY-81, inflation as measured by the GNP deflator was almost 10 percent and 3-month bill rates averaged about 14 percent. Both of these items caused government expenditures to move sharply higher. Cost-of-living adjustments in many government programs were huge, especially in areas such as HHS. The Federal Reserve kept money very tight until well into CY-84 when inflationary pressures eased substantially. Lower oil prices, lackluster economic growth at home and abroad (especially since mid-CY-84), a stronger dollar up to the first quarter of 1985, and a deterioration of the United States' international competitiveness which limited price increases and the bargaining power of labor, all contributed to holding down inflation.

These forces allowed the Federal Reserve to substantially ease from late CY-84 through late CY-86. In the latter year, the GNP deflator averaged less than 3 percent and interest rates on three-month bills were slightly under 6 percent.

Congress also should receive some credit for holding down spending during the last several years, although its record in the late 1970s and

FIGURE I-8.1 Federal Expenditures Related to Interest Rates and the CPI

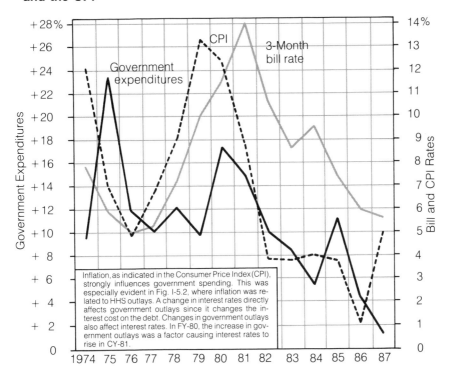

Inflation, as indicated in the Consumer Price Index (CPI), strongly influences government spending. This was especially evident in Fig. I-5.2, where inflation was related to HHS outlays. A change in interest rates directly affects government outlays since it changes the interest cost on the debt. Changes in government outlays also affect interest rates. In FY-80, the increase in government outlays was a factor causing interest rates to rise in CY-81.

Year	Government Expenditures	3-Month Bill Rate CY Avg.	CPI Dec.-to-Dec.
1974	+ 9.6%	8.10%	+12.2%
1975	+23.4	5.96	+ 7.0
1976	+11.9	5.12	+ 4.8
1977	+10.1	5.42	+ 6.8
1978	+12.1	7.42	+ 9.0
1979	+ 9.8	10.46	+13.3
1980	+17.4	11.96	+12.4
1981	+14.8	14.71	+ 8.9
1982	+10.0	11.06	+ 3.9
1983	+ 8.4	8.94	+ 3.8
1984	+ 5.4	9.89	+ 4.0
1985	+11.1	7.73	+ 3.8
1986	+ 4.6	6.15	+ 1.1
1987	+ 1.4	5.09p	+ 4.4

p = preliminary.

Sources: *Budget of the U.S. Government, Economic Indicators, Economic Report of the President, Federal Reserve Bulletin*

early 1980s was far from exemplary. When tax receipts collapsed in FY-82 and FY-83, caused mainly by the Reagan administration's 1981 tax law changes, the deficit exploded.

The Congressional Budget Office's longer-term deficit estimates were so large Congress had to act. The main response was to limit the growth of government spending, and the key vehicle used was Gramm-Rudman-Hollings and its philosophy. While this is hardly a well-thought-out piece of legislation, even in its revised form, it has helped in holding down the growth in outlays.

The role of the Reagan administration in reducing government spending should not be misinterpreted as being inconsequential. However, in order of effectiveness, the administration is definitely behind the Federal Reserve, and it is arguable whether it has done more or less than Congress. While Congress has been willing to be more generous in nondefense spending, the administration has been pushing for higher defense outlays. Trying to add with one hand and take away with the other makes it difficult to measure the administration's net contribution to the slowing of spending.

9. Is there a "party-in-power" factor which correlates with the deficit increase since FY-74?

The Republicans had control of the White House for nine of the years from FY-74 through FY-86, and two deficit-explosion periods (FY-75/76 and FY-82/83). Cursory analysis would hold the Republicans responsible for the adverse budget picture, but several factors argue for a broader distribution of the blame.

Inasmuch as Carter was the only Democratic president during this period, some might contend that a Democratic White House did not have much of an opportunity to contribute to the deficit explosion. Moreover, during President Carter's one term, his party had control over both the House and the Senate, while the Republicans controlled no more than one house during any of their administrations. (The relative position of each party in Congress is presented in Figure I-9.1.) Also, the budget numbers are a reflection of past as well as current decisions. For example, during the Carter years, many spending programs were put in place which did not reach fruition until the Reagan administration.

During the first deterioration period, when the deficit went from $6 billion (FY-74) to $53 billion (FY-75) to $74 billion (FY-76), the Republicans controlled the White House, but the Democrats controlled both houses of Congress. In this period it was Congress which must bear the responsibility for the large advances in nondefense spending—the primary cause of the deficit increase. Yet this was also the Watergate period and the Republicans lacked budget leadership since they had to contend with more pressing political concerns which eclipsed the comparatively mundane areas of budget control. Thus, culpability cannot be laid at the door of any one group; both the Republicans and the Democrats were to blame. Nor was the problem brought about by the sole action of either the White House or Congress.

In the FY-82/FY-83 period, the budget deterioration was much more serious and the factors more complex than in the FY-74/FY-76 period. Large spending increases were set in motion in the early 1980s by President Carter in both the defense and nondefense areas. President Reagan was more than willing to move ahead in spending on the defense side but found little initial success in slowing nondefense outlays. Control of the House of Representatives by the Democrats proved to be a major stumbling block in cutting nondefense spending.

Yet, when the deficit rose from $79 billion (FY-81), to $128 billion (FY-82), to $208 billion (FY-83), the primary culprit was the

FIGURE I-9.1 Political Profile

Congress	Years	House of Representatives			Senate			President
		Majority Party	Minority Party	Other	Majority Party	Minority Party	Other	
93rd	1973-74	D-242	R-192	1	D-56	R-42	2	Nixon/Ford
94th	1975-76	D-291	R-144	—	D-60	R-37	3	Ford
95th	1977-78	D-292	R-143	—	D-61	R-38	1	Carter
96th	1979-80	D-277	R-158	—	D-58	R-41	1	Carter
97th	1981-82	D-242	R-192	1	D-53	R-46	1	Reagan
98th	1983-84	D-267	R-167	1	R-55	D-45	—	Reagan
99th	1985-86	D-253	R-182	—	R-53	D-47	—	Reagan
100th	1987-88	D-260	R-175	—	D-55	R-45	—	Reagan

There was only one time during the above period when both houses of Congress and the White House were controlled by the same party–from 1977 through 1980–by the Democrats and President Jimmy Carter. The Democrats controlled the House by large amounts throughout the time span. In the Senate, the Democrats had control for five of the sessions and the Republicans for three.

Source: Information Please Almanac.

receipts shortfall, and the bulk of the blame falls on President Reagan's 1981 tax law changes. In the case of the FY-82 receipts shortfall, some of the responsibility must be shouldered by the Carter administration. On January 15, 1981, the Carter administration submitted an economic forecast and receipts growth estimates which were totally unrealistic—a 13.1 percent increase in GNP and an 18.6 percent increase in tax receipts.

Of course, the Carter administration knew it would not be around to answer for these wildly optimistic estimates. The actual GNP increase came in at only 3.7 percent and the growth in tax receipts at a mere 2.5 percent. (See Figures I-9.2 and I-9.3.) Yet, FY-82 began close to a year after Reagan was elected, and ended almost two years after the election. Thus, while he is not responsible for the improper estimates, his administration must be held responsible for the dismal results.

In FY-83, both the estimates and the results can be fully attributed to the Reagan administration. Tax reductions and reforms decimated tax receipts.

It is difficult to judge what portion of the receipts shortfall was due to tax reductions and what portion was the result of ill-conceived tax reforms, but both were consequential factors. In fairness to the Republican party, these tax changes seemed to be more indigenous to "Reagonomics" than to Republican economic policies.

The analysis suggests, from a budget-performance perspective, it is not which party is in control of the White House or which party controls Congress. The keys are the individual players and their interactions. There seems to be a propensity for Democrats to be more willing to spend than Republicans (especially in nondefense areas) and to accept higher taxes. However, that perception is no more than a generality. Each president has his own priorities, and each Congress has its own propensities. Some presidents have tried to exert strong control over the budget; others have not. Congress has at times been dominated by a strong-willed leadership and at times has been rudderless.

In the two periods under examination—FY-75/FY-76 and FY-82/FY-83—while the circumstances were quite different, the interaction of the individuals involved and their policies proved highly detrimental to the budget.

In FY-75/FY-76, Congress seemed to be the dominant player and was controlled by Democrats who were quite willing to go forward with nondefense outlays. The Republican White House, despite numerous presidential vetoes, was unable to stem the tide.

FIGURE I-9.2 Economic Assumptions Versus Actuality (Estimates Are for Calendar Years)

Year	President Presenting Budget	GNP Current Dollars	GNP Deflator	Unemployment Rate (4th Qtr.)	91-Day Treasury Bill Rate	10-Year Treasury Note Rate
		Assumptions*				
1974	Nixon					
1975	Nixon	+ 8.5%				
1976	Ford	+12.6	+7.5%	7.9%	6.40%	
1977	Ford	+12.2	+6.2	6.9	5.50	
1978	Ford	+11.3	+5.9	6.6	4.40	
1979	Carter	+11.2	+6.2	5.9	6.10	
1980	Carter	+ 9.5	+6.8	6.2	7.60	
1981	Carter	+10.7	+8.8	7.4	9.00	
1982	Carter	+13.1	+9.3	7.5	11.00	
1983	Reagan	+11.5	+6.0	7.9	10.50	
1984	Reagan	+ 9.2	+5.2	9.9	7.90	9.80%
1985	Reagan	+ 9.1	+4.8	7.6	7.70	9.20
1986	Reagan	+ 8.5	+4.3	6.8	7.90	10.30
1987	Reagan	+ 8.3	+4.2	6.5	6.50	8.50
1988	Reagan	+ 7.3	+3.5	6.2	5.60	6.60
1989	Reagan	+ 7.3	+3.7	5.5	5.20	7.40

*Estimates are made almost a year before the calendar year begins.

The largest errors in the official estimates were in forecasting interest rates. There were only four years where the forecasts were close to the mark. Inflation estimates from 1977 through 1981 came in stronger than expected. From 1982 through 1987, inflation was overstated.

Sources: *Budget of the U.S. Government, Economic Indicators, Economic Report of the President, Federal Reserve Bulletin*

Congress was acting and the executive branch was reacting, which does not lead to effective budget control. That the economy was just coming out of a recession, and inflation and interest rates were high, also complicated matters.

Despite very different circumstances in FY-82/FY-83, the ultimate outcome was the same—a sharp deterioration in the budget. In this period, President Reagan had strong feelings concerning the budget and tried to exert his will on Congress. However, the Democrats controlled the House, which meant there was no rubber stamp for the president's proposals. When it came to budget matters, the Democrats in Congress seemed stronger willed and more united in their views than their Republican counterparts. These circumstances were extremely adverse for

		Actuality				
GNP Current Dollars	GNP Deflator	Unemployment Rate (4th Qtr.)	91-Day Treasury Bill Rate	10-Year Treasury Note Rate	President Presenting Budget	Year
8.3%	+9.1%	5.5	7.89%	7.56%	Nixon	1974
8.5	+9.8	8.3	5.84	7.99	Nixon	1975
11.5	+6.4	7.6	4.99	7.61	Ford	1976
11.7	+6.7	6.9	5.27	7.42	Ford	1977
13.0	+7.3	6.0	7.22	8.41	Ford	1978
11.5	+8.9	5.8	10.04	9.44	Carter	1979
8.9	+9.0	7.0	11.51	11.46	Carter	1980
11.7	+9.7	7.5	14.03	13.91	Carter	1981
3.7	+6.4	9.5	10.69	13.00	Carter	1982
7.6	+3.9	9.5	8.63	11.10	Reagan	1983
10.8	+3.7	7.4	9.58	12.44	Reagan	1984
6.3	+3.2	7.1	7.48	10.62	Reagan	1985
5.6	+2.6	6.9	5.98	7.70	Reagan	1986
6.0	+3.0	5.8	5.60e	8.30e	Reagan	1987
					Reagan	1988

budget control. And this was above and beyond the problems caused by the policies themselves.

The diversity of fiscal opinion and philosophy proved to be a disaster. President Reagan pushed very hard to lower taxes, increase defense spending, and sharply curtail nondefense outlays. He was powerful enough to get his way on lower taxes and high defense spending, but the Democrats were powerful enough to get their way on nondefense spending. Thus, the United States had the worst of all possible budget worlds—a sharp rise in spending across the board and a cut in receipts.

Other factors added to the budget problem. There were large advances in outlays not controllable in the short run, such as interest

FIGURE I-9.3 GNP Current Dollar Growth—Assumptions Versus Actuality

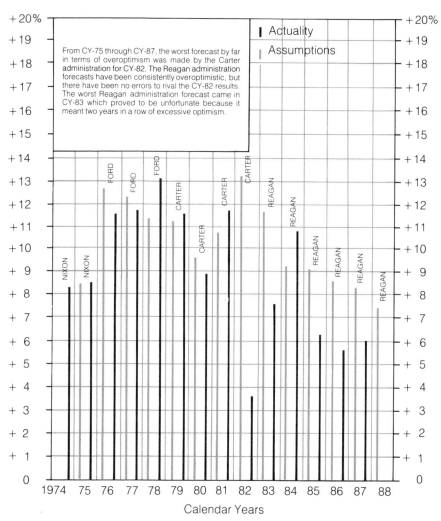

From CY-75 through CY-87, the worst forecast by far in terms of overoptimism was made by the Carter administration for CY-82. The Reagan administration forecasts have been consistently overoptimistic, but there have been no errors to rival the CY-82 results. The worst Reagan administration forecast came in CY-83 which proved to be unfortunate because it meant two years in a row of excessive optimism.

Calendar Years

Source: *Budget of the U.S. Government*

costs and spending programs initiated by the Carter administration. The economy put in a disappointing performance as a recession occurred in CY-82. Finally, inflation and interest rates were at very high levels which added to the growth of government spending.

Where does most of the blame lie for the FY-82/FY-83 budget disaster? It must be at the door of the White House, not just because of flawed policies, but also because of an inability to grasp what was happening to the overall budget. The administration seemed more intent on cutting taxes and raising defense spending than on holding down the size of the deficit. Perhaps the most damaging factor of all was that from the start, official budget estimates were totally unrealistic, especially on the receipts side, and these unrealistic estimates continued for an incredible period. Supply-side proponents had much to do with this extended optimism. If the administration had corrected its receipts estimates much earlier, Congress might have moved toward frugality at an earlier date.

While the voter can elect a president who reflects his or her budget philosophy, the same degree of control is not present when it comes to Congress as a whole.

Voters cast ballots for only a few congressional candidates out of the many who are elected. Therefore, no one really knows until after the new Congress is in place what its budget leanings will be and how they will be pursued.

To ameliorate the problem, it might prove useful if, every two years, after a new Congress convenes in early January, several days are devoted entirely to budget topics. The Congressional Budget Office would set up the agenda and topics to be discussed. The presentations would give an administration, and the public, some indication as to how the members feel about upcoming budget items. The result would also indicate what is politically possible and where major conflicts will arise.

The usefulness of these meetings would be enhanced if the budget for the new year is submitted at the beginning of June (not January or early February as is presently the case) and by the newly incumbent administration (not the one in power before the November election). Thus, the administration submitting the budget would have a period in which to adjust its budget proposals in order to take into consideration the political realities.

10. How obvious were the official budget estimating errors when they were made, and immediately thereafter?

The handwriting was clearly on the wall.

In the two key periods studied—FY-75/FY-76 and FY-82/FY-83—it was obvious that the deficits were substantially underestimated. There was ample information available, either previous to or early in these periods, for public officials to recognize the deficits were out of control and something should be done about the situation. Unfortunately, it took both the Ford and Reagan administrations a long time before admitting to the deterioration. If they had recognized—or acknowledged—the problem earlier, there would have been time to take some corrective action to moderate the sharp increases in the deficit.

To substantiate these claims, see the appendix, which presents excerpts from weekly financial reports written by the author and William Griggs during the two troubled periods.

11. What is the budget deficit outlook in the years ahead?

For purpose of analysis, a three-year period is used, beginning with FY-88. During this time, the numbers will still be significantly influenced by current budget considerations.

The budget policies of the Reagan administration are likely to remain a dominant force in FY-89 and into FY-90. Only in FY-91 will the new administration have had sufficient time in office to appreciably influence budget results. Since an administration can influence receipts more quickly than outlays (because so much of the latter is uncontrollable in the short term) the key years for analyzing the two are different. In the case of the Reagan administration, measuring its receipt performance should be from FY-82 through FY-89. In the case of expenditures, the important years are FY-83 through FY-90.

EXPENDITURES. In the four years from FY-83 through FY-87, the annual growth in nominal GNP (real growth plus the increase in prices) was relatively steady at about 6 or 7 percent. Government outlays, however, showed a declining growth rate, starting the period above the GNP advance but increasing by only 1.4 percent in FY-87. This performance contrasts sharply with the FY-74 through FY-82 period when government outlays rose 180 percent, while nominal GNP increased only about 115 percent.

Looking ahead, the key question is which trend is likely to occur? If the growth in annual outlays exceeds or mirrors the advance in nominal GNP, the likelihood of moving the deficit sharply lower in the years ahead is slim. The growth in expenditures must stay well below the GNP advance for a substantially lower deficit to occur.

To determine whether the most recent relationship between government outlays and GNP will hold true, major spending categories need to be examined. Old age and survivors insurance (OASI) is by far the largest component of health and human services (HHS). The keys to future spending in this area are inflation and cost-of-living adjustments. It appears the CPI slowing came to an end late in CY-86 and by CY-87, there was a higher underlying level.

However, because of time lags, a meaningful inflation impact in OASI is not likely to appear until FY-89 or FY-90. Moreover, when it does affect spending, the advances are not likely to be anywhere near as large as in the early 1980s. From FY-88 through FY-90 the growth rate in HHS spending should move steadily higher with a larger rate of advance in FY-90 than in FY-87.

In the defense area, procurement and personnel costs (including retirement) are the two key components which determine spending increases. With the large advances in procurement in recent years, many of the military readiness targets are well on their way to completion. Inflation may pick up, but it is not likely to affect costs significantly from FY-88 through FY-90, since many projects are already in place.

There also appears to be some slowing of cost increases on the personnel side, a good part of which is due to a major effort some years ago to make military compensation more attractive. After these large initial personnel cost increases, subsequent advances have moderated. In the military retirement area, however, increases are likely to be substantial for some time as these large pay advances inevitably result in considerable retirement outlays. Inflation, of course, is a factor, but while it is likely to add to costs later in the three years under study, the amount should not be especially large.

Interest costs may be the most difficult area to estimate for this three-year period. So much depends on interest rates which, to a large extent, are outside the control of the government. While estimating future rate levels is no more than guesswork, it is reasonable to assume the astronomic rate levels of CY-79/CY-82 will not return, and that the combination of events which took place then will not reoccur in FY-88/ FY-90 (double-digit inflation, the Federal Reserve's monetarist approach which allowed interest rates to move substantially higher, and a budget deficit moving sharply upward). Even if interest rates stay at their early-FY-88 levels (about 9   percent on longer maturities), this should not cause a large surge in interest costs for quite a few years. There are still many high-coupon issues to be refunded.

Finally, there is the agricultural situation, which is unclear (especially since FY-87 spending declined). The problems in this area are deep-seated and the government will no doubt be a major provider of assistance, especially when it comes to the Federal Farm Credit System. Fortunately, in terms of dollar amounts, this component is relatively small compared with the other three spending areas, and there is some evidence that the agricultural outlook is improving.

Looking at spending in a broader perspective, it is politically difficult to hold government expenditure growth to well under the general economic growth rate on a continuing basis. It is much easier to substantially reduce the increase in spending from very high growth levels, such as 17 percent in FY-80 and 15 percent in FY-81, than it is to sustain a spending growth of 1.4 percent in FY-87. It is easier to find waste the first few times spending is being pared than after expenditures have already been squeezed.

The spending analysis suggests that the 1.4 percent increase for FY-87 will be the smallest growth rate for many years to come. The spread between the growth in government spending (1.4 percent) and nominal GNP (between 6 and 7 percent) should also be the largest for quite some time. By FY-90 the annual growth in government spending should be between 3 and 5 percent, which should significantly narrow the gap with GNP growth. These estimates suggest if the deficit is to be significantly reduced, a large growth in receipts must be a key ingredient.

RECEIPTS. The receipts outlook for FY-88 to FY-90 does not indicate steady and major inroads can be made to reduce the deficit. Receipts must grow at substantially more than nominal GNP for this to happen. Yet, the economy does not run forever without a recession and a receipts dropoff. Thus, in nonrecession years, receipts must grow very rapidly to compensate for the softness in recession years. Since by early FY-88, the economic recovery had already finished its fifth year and had not generated enough receipts to lower the deficit significantly, the receipts potential through FY-90 does not look encouraging. It is also reasonable to assume there will be one recession period between FY-88 and the end of FY-90.

Another important factor in the future tax receipts performance is the Tax Reform Act of 1986. This is a very complex document which makes it difficult to measure its impact on receipts, and its ultimate effect on the budget. There are two primary time periods involved:

1. In the first period, from October 1986 through December 1987 (FY-87), the Treasury acquired $30 billion to $40 billion of one-time receipts—more than twice what it expected—some of which will take away from future tax payments. An important consideration in bringing forward receipts into FY-87 was to minimize the deficit and to make it relatively close to the Gramm-Rudman-Hollings target.

   The additional inflows came mainly from two sources: corporate income taxes and nonwithheld individual income taxes. They more than offset the reduction in withheld individual income taxes which began on January 1, 1987.

   Corporations as a group now pay more taxes than before, primarily because of the loss of the investment tax credit and reduced depreciation benefits. That was evident in the quarterly payment of taxes from December 1986 to December 1987.

The Treasury also received additional funds from nonwithheld individual tax payments. That was especially evident on April 1987. The Treasury benefited from some fortuitous circumstances as the capital gains tax advantage came to an end at the close of CY-86 at a time when a bull market in stocks was well underway. These two factors led to profit taking by investors. In April 1987 alone, the extra tax inflow was more than $20 billion, with most of it in nonwithheld individual taxes.

2. In the second period, which began January 1988, the big-bulge receipts came to an end. By the same token, the drag on economic activity from the one-time payments was also over. The budget deficit, which was $221 billion in FY-86 and $150 billion in FY-87, was heading higher.

Not only did the big bulge of tax receipts end, but in January 1988 individual tax reductions were phased in. That is when the net revenue loss from tax reform began. FY-88 will not receive the full brunt of the receipts shortfall; that will show up in FY-89. Thus, analysts will have considerable difficulty measuring the receipts and budget impact of the Tax Reform Act until late FY-89.

The size of the net tax loss in tax receipts in FY-88 will be difficult to judge. An obvious problem is trying to measure the net impact on economic activity stemming from the tax reform legislation. Other problems are trying to determine the extra receipts from the November 1987 GRH agreement and how adept individuals and corporations will be in figuring out ways to limit any newly acquired tax liability. Irrespective of the exact amounts involved, one thing seems likely: the Tax Reform Act moved the deficit closer to the GRH target in FY-87, but it will widen the gap versus the GRH target in FY-88.

Assessing overall receipts in FY-87, tax revenues grew $85 billion. Of that, $30 billion to $40 billion was a direct result of the Tax Reform Act. If the remaining $50 billion or so represented the entire growth in receipts, it would have meant only about a 6 percent advance. By excluding the one-time payments, a better reflection of the underlying receipts growth is achieved.

Since from FY-88 through FY-90 tax reform will reduce receipts and a recession is a reasonable possibility, the presumption is for annual receipts growth to average no more than 6 percent, and probably less.

The receipts outlook for the three-year period would not be complete without looking at a broader group of considerations. Since the rate of inflation in CY-87 was above the CY-86 advance, this should cause an increase in both spending and receipts. However, if FY-80/FY-81 data are indicative of the future, inflation should give more of a lift to outlays than to receipts. Moreover, when inflation increases, monetary policy becomes less accommodative and economic growth is limited, and so are tax receipts.

Another factor to consider is that much of the tax receipts' benefit from inflation occurs when individuals are pushed into higher tax brackets in a sharply rising marginal tax rate system. Under the Tax Reform Act, the tax rates have been lowered substantially. For example, as of CY-88, there are two brackets for individuals. That means only limited receipts growth if inflation should pick up substantially.

There is, of course, the option of the government increasing taxes to raise a meaningful amount of money. However, this is easier said than done. It is never politically popular to raise taxes, and in the case of the Reagan administration, it has been almost totally unacceptable. Candidates who have supported tax increases often experience an abrupt curtailment of their political careers. Former Vice President Mondale surely would concur.

In addition, there are supply-siders in the administration who believe total receipts will ultimately rise by cutting tax rates. They have adhered to that line of thinking although the numbers disprove their reasoning. From FY-81 through FY-87, based on their theories, substantially higher receipts should have materialized. Yet, this did not happen.

Officials willing to present the case for a tax increase to the public are clearly in the minority. Even among those who think taxes should be higher, there are considerable differences of opinion as to how this should be accomplished. It is little wonder, therefore, that it is difficult to get broadbased backing for any one approach.

The situation was vividly demonstrated in the November 1987 GRH compromise where receipts were raised only a token amount for FY-88 and FY-89. None of the increases came from broadly based taxes.

Based on current tax law, economic conditions, and political reality, this analysis strongly suggests that from FY-88 through FY-90, receipts will be insufficient to hold the deficit to its FY-87 level. The economy will not be strong enough and the tax-take will be less than in past years. (Figure I-11.1 shows past results.)

THE DEFICIT. In FY-87, the budget deficit experienced a major reduction to $150 billion from $221 billion; the result, primarily, of the one-time tax benefit discussed earlier. Some of the deficit reduction was due to relatively low inflation and interest rate levels in the previous two years, which held down spending growth to a small, but unsustainable,

FIGURE I-11.1 Tax-Take

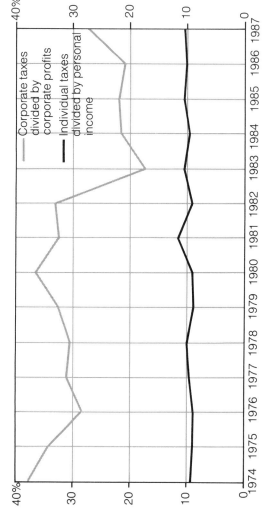

Corporate tax payments as a percentage of corporate profits dropped sharply in 1983, due in large part to the change in the tax laws in 1981. The increase in the tax-take in 1987 was due to the Tax Reform Act of 1986 where corporations assumed a larger tax burden. Individual tax payments as a percentage of personal income have stayed quite constant from FY-74 through FY-87. However, because personal income is so large, a 1 percent change in the tax-take is worth about $4 billion in tax payments.

Sources: Budget of the U.S. Government, Economic Report of the President

60

level, and a small portion resulted from adherence to the GRH philosophy.

There is a danger that public officials will view this improvement as the start of a trend and conclude little else remains to be done. Adding to this danger is undue reliance on GRH, which now appears constitutional but is not likely to prove fully effective. The parties involved may try to circumvent its purpose. There is also a realistic concern that the conflicting policies of the administration and Congress will be far from conducive for reducing the deficit.

President Reagan is proud of the lower income tax rates passed in CY-86 and would no doubt veto any meaningful tax increases. A notable increase in defense spending has been one of his priorities. Congress will strongly resist any major incursions in nondefense outlays because large cutbacks have already occurred. With Congress now dominated by the Democrats, the president winding down his term in office, and his administration plagued by internal conflicts and scandals, the chances for major additional cutbacks in nondefense spending are slim.

Thus, the next opportunity to initiate deficit-reduction policies in a significant and sustained manner will occur in CY-89 when a new president and Congress take office. What can be done then will depend on whether the new president is willing to support revenue-raising measures and can reach an agreement with Congress on total expenditure containment.

To achieve such an objective, the executive and legislative branches will have to take a more evenhanded approach in defense versus nondefense spending.

If the FY-88/FY-90 outlook proves reasonably accurate, the budget results for President Reagan's two terms in office will be adverse and disappointing, especially for one with such strong conservative leanings. On the positive side for his administration, considerable improvements will have been made in tax equity and a major slowing in the growth of total government spending (for which his administration will be only partially responsible). Yet these pluses will be more than offset by very large increases in both the deficit and public debt outstanding over the entire period.

If the preceding estimates prove out, by the end of FY-90, the government debt (which includes investments of government trust accounts) will be about $3 trillion, compared with about $1 trillion at the end of FY-81, and annual budget deficits will still be in the vicinity of $150 billion to $200 billion—a very poor budget legacy.

12. What price is the United States paying for its huge budget deficit?

The costs of the deficit seem so obvious, yet are impossible to quantify. There are three primary reasons for this analytical problem. First, economic problems exist in the United States which are caused by a multiplicity of factors, one of which is the budget deficit. Second, there are potential problems which have yet to surface where the budget deficit will be a meaningful adverse force. Finally, there are the lost opportunities and inflexibilities which exist because of the deficit.

For example, when the economy is weakening, a huge budget deficit seriously curtails any attempts at economic stimulation. The government is reluctant to spend when the deficit already is at a high level. Thus, the ability to implement countercyclical fiscal policies to extricate the economy from a recession is severely limited.

From the mid-CY-84 to the end of CY-87, economic growth in the United States averaged about 3 percent. This was not an especially good performance, since at the beginning of this period, the economy had considerable unutilized resources. Yet, there was no thought of using stimulative measures on the spending side. Using fiscal policy as a countercyclical device is questionable (and is discussed in the last part of this book); to abandon it by choice is one thing, to abandon it by budget necessity is another matter.

When major domestic or international problems arise which require additional spending, huge budget deficits limit the willingness of the government to act. Domestically, this has been illustrated recently in the areas of agriculture, education, and export stimulation.

On the international level, direct economic, financial, social, and political assistance are now limited, as is U.S. support for international institutions. The lack of assistance for the latter comes at a time when international organizations offer the best opportunity to help combat some domestic financial difficulties, such as the inability of foreigners to repay debt and interest to U.S. financial institutions.

A large and excessive budget deficit has often induced the Federal Reserve to follow a monetary policy which is tighter than economic growth conditions warrant. An imbalance between monetary and fiscal policies has not been conducive to sustained economic growth, or to maximizing the underlying real rate of growth. Yet, excessive inflation and an ultimately tighter monetary policy could result if the Federal Reserve totally ignores the huge budget deficit in its policy deliberations.

When Paul Volcker was chairman of the Federal Reserve (mid-CY-79 through mid-CY-87), there were two distinct policy periods. From the fall of 1979 to the middle of 1984, monetary policy erred strongly on the side of tightness, in part to limit the adversities resulting from rapidly increasing budget deficits. That had an unfortunate impact on economic activity, tax receipts, and naturally, on the size of the deficit.

From mid-1984 to early 1988, however, monetary policy gravitated toward a much more accommodative stance. The size of the budget deficit, while still important, seemed to have been downplayed in monetary policy decisions. Yet, despite the sharp increase in Federal Reserve accommodativeness, the budget picture remains grim.

Huge budget deficits also create a fear in the minds of many investors that unacceptable inflation will ultimately result. Bond investors demand an additional rate of return to compensate for such a risk. The financing needed to cover the deficit also adds upward pressure to interest rates. In the fall of CY-87, the budget deficit for the fiscal year then concluded was $150 billion, inflation was running at about 4 percent and yet, long-term Treasury bonds were trading at about 9 percent. (A real rate of return between 3 or 4 percent has generally been considered normal.) The additional return demanded by investors appears to be due in large part to expectations of higher inflation.

Moreover, annual interest payments of about $200 billion are not the most productive way for the government to spend money. Not only do they add $200 billion to the amount of government financing, but because of compounding, the annual number will move substantially higher. For example, if the budget were in balance except for interest costs, the interest rate level was 8 percent, and the amount of debt outstanding was $2.5 trillion, the annual interest cost would be $200 billion. In the following year the debt outstanding would be $2.7 trillion and at an 8 percent rate, interest costs would be $216 billion which, in turn, would be added to the debt outstanding.

With foreign ownership of government securities growing at a very rapid pace, the ever-increasing interest payments they receive add to the very large current account deficit. This tends to put downward pressure on the dollar, adds to inflationary pressures, and reduces the ability of the United States to control its currency.

Yet, there has evolved a greater willingness to rely on foreign money to finance the budget deficit. This can be a dangerous proposition if foreigners decide to withdraw funds from U.S. markets, especially from the long bond market. (Signs of that were evident in the summer and fall of 1987.) By using foreign financing as a crutch, the United States is trying to avoid the painful but correct approach of rebuilding its savings rate.

In terms of international bargaining, actual and potential budget problems reduce the ability of the United States to maximize its political and economic influence, and reduce the chances of international agreements. The argument by foreigners that the United States should resolve its own budget problems before lecturing others on how to run their domestic economies appears to be a major stumbling block to international cooperation.

Huge and seemingly uncontrollable budget deficits also sap the American people's confidence in their government. One of the main causes of the stock market debacle in October 1987 was the inability of government to come to grips with the budget problem.

While there is a running argument as to whether it is Congress or the executive branch which is primarily responsible, any lack of confidence, regardless of where the blame lies, is a negative force for economic activity. The lack of confidence creates a degree of uncertainty as to what future government policies may bring, and discourages individuals and businesses from making long-term commitments.

Trying to measure the impact on long-term spending commitments is impossible, since so many factors contribute to private decisions. All that can be said is that in calendar years 1985, 1986, and 1987, despite very large budget deficits, real economic growth fell short of its potential and this was not due to either labor or capacity shortages. The primary culprits appear to be the twin deficits—budget and foreign trade.

Both the executive and the legislative branches also expend considerable time and effort looking for means by which to eliminate, or at least limit, the deficit and Treasury debt. That reduces the time which could be spent in other areas. As a result of the considerable pressure to cut back on spending, reductions tend to occur in areas which will generate the least political risk. Such an approach surely does not result in the government focusing on real solutions to its financial problems.

Finally, financially difficult times for the federal government tend to hurt state and local governments and their instrumentalities, as well as federal agencies and federally sponsored agencies. That is not to suggest it is proper for money to be thrown at these organizations, but rather the amount of federal assistance should be based on need rather than political expediency.

There is little doubt the quality and level of services provided by state and local governments have been hurt by cutbacks in federal assistance.

PART TWO

TAX REFORM AND TAX RECEIPTS— MORE WORK IS NEEDED

13. What were the prerequisites used in designing the 1986 Tax Reform Act, and were they the proper ones?

There were two basic prerequisites to the Tax Reform Act—reductions in income tax rates and revenue neutrality.

Since the rate cut reduced the tax-take, money had to be raised in other ways to attain revenue neutrality. The amount was sizable due to the substantial cutback in marginal income tax rates (the maximum rate for individuals being reduced to 28 percent from 50 percent). By concentrating on revenue-raising measures which would ensure the legislation was revenue neutral, important broader economic issues were ignored. Thus, a major opportunity was lost. The real need was for tax reform legislation to attack directly three basic U.S. economic problems. There is little doubt there is a need for greater savings and reduced borrowings. One of the aims of tax reform should have been to increase net savings.

The second should have been to stimulate exports. Tax laws can be quite effective in this area, even those remaining within the confines of the General Agreements on Tariffs and Trade (GATT).

The third should have been to raise budget receipts (not necessarily via higher marginal income tax rates), thus narrowing the budget deficit. These three objectives directly address the major shortcomings in the U.S. economy; the two which were used were tied more to philosophical preferences than to broad economic objectives.

The need to improve savings and reduce borrowings could have been achieved in several ways. For example, the inducement for individuals to save for retirement should have been enhanced, not reduced. Full IRA deductibility should have been retained; the maximum amount to be saved should have been placed on a rising scale based on age. Thus, an individual in the 50-to-60-year age bracket should have been allowed to save in excess of $2,000 annually and receive full tax benefits.

Capital gains tax benefits should have been kept, not only as an inducement to save, but also to make capital more mobile. As a suggestion, capital gains on investments held for two years or less should receive no special benefit, but those held over two years would be taxed at 20 percent or the individual's highest marginal tax—whichever is lower. A period of two years is used, rather than six months or one year, to ensure the benefit accrues to investors and not to traders; the period is distant enough to limit revenue losses to the Treasury, and a maximum 20 percent rate can hardly be considered punitive.

The tax deductibility of interest payments could have been even more severely limited to encourage savings versus borrowing. The government could also substantially expand its savings bond program with more attractive interest rates and an improved system for purchasing the bonds. The 1986 cutback in savings bond rates moved the program in the wrong direction.

On the corporate side, a strong case can be made that firms should be induced to raise more equity funds and to reduce the amount of debt they have outstanding. That could have been achieved by allowing partial or even full tax deductibility for dividends paid, while cutting tax deductibility on interest payments. Thus equity financing would be more attractive for both the issuer and the buyer (who would have a capital gains benefit). Such an approach also would have eliminated many of the benefits of leveraged buyouts (a disturbing portion of which are on shaky economic ground).

The second strategy—an improved trade balance—could have been achieved by extending some tax relief to businesses heavily engaged in exports. More generous depreciation rules could have been instituted and the investment tax credit could have been maintained. Tax reform should be used to stimulate exports, not inhibit imports. The export approach would be far more palatable to the nation's trading partners and make more economic sense.

Moreover, to make major inroads in the $171 billion trade deficit for 1987, most of the help must come on the export side. Suppressing the growth of imports cannot achieve enough of an improvement in dollar terms.

The last strategy should have been to reduce the budget deficit by raising receipts. That could have been accomplished by such techniques as making the minimum tax laws even more stringent, limiting exemptions and deductions to a greater extent, further minimizing interest deductibility, and reducing or eliminating most of the special tax advantages for individuals, companies, and industries.

The individual income tax surcharge recommended on page 78 of this book could also be instituted. The surcharge would apply only when the budget deficit increases from the preceding year, the deficit exceeds 1 percent of nominal GNP, and the economy shows positive real growth. Thus, if the budget deficit is narrowing, or is at a relatively low level, or there is no real growth, there would be no surcharge.

Whatever techniques are used to raise receipts, the changes must be equitable and politically palatable. Most important, they must not conflict in any major way with the other two prerequisites of tax reform—increased savings and export inducement.

These proposals might seem to be an exercise in wishful thinking since the Tax Reform Act of 1986 is not only in place, but is, in many ways, contradictory to these suggestions. But tax legislation is not carved in stone. Many of the tax changes instituted in 1981 were revised or eliminated in 1986, even though initially it appeared the changes would last for an extended period. After several years, politicians finally realized the 1981 adjustments were not as positive as originally thought. The same fate is probably in store for parts of the 1986 Tax Reform Act.

Yet, the current political and philosophical climate is not conducive to developing the tax reforms suggested here. It would require not only an agreement by both the executive and legislative branches on the three strategies, but also on how they would be carried out. The latter would be the more difficult task since there are so many techniques which can be used to implement each of the strategies. Even if the political and philosophical atmosphere were more positive for such reforms, it should not be presumed there would be no controversy.

The most potent factors favoring new tax reforms would be disappointing economic growth and budget deficits which are far above Gramm-Rudman-Hollings targets—both likely occurrences.

14. Can the budget deficit be reduced substantially without a major increase in receipts?

Mathematics suggest receipts must show considerable growth merely to stabilize the deficit. Since receipts levels are considerably smaller than outlay figures, it takes about 2 percent more rapid growth in receipts to arrive at the same dollar increase in outlays. While achieving a larger rate of advance in receipts may not be all that difficult in any one year (FY-87 for example), it is quite difficult over an entire business cycle because of recession years and the reduced progressiveness in income tax rates. For example, it may now take an annual advance in nominal GNP of about 6 or 7 percent over a business cycle to generate an 8 percent increase in tax receipts.

To avoid deficit deterioration, it is necessary to hold the growth in government spending at less than the rate of growth in nominal GNP. If receipts exceed GNP by more than 1 percent, and expenditures advance at less than 1 percent, the deficit should be relatively stable in dollar terms.

FY-87 was not a representative year in regard to underlying trends. The deficit declined $71 billion, of which $30 billion to $40 billion represented the one-time receipts benefit of the Tax Reform Act of 1986. Most of the remainder was due to a government spending advance of only 1.4 percent, or roughly one-fifth the increase in nominal GNP. In future years, the one-time tax reform benefit will be unavailable and the small growth in government spending compared with the advance in GNP will not be repeated.

It cannot be presumed the growth rate in government expenditures will be cut back yearly. The first several years of such cutbacks are the easiest; it then becomes more difficult—from both an economic and political standpoint—to find the so-called waste and fat. Moreover, future administrations are not likely to be as adamant about suppressing nondefense outlays.

Since the government does not want merely to hold the deficit at a dollar amount, but wants to cut it substantially, receipts become an even more important factor. A major advance in receipts is necessary, one which is much larger than the rate of growth in GNP. The key reason: with spending already less than the GNP growth rate, but with the differential likely to narrow, there is limited room for additional help from cutting outlays. Yet, receipts growth in recent years has been hindered, not only by relatively slow economic growth, but also by a very small tax-take per dollar of income.

In CY-74, for example, corporate profits were slightly more than $100 billion, while net corporate income tax payments in FY-74 were about $39 billion, or a 38 percent tax-take. In CY-87, corporate profits were approximately $300 billion, while net corporate income taxes for FY-87 were about $84 billion, for a yield of roughly 28 percent. Thus the percentage tax-take fell substantially.

As for individuals, in CY-74, personal income amounted to about $1.2 trillion and net individual income tax receipts were $119 billion, for a tax-take of about 10 percent. In CY-87, personal income was over $3.7 trillion and net individual tax receipts were close to $400 billion, still an annual tax-take of roughly 10 percent.

The latter percentage is especially disappointing since, from FY-74 to FY-87, the growth in unreported cash and the underground economy has probably been much greater than the increase in reported personal income. Thus, it should not be surprising that the budget deficit is so large, with individuals paying only about 10 percent of reported income in the form of federal income taxes.

There is a positive side to this receipts analysis. With the tax-take so low as a percentage of income, it would not require a very large percentage increase to improve receipts substantially. For example, if the take from individuals averaged 15 percent rather than 10 percent, it would roughly eliminate the deficit. Unfortunately, the Tax Reform Act of 1986 apparently will not improve the tax-take. While numerous changes were made to improve receipts, the decline in marginal income tax rates offsets other benefits.

There appears to be no way around the hard facts of budget life. If the government wants merely to stabilize the dollar amount of the deficit, it might be sufficient to have receipts grow moderately above the GNP growth rate, and to have spending advance moderately below that rate. If, however, the government wants a large decline in the deficit (which is presently the case), most of the support must come from the receipts side. A more rapid growth in economic activity is necessary, but a larger tax-take should be an integrated part of any plan, especially since the rate of economic growth is not directly under the government's control.

15. *If receipts-raising measures are necessary, why haven't they been instituted?*

There are two primary reasons why receipts-raising measures have not been implemented. One is that President Reagan has very strong feelings against raising taxes, especially income taxes. There is a belief among members of his administration that the best way to control the growth in spending is to keep taxes down; the logic being that government will not spend what it does not have. This faulty philosophy is not likely to change during the remainder of his term, despite the probability that the hoped-for improvement in the budget deficit in FY-88 will not materialize. Deficit spending has been a way of life in the United States for decades.

The second reason why receipts-raising measures have not been implemented is political unpopularity, especially with those who have to pay the taxes. The broader the tax base, the easier it is to raise money, but the greater the number of people who are adversely affected. Every method of raising receipts has disadvantages from either an economic or political standpoint. In many cases it is also very difficult to measure the net benefit or the cost of any major tax change. That has been especially evident in the various tax reforms implemented in recent years.

Increasing tax rates or initiating new taxes are the most obvious methods of raising revenue. The most commonly discussed rate increases are on individual income taxes, corporate income taxes, excise taxes (principally on tobacco and alcohol), and gasoline taxes. The two most frequently discussed new taxes are value added and an oil import tax.

Raising individual income tax rates has the advantage of being able to take in relatively large amounts of money with small rate increases because the tax is so broadly based. That method also tends to be comparatively equitable and is simple to administer. The primary economic disadvantages are that it limits the ability of individuals and businesses to invest, it could result in taxpayers spending more time and effort in seeking out tax-favored investments, and it does not encourage discipline with regard to controlling budget outlays.

Yet, political considerations are the major dissuasive force for individual income tax increases. Stimulation of the economy was the justification for the large tax reductions of the 1980s. It would be politically embarrassing to disavow that philosophy, especially since the 1986 Tax Reform Act reduced or eliminated many individual tax benefits to make possible the overall rate reduction.

An increase in corporate income taxes is another method of raising receipts. However, it is not as broadly based as individual income taxes, and therefore the amounts which can be raised are considerably less. Moreover, while the corporate income tax rate was reduced as a result of the 1986 Tax Reform Act, other changes were made which substantially increased overall corporate tax payments. Since corporate profits in recent years have been far from robust, and corporations have been holding back on new plant and equipment outlays, another tax increase could have an adverse impact on both short- and long-term profitability.

Thus, while it is more politically palatable to raise money from the corporate rather than the individual sector, the net benefit could be quite disappointing.

Excise tax increases, especially on tobacco and alcohol, have always been an extremely popular method of raising receipts. The purchaser is the one directly affected, the money is spent on items which have no recognizable social value, and there is always the hope the tax will reduce indulgence. Yet, from a budgetary viewpoint, the receipts gained may be only several billion dollars, whereas tens of billions are needed. That suggests the tax rates on alcohol, tobacco, and related products of "sin" should be based primarily on social considerations: how strongly the public feels about restricting the usage, rather than the amount such taxes contribute toward reducing the budget deficit.

An additional gasoline tax and an oil import tax are suggestions which have received considerable attention in recent years. An increase in the gasoline tax has the economic advantage of being paid for by the ultimate user of the product. Moreover, the higher the cost of gasoline, the greater the petroleum conservation and the more individuals would be induced to use car-pooling and mass transportation. However, both federal and state gasoline taxes already seem high to most Americans, and an increase would adversely affect a large number of individuals, and the trucking industry as well, in direct and obvious ways. It could also bring about price increases in numerous other areas. Meanwhile, the benefits derived from such a tax are much less direct and obvious.

An oil import levy can be beneficial to domestic oil producers, especially when their industry (and a major region of the country) is in considerable difficulty. Higher oil prices, resulting from an import charge, would induce greater domestic exploration and development, and, by improving domestic production, limit the influence of foreign producers and their governments on U.S. policies and economic activity. If the tax rate is relatively high, it can raise a fairly large amount in the short term for federal, state, and local governments.

Nevertheless, it would have little justification during a period when the U.S. petroleum industry is strong, would invite trade retaliation on the part of foreign governments, would discourage international free trade, and would harm the economies of countries, such as Mexico and Venezuela, which already have problems repaying international loans. (That could have nasty internal political ramifications for the United States, especially in light of existing problems in Central and South America.) It would mean reduced conservation of domestic supplies, which in the long run could lead to a greater dependence on less reliable sources from abroad.

The domestic political aspects are also, on balance, negative for an oil import tax. There are more consumers of oil and its byproducts than there are producers, and there are more congressmen, senators, and electoral votes from oil consuming states than from oil producing states.

Perhaps the most frequently discussed revenue-raising measure in recent years has been the value-added tax (where the government taxes the value added to a product at each stage of production and distribution). It is a derivation of a national sales tax, is broadly based, can raise huge amounts of money with most individuals not feeling as much of the pain as in the case of income taxes, and would probably have less of an adverse impact than income taxes on economic incentives for middle- and higher-income people. Inasmuch as such a tax is not currently in place, the potential revenue increase is very large, and since individuals are already accustomed to paying sales taxes, its adverse impact would be dulled to some degree.

The argument of a value-added tax being regressive and hurting lower-income individuals to a disproportionate degree has lost some of its impact. There are few highly progressive taxes left in the United States. The days of high marginal income tax rates are gone and the difference in impact of a value-added tax on various income groups would be much less than at the beginning of the decade.

There are important arguments, however, against the use of a value-added tax. Once such a tax is in place, the likelihood is the rate will move in only one direction—up. The amounts which can be raised are so large it could substantially discourage budget frugality. The tax is not based on ability to pay, and even the unemployed pay.

Assuming the tax causes an increase in prices—which seems likely—it would add to inflation and reduce real consumer spending power. It also impinges on an important form of state revenue and could prove to be a rather expensive tax to collect, with considerable administrative headaches involved. Assuming a value-added tax is not deductible for federal income tax purposes, the pain for consumers is obvious, especially on expensive but not necessarily "extravagant" items. A lack of tax deductibility would be a major political negative as the tax directly and adversely affects virtually all individuals.

The government's choices in raising revenue can be classified by gradations of political pain. The most onerous are tax increases which affect everyone directly, and the most burdensome of these for middle- and upper-income individuals is the income tax. A nondeductible value-added tax would also fall into this category and would adversely affect all income levels.

The second category is comprised of taxes which are not as broadly based as in the first group, and are largely related to use. That includes taxes on oil imports, gasoline, tobacco, and alcohol.

The third category is where the amount to be taxed is adjusted rather than the tax rate itself. That can be done through changes in deductions, exemptions, and capital consumption allowances. That approach is the least obvious and the least politically painful.

If an administration (such as President Reagan's) makes clear its opposition to a tax increase and that philosophy is of paramount importance in overall domestic policies, it is politically very difficult to reverse gears and seek a tax increase in the first category. A tax increase from the second category would be less painful since it can be argued it is necessary for reasons other than revenue raising. Changes in the third category, typically, are not very painful since it can be argued they are no more than selective adjustments brought about by equity or technical considerations. The problem is the Reagan administration has already extensively used the third category to raise receipts and there are fewer sources available for raising large amounts of money from that group.

Rather than raising taxes, there is a less-obvious approach to enhancing receipts: reduce the benefits that individuals and businesses derive from tax deductions, exemptions, and capital consumption allowances. The amounts involved in these areas are quite considerable and can have a major impact on receipts.

The 1986 Tax Reform Act used this approach, but mainly to offset the revenue loss from marginal income tax rate reductions. In this tradeoff, the political gain from the well-publicized, large and direct reductions in income tax rates were far greater than the political cost of discreetly and indirectly adding to tax payments.

16. *What type of revenue-raising measure would make the most sense?*

What needs to be done is to find a measure which can raise a large amount of money in a relatively painless way; one which is politically palatable, equitable, simple to understand, easily administered, has no major adverse side effects, and can induce the government to control outlays rather than increase them.

While such a combination may sound impossible, that may not be the case. There is an approach which could achieve these objectives—a surcharge on individual income taxes. It would be applied in the next calendar year if:

- in the fiscal year just ended, the deficit was higher than in the previous fiscal year;
- the deficit in the fiscal year exceeded 2 percent of nominal GNP; and
- there was positive, real growth in the previous fiscal year.

The surcharge would raise an amount equal to the difference in deficits between the two years. For example, in FY-86 (which ended September 30, 1986), the budget deficit was $221 billion, compared with $212 billion in the previous fiscal year. The FY-86 deficit was almost 5 percent of nominal GNP and real GNP growth was close to 3 percent. In this case an income tax surcharge would be instituted in calendar year 1987 to raise $9 billion. Based on the $349 billion of income taxes collected (both withheld and nonwithheld) a surcharge of 3 percent would be imposed. (For simplicity's sake, a number rounded to the nearest 1 percent should be used.) Looking to CY-88, no surcharge would be required since the deficit for FY-87 of $150 billion was less than that for FY-86.

A large amount of money could be raised with the surcharge because the tax base is so broad. Yet, the surcharge percentage is likely to be rather nominal, so the individual burden would be minimized. In the example, an individual who would normally pay $10,000 in income taxes in calendar 1987, would pay a $300 tax surcharge during the year. That would not be a great burden because the surcharge would be fairly modest and because there would be many years when it would not apply. Moreover, if Congress and the administration were to work steadily to reduce the deficit, the surcharge would not have to be used at all, making it a much more attractive alternative than a continuing tax.

Using the concept of the deficit being more than 2 percent of nominal GNP (rather than a balanced budget triggering point) would also tend to limit the use of the surcharge. That method can also be justified on the basis that its purpose is not to drive down the deficit indiscriminately, but rather to stop the deficit from moving to unacceptable and unmanageable levels. The reason for not having a surcharge if there is negative real GNP growth in the previous year is to avoid having a tax increase at a time when policy should not be hindering an economic recovery.

The surcharge approach is reasonably equitable since everyone would pay the same percentage increase on their income taxes. Thus, individuals with the highest incomes would pay the largest dollar amounts. If the basic income tax system is equitable, the surcharge system would be equitable. The surcharge approach also is easy to understand because it relates to paying for a specific budget shortfall for a definite period. Typically, when income taxes are raised, the increase is usually viewed as being permanent, not directly related to any budget shortfall, and might even be considered an inducement to future spending increases.

The surcharge approach would be simple to administer since all it would require is an extra line or two at the bottom of the income tax forms. The ability to inform individuals about the surcharge adjustment should be no great problem since the fiscal year ends on September 30 and the deficit is known by the end of October. Therefore, the surcharge percentage could be determined two months before the start of the next calendar year, which is when it would go into effect. In determining whether the deficit is above 2 percent of GNP or whether there was negative GNP growth, the data will also be available in late October.

Higher taxes do not enhance a politician's popularity, and while Americans agree large deficits are detrimental, they are not exactly sure how they pay a price. A surcharge will make their individual involvement both direct and comprehensible. If there were ever an inducement for government to hold down spending, this would be it.

The surcharge approach is compatible with both Gramm-Rudman-Hollings (GRH) and the balanced budget amendment because its objective is to contain spending and reduce the deficit. The surcharge approach attempts to cut spending, as does GRH, and it attempts to reduce the deficit, as does a balanced-budget amendment.

A good case can be made, however, that the surcharge should be used as an alternative, rather than a supplement, to GRH and the balanced-budget amendment because of their inherent shortcomings. The biggest advantage of the surcharge over the other two is its flexibility. GRH requires huge reductions in the budget deficit for consecutive years until the deficit is extinguished. A balanced-budget amendment requires the budget to be in continual balance which is both impractical and illogical. The surcharge, however, does not try to drive down the deficit irrespective of the problems encountered or created.

GRH and a balanced-budget amendment run the risk of putting the economy into a recession, or making it difficult to escape from one because of the fiscal drag from the attempt to cut the deficit. The surcharge, however, attempts only to put a cap on the deficit. It still relies on the executive and legislative branches to use good judgment as to how the deficit should be brought down, and how long the process should take.

Reducing the deficit to manageable proportions and holding it there cannot be accomplished just through legislation—whether it be GRH, a balanced budget amendment, or a surcharge. What is needed is to have the economy average between 3 and 4 percent real growth, and at the same time keep the growth rate in government outlays less than nominal GNP. None of the three approaches is a substitute for economic strength, and none can guarantee such overall results. As a matter of fact, if both GRH and the balanced-budget amendment were in place, it would be very difficult to achieve a 3 to 4 percent real growth on an ongoing basis.

The occasional surcharge, however, should not have a major adverse impact on economic growth. While there are times, mainly during economic weakness, when it would be procyclical (pushing the economy in the direction it is already heading), the impact of the surcharge on GNP would probably be negligible in most instances.

The dollar amounts would be quite small when compared with the size of the economy or total tax receipts. Moreover, it would be far less procyclical than the other two approaches, and is unlikely by itself to push the economy into a recession.

Assuming the surcharge acts as an inducement to hold down spending, and substantially reduces the possibility of the deficit moving out of control, its modest retardation of economic growth is a small price to pay.

17. Should the government offer some form of amnesty to those who either do not report, or underreport, their income?

Tax amnesty is an active topic of discussion because quite a few states have tried it with good revenue results. The revenue inflow, of course, is the primary argument supporting this approach, yet such a program has other merits. When individuals finally pay what they owe, it can be argued they will pay their proper taxes in the future inasmuch as they are starting off with a clean slate. That could lead to a long-term inflow of tax receipts. An amnesty approach does not require either a large administrative staff or substantial cash outlays, nor is it time consuming, especially when compared with the amount of tax revenues collected. Finally, the currently low tax-take as a percentage of personal income suggests there is a huge amount of tax dollars to be collected from an amnesty program.

Yet, the federal government has resisted such an approach, in part because it fears giving the appearance people are in some way being rewarded for cheating. It is believed if people are not severely penalized for not paying taxes, it might be an inducement for others to cheat. The IRS is being given more money, personnel, and sophisticated computer systems and is developing an improved exchange of information with state and foreign governments to uncover tax delinquents. The argument is the more tax receipts which can be raised this way, the less need there is for an amnesty program.

The key question is: can a system be developed which encourages individuals to pay a substantial amount of back taxes, without feeling they have gotten away with something, and without inducing others to believe they can benefit by cheating?

The answer is yes.

When an individual voluntarily reports previously undisclosed income, there would be no penalties, only an interest charge. Back interest would be assessed at the same rate as the Treasury's quarterly auctions on 10-year notes. Interest would be compounded quarterly, which matches the auction pattern. The individual could choose a payment program of as long as three years. During this period, interest, as computed above, would be added to the overall payment.

The use of a 10-year maturity in the interest computation gives the

Treasury a favorable rate of return. It is typically one of the most expensive financing areas for the Treasury on the yield curve. Moreover, auction rates tend to be higher than market yields and quarterly compounding adds to the Treasury's return.

Back taxes and interest payments could be added to the normal payments the individual regularly makes. If a person normally pays only withheld taxes, an additional amount could be withheld from each paycheck. If an individual usually pays on an estimated basis, an amount could be added to each payment. If the payments are a combination of withheld and estimated taxes, they could be divided between the two methods. If the full amount has not been paid at the end of three years, then a penalty would be invoked.

Even if an individual has been diligent in paying the shortfall, that would not preclude a future audit on the newly reported amounts. However, one would not automatically be subject to additional audits as a result of participation in the amnesty program; such a course of action would make people even more reluctant to come forward and admit they had been cheating. Finally, while individuals can report previously undisclosed income at any time, to facilitate the process, an amnesty section could be added to the annual tax payment form.

In order for this program to reach its full revenue potential, it is necessary for the IRS to have a larger budget and more aggressively seek out and punish those who fail to report income. There must be severe penalties for those who have not voluntarily disclosed unreported income, as opposed to no penalties for those who have reported.

This amnesty approach fulfills the requirement of providing an inducement to pay with no inducement to cheat. The longer one procrastinates in reporting, the greater the interest cost and the greater the risk of being caught and paying severe penalties. The 3-year payment period should act as an inducement for those individuals who are concerned about their ability to pay. Since the amounts due would be added to future regular tax payments, administrative problems would be minimized and errors reduced.

Another advantage of the program is that it will not be turned on and off. Rather, it would be ongoing, bringing in taxes on a continuing basis. The longer the program is in effect, the more cost-efficient the system is likely to become. It is a program which is easy to understand, appears reasonable and equitable, could be systematically carried out, and should avoid the shortcomings of state programs.

Of all the suggestions in the book, this could be one of the most important. The revenue-raising potential of a properly designed amnesty program is very substantial, and most important, it is politically popular to soak the tax cheats.

PART THREE

DEFICIT FINANCING AND CASH MANAGEMENT— HOW IT IS DONE AND HOW IT CAN BE IMPROVED

18. Has the Treasury's debt management approach changed significantly since FY-74?

Given the huge budget deficits from FY-74 through FY-87, it should not be a surprise Treasury debt grew to more than $2.3 trillion at the end of FY-87, from less than $500 billion at the end of FY-74. Of the $1.9 trillion increase, about $1.4 trillion was in marketable debt, primarily in the note and bond areas (maturities of more than one year).

Figure III-18.1 shows the annual changes of marketable debt by maturities. Figure III-18.2 is a pie chart illustrating the maturity changes from CY-74 through CY-87.

During this period, the Treasury relied heavily on three techniques in adding to its outstanding debt. First, it added to the list of maturities and the frequency with which they were issued. Second, it put financings on a more routine basis so investors would know when various maturities would be auctioned. Third, it placed greater emphasis on issuing intermediate- and longer-term maturities. These three techniques made sense, and in combination, worked very well.

The budget deficit reached $100 billion only as recently as FY-82 and it was then that these three techniques were used in combination. In recent years, the offerings of 7-, 10-, and 30-year maturities accounted for more than half the new money raised by the Treasury in a year. Much money was raised in these maturities because each was issued quarterly, each ran in the area of $8 billion to $10 billion, and few issues with these same maturities came due, since regular sales were started only around the beginning of the decade. Thus, the greatest benefit to debt managers from these techniques accrued to those who first used them.

A financing point worthy of note is that through August 1972, in refunding maturing coupon issues, the Treasury used both rights and advance refunding techniques[1] as well as cash auctions. In a rights offering, considerable emphasis is placed on enticing holders of maturing issues to reinvest their funds. Since 1972, the Treasury has moved entirely to cash offerings since it could not afford paydowns in its refundings. (Figure III-18.3 shows the evolution of the various maturity offerings.)

A chronology beginning with CY-74 shows how the Treasury

---

[1]A rights technique is where holders of maturing notes and bonds are allowed to exchange their securities for new Treasury issues. An advance refunding technique is where holders of specified Treasury issues that are *not* maturing, are offered the opportunity to exchange them for new Treasury issues.

FIGURE III-18.1 Marketable Treasury Debt Outstanding (Billions of Dollars)

End of December	Held by Private Investors						Held by Federal Reserve	Others	Total Marketable Debt	Average Maturity	
	Within 1 Year	1 to 5 Years	5 to 10 Years	10 to 20 Years	20 Years and Over	Amt. Outstanding (Privately Held)				Years	Months
1974	100.3	54.2	13.5	8.7	4.3	181.0	80.5	21.4	282.9	2	11
1975	150.1	74.7	16.7	8.5	5.9	255.9	87.9	19.5	363.2	2	8
1976	157.5	103.7	31.0	7.4	8.2	307.8	97.0	16.5	421.3	2	7
1977	171.4	118.9	32.7	8.3	11.6	343.0	102.5	14.4	459.9	2	11
1978	174.2	128.3	33.6	13.8	15.3	365.2	109.6	12.7	487.5	3	3
1979	190.4	133.2	36.6	19.8	22.3	402.2	117.5	11.0	530.7	3	7
1980	239.7	159.6	41.2	27.3	24.6	492.3	121.3	9.6	623.2	3	9
1981	275.3	188.4	50.9	34.1	32.0	580.7	131.0	8.6	720.3	4	0
1982	346.3	239.3	77.6	35.7	37.3	736.1	139.3	6.1	881.5	3	11
1983	394.1	298.3	106.0	43.1	52.5	894.0	151.9	5.0	1050.9	4	1
1984	455.8	365.8	136.1	52.1	71.8	1081.5	160.9	5.0	1247.4	4	6
1985	490.2	423.6	163.0	66.0	94.4	1237.3	181.3	19.1	1437.7	4	11
1986	511.1	481.8	197.6	70.7	127.6	1388.7	211.3	19.0	1619.0	5	3
1987	502.9	528.3	222.8	73.9	155.8	1483.6	222.6	18.5	1724.7	5	9

The largest rate of growth in marketable debt outstanding has taken place in maturities of five years and over. Much of the advance in the maturities of five years and over has taken place since CY-83, especially in the twenty years and over area.

Sources: *Economic Report of the President, Federal Reserve Bulletin, Treasury Bulletin*

FIGURE III-18.2 Maturity Distribution of Marketable Debt Held by Private Investors

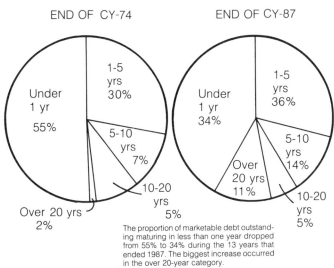

END OF CY-74

END OF CY-87

Under 1 yr 55%

1-5 yrs 30%

5-10 yrs 7%

10-20 yrs 5%

Over 20 yrs 2%

Under 1 yr 34%

1-5 yrs 36%

5-10 yrs 14%

Over 20 yrs 11%

10-20 yrs 5%

The proportion of marketable debt outstanding maturing in less than one year dropped from 55% to 34% during the 13 years that ended 1987. The biggest increase occurred in the over 20-year category.

Source: *Treasury Bulletin*

financed most of its huge budget deficit needs. First, the review indicates how small the individual financings were at the beginning of the period and how rapidly they grew. Second, a picture unfolds as to the greater frequency of offerings and the use of more maturities. Third, the history shows how the Treasury responded in its financings when the budget deficits changed substantially from year to year. Finally, the changes over the years indicate trends and propensities Treasury managers might use in the future.

In CY-74, the budget was close to balance and there was little need for an aggressive approach to financings, especially of the long-bond variety. The 2-year note was sold on a quarterly basis, there were three offerings during the year of 3-, 7-, and 25-year maturities, plus a few other note and bond offerings. The 3-year maturity ran about $2 billion, the 7-year about $1.5 billion, and the 25-year a mere $500 million. Bill financings played an important role, which held the average maturity on the public debt to only about three years.

In CY-75, the budget deficit moved sharply higher, by an unexpected amount. The Treasury responded by adding considerably to maturities in the shorter end of the market. There was a sizable increase in bills, five coupon issues were sold with less than 2-year maturities,

FIGURE III-18.3 Treasury Offerings of Notes and Bonds for Cash by Maturities Beginning in 1974 (Billions of Dollars)

Maturities	1974	1975	1976	1977
Under 2 Years		.8 1.7 1.6 1.5 1.6	2.6	
2 Years	1.5 2.0 1.8 2.2	1.7 2.6 1.6 2.1 2.2 1.5 2.0 3.2 2.1† 2.5 3.2 2.5	2.6 2.5 3.1 2.3 2.5 2.6 2.9 2.7 2.8 2.8 2.8 3.1	2.9 2.7 3.0 1.9 1.9 2.0 3.1 3.4 3.8 4.1 4.7
3 Years	2.3 2.4 1.1	3.3 2.9 3.1 2.5	3.0 2.1 3.3	3.3 3.7 3.9
4 Years	1.9	1.3 1.8 2.1	2.0 2.1 2.2 2.7	2.8 2.5 3.0 3.4
5 Years	1.0		2.0 2.6 2.6 2.5	2.7 2.6 2.7
7 Years	1.5 1.8* 1.8	1.8* 1.8 1.5 2.0 2.5	6.0 2.2	2.0 2.9 2.5
10 Years			4.7 8.0	2.0
15 Years		1.2		1.5
20 Years	.3			
25 Years	.3 .4 .6	.8 .8 .8 1.0	.8 1.0 1.0	
30 Years			.4	.8 1.0 1.0 1.3

*6 years   †29 months

Maturities	1978	1979	1980
Under 2 Years			
2 Years	3.6 3.6 3.8 3.7 2.7 2.9 3.6 3.7 3.3 3.4 3.6 2.9	3.0 2.9 2.5 2.9 2.8 2.3 2.8 3.0 3.3 3.3 3.9 4.3 3.5	4.0 4.0 3.5 4.0 4.0 4.3 4.5 4.5 4.5 4.3 4.5 4.5
3 Years	2.5 2.8 2.5‡	2.8 2.8	3.3 3.5 4.0 3.8‡
4 Years	2.8 2.3 2.3	2.7 2.9 2.8 2.5 2.5	2.5 3.2 3.0 3.3
5 Years	2.6	2.5 2.5	2.5 3.0 3.0 3.0
7 Years	3.0 3.3	2.3 2.5‡	2.0
10 Years	2.5 2.5	2.3 2.0	2.0 2.8 2.3
15 Years	1.5 1.8 1.5	1.5 1.5 1.5 1.5	1.5 1.5 1.5 1.5
20 Years	1.5§	2.0	
25 Years	1.3‖		
30 Years	1.5 1.8	2.0 2.0 2.0 2.0	2.0 2.0 1.5 2.0

‡3 years, 6 months   §22 years, 3 months   ‖27 years, 3 months

91

FIGURE III-18.3 (cont'd.) Treasury Offerings of Notes and Bonds for Cash by Maturities Beginning in 1974 (Billions of Dollars)

Maturities	1981	1982	1983
Under 2 Years			
2 Years	4.5 4.8 4.8 4.3 4.3 4.5 4.8 4.8 4.8 4.8 4.8	5.3 5.3 5.3 5.3 5.5 5.5 6.0 6.5 6.5 6.8 6.8 7.0	7.3 7.5 7.8 7.8 8.0 8.0 8.0 8.0 8.0 8.3
3 Years	3.9* 3.0 4.3 4.5	6.5 6.5 6.8 6.5	6.5 6.5 6.5 6.5
4 Years	3.5 3.3 3.3 3.3	5.3 5.8 5.8 6.0	6.0 6.0 7.0 6.2
5 Years	3.3 3.0 3.3 3.3	5.5 5.8 6.0 6.0	6.0 6.3 6.5 6.8
7 Years	2.5 2.8 3.0 3.0	4.5 4.8 5.0 5.0	5.3 5.3 5.5 5.5
10 Years	2.5 1.8 2.3 2.3	4.5 4.8 5.0 5.3	5.3 5.3 5.5 5.8
15 Years			
20 Years	1.5 1.8 1.8 1.8	3.0 3.5 3.5 3.5	3.8 3.8 4.0
25 Years			
30 Years	2.3 2.0 2.0 2.0	3.5 3.8 3.8 4.3	4.5 4.8 4.8 5.3

*3 years, 6 months

Maturities	1984	1985	1986	1987
Under 2 Years				
2 Years	8.3 8.3 8.3 8.3 8.5 8.5 8.5 8.8 9.0 9.0	9.0 9.0 9.0 9.0 9.0 9.3 8.9 9.3 9.3 9.5 9.5	9.5 9.5 9.5 9.8 9.8 9.8 10.0 10.0 10.0 10.3 10.3	10.3 10.0 10.0 10.0 9.8 9.8 9.8 9.8 9.3 9.3 9.3 9.3
3 Years	6.5 6.5 6.5 6.5	7.3 8.0 8.5 8.8	9.0 9.0 9.5 10.0	10.0 10.0 9.8 9.8
4 Years	6.0 6.0 7.0 6.2	6.3 6.5 6.8 7.0	7.0 7.4 7.5 7.8	7.8 7.5 7.3 7.0
5 Years	6.0 6.3 6.5 6.8	7.0 7.0 7.3 7.5	7.5 7.8 8.0 8.3	8.3 8.0 7.8 7.5
7 Years	5.3 5.3 5.5 5.5	5.8 5.8 6.0 6.3	6.5 6.5 6.8 7.0	7.3 7.3 7.0 6.8
10 Years	5.3 5.3 5.5 5.8	6.0 6.5 6.8 7.0	7.0 9.0 9.5 9.8	9.8 9.8 9.3 9.3
15 Years				
20 Years	3.8 3.8 4.0 4.0	4.3 4.3 4.5 4.8	4.8	
25 Years				
30 Years	4.5 4.8 4.8 5.3	5.8 6.0 6.5 6.8	7.0 9.0 9.5 9.3	9.3 9.3 9.0 4.8

Large and regular financings of notes and bonds have allowed the Treasury to finance the huge deficits with less difficulty than expected. When the deficit changes, the Treasury in recent years has adjusted its financings by the amounts offered rather than by new maturities or techniques.

Source: *Treasury Bulletin*

93

and the 2-year note auctions were expanded from quarterly to monthly, which raised a considerable amount of funds. The 3-, 7-, and 25-year maturities were used somewhat more frequently, but in actual dollar amounts, the changes and the totals were rather modest.

In CY-76, the deficit unexpectedly moved much higher, and once more the shorter end of the market dominated the scene. The most important additions were the sale of four issues with 5-year maturities and two issues with 10-year maturities. By this time, the 25-year bond offerings had finally been increased to $1 billion. With the emphasis on shorter maturity, the average public debt maturity had declined to close to 2½ years.

In CY-77, the budget picture brightened and the Treasury was under less financing pressure. The most important financing factor during the year was the sale of four issues of 30-year maturities. In the three preceding years, there had been only one such offering. However, there were no 25-year maturities sold during 1977. With the 30-year offerings, the average public debt maturity was lengthened—a trend which has continued to the present.

The following year was not much different from 1977 in terms of the deficit or budget financing. Yet it was becoming apparent the Treasury was going to make more frequent use of the longer market as a source of funds. In the previous year, the Treasury sold five issues with 15-year-or-longer maturities; in CY-78 there were seven such offerings.

The budget deficit declined again in CY-79, and as one might have expected, the financing pattern and the size of the individual offerings were not greatly different from the previous year.

In CY-80, the budget picture deteriorated, and Treasury financing needs rose. The Treasury responded by increasing the size of 2-year notes, by selling four issues each of 3- and 5-year notes (in 1979 it sold only two of each), and by adding a fourth offering to the 30-year obligations.

The deficit deteriorated moderately in CY-81. From a financing view, the most important item was the inauguration of a much more standardized schedule of coupon offerings. There were now quarterly financings of 3-, 4-, 5-, 7-, 10-, 15-, and 30-year maturities. While there were a large number of regular offerings, the size of individual issues remained quite small. A typical 30-year bond offering ran only about $2 billion.

In CY-82 the budget deficit exploded, and so did Treasury financing. Since the "routinization" of financing was already in place, much of the additional money was raised by increasing the amount of the individual offerings. That was especially evident in the 3-through-10-

year maturities where issues were often about $2 billion more than what was sold in the previous year. Long-bond issues also grew substantially in size, despite relatively high rates and a market where trading was relatively thin.

In CY-83, Treasury financings took another quantum leap: no maturity was spared in the offerings. An exceptionally large increase took place in the 2-year note, and with these financings occurring monthly, substantial amounts of new money were raised. The Treasury also did more financing in the long market, yet the size of individual issues was generally still less than $5 billion.

In CY-84, the deficit edged lower, but was still very large. The slight moderation allowed the Treasury to stay with the same number and schedule of offerings as in 1983. Moreover, the increases in the individual offerings moderated considerably.

In CY-85, the deficit moved noticeably higher and the Treasury needed to be more aggressive than in 1984. All of the regular note and bond offerings were increased considerably; especially notable was the increase in the 30-year bond. Individual issues were now more than $6 billion, and were running more than $1 billion above the offerings of a year earlier. A combination of Japanese buying interest and substantial U.S. pension and retirement fund participation helped make the large increase possible.

In CY-86, the deficit again moved higher, and Treasury financing also rose. The Treasury decided to discontinue 20-year bond offerings, apparently because the issue was viewed as being too expensive since it was higher on the yield curve than the 30-year obligation. These deficit and financing factors meant large increases across the board in other intermediate and longer-term maturities. The 10-year and 30-year offerings experienced especially large additions, which was to be expected in view of the 20-year maturity being no longer available, and with strong foreign and domestic demand still present.

In CY-87, the budget deficit declined substantially. The Treasury's adjustment came in the form of smaller financings; first in bills and then in notes and bonds. Weekly bill auctions was reduced to less than $13 billion, from $16 billion. The size of most note and bond offerings was reduced $500 million to $1 billion, from peak levels. Except for the termination of the 20-year offerings in the previous year, no change had occurred in the basic Treasury financing schedule since 1982. Large swings in the deficit were handled by changes in the size of individual offerings rather than by adopting new financing techniques. Debt and bond ceiling problems created unusual headaches for Treasury debt managers.

One key factor in recent years which substantially affected the size of marketable financings has been the purchase by state and local governments of nonmarketable Treasury issues. The official title of these issues is "State and Local Government Series," but the market refers to them as "SLUGS." In the early 1980s, state and local governments borrowed money at historically high interest rates. Most of these issues were callable in the late1980s and early 1990s. When interest rates declined in the mid-1980s, state and local governments borrowed more money but at lower rates. The proceeds from the second financing were invested in SLUGS. The maturities of these investments usually corresponded with the first call date of the high interest cost initial offerings. When the call date on that first issue occurs, the state and local governments will pay them off with the money available from the maturing SLUGS.

In the three years ended December 31, 1987, the amount of money raised by the Treasury via this vehicle was $95 billion. If this increase had not taken place, each regular marketable note and bond offering would have been about $2 billion larger.

Figures III-18.4 and III-18.5 show nonmarketable debt outstanding (which includes SLUGS).

FIGURE III-18.4 Nonmarketable Treasury Debt Outstanding (Excluding Government Account Series and Minor Items)

End of December	Savings Notes and Bonds	Foreign Government and Public Series	State and Local Government Series	Total
1974	63.3	22.8	.7	86.8
1975	67.5	21.6	1.3	90.4
1976	71.9	22.3	4.5	98.7
1977	76.6	22.2	14.0	112.8
1978	80.5	29.0	24.4	133.9
1979	79.5	28.8	24.6	132.9
1980	72.2	24.0	23.5	119.7
1981	67.8	19.0	23.0	109.8
1982	67.7	14.7	25.7	106.1
1983	70.5	10.4	36.7	117.6
1984	73.1	9.1	44.4	126.6
1985	78.0	7.5	87.5	173.0
1986	90.6	4.7	110.5	205.8
1987	99.2	4.0	139.3	242.5

The growth in the nonmarketable debt outstanding has been much smaller than in the marketable area. Moreover, virtually the entire advance has come in the state and local government area (SLUGS) and most of that occurred from 1985 through 1987.

Source: *Monthly Statement of Public Debt of the United States*

FIGURE III-18.5 Nonmarketable Treasury Debt Outstanding as of 12/31/87 (Excluding Government Account Series and Minor Items)

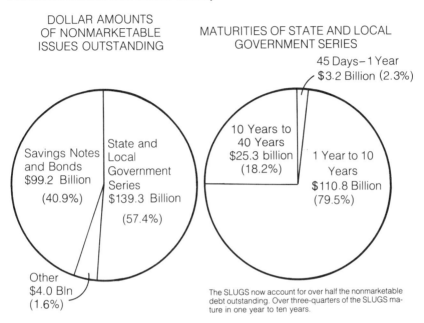

DOLLAR AMOUNTS OF NONMARKETABLE ISSUES OUTSTANDING

Savings Notes and Bonds $99.2 Billion (40.9%)

State and Local Government Series $139.3 Billion (57.4%)

Other $4.0 Bln (1.6%)

Total: $243 Billion

MATURITIES OF STATE AND LOCAL GOVERNMENT SERIES

45 Days–1 Year $3.2 Billion (2.3%)

10 Years to 40 Years $25.3 billion (18.2%)

1 Year to 10 Years $110.8 Billion (79.5%)

The SLUGS now account for over half the nonmarketable debt outstanding. Over three-quarters of the SLUGS mature in one year to ten years.

Source: *Monthly Statement of Public Debt of the United States*

State and local governments, at the end of CY-87, held $139 billion of these nonmarketable Treasury issues. A large portion will be cashed in during the late 1980s and early 1990s when state and local governments call in and redeem high-coupon issues marketed in the early 1980s. From a timing perspective, many of these redemptions will occur when gross marketable Treasury note and bond maturities increase substantially—thus adding to the government's overall refinancing problems.

19. How will Treasury financings from 1974 through 1987 affect future debt management?

Large Treasury deficits began only as recently as FY-82, followed by sizable offerings of long-term debt in 1983. Therefore, the amounts to be refunded of previously offered long-term debt are currently not very large, as is apparent in Figure III-19.1. However, if very large deficits continue, and there is considerable emphasis on debt extension (both of which are likely), the refunding burden will increase substantially.

There are four approaches which can be used to estimate future Treasury financings.

One is a fantasy: the deficit disappears in the late 1980s or early 1990s, the budget stays roughly in balance, and debt managers live happily ever after.

The other extreme is a nightmare: the budget deficit, which in FY-87 was about 3½ percent of nominal GNP, stays at that level indefinitely. Thus, if GNP advances by 5 times in the next 30 years, the same would happen to the dollar amount of the budget deficit. This scenario is highly unlikely since a deficit of $750 billion to $1 trillion per year is politically unacceptable and extremely difficult to manage financially.

There are two other assumptions which seem more probable. One is the reduction of the deficit/GNP ratio to a relatively tolerable 2 percent during the next decade, with it remaining near that level thereafter. The other approach is to presume the dollar deficit stays close to the FY-87 level of $150 billion for an indefinite period. By holding the deficit steady on a dollar basis, it would continue to decline as a percentage of GNP.

The deficit/GNP ratio approach is difficult to deal with analytically since guesses have to be made as to GNP growth, and changes in the ratio. Therefore, for the sake of analytical simplicity, holding the annual dollar deficits close to the FY-87 level is the approach used. It may not be as probable as the 2 percent deficit/GNP ratio approach, but it has a much better chance of occurring than either the balanced-budget scenario or the deficit running 3 percent to 4 percent of nominal GNP.

Even after an analytical approach for determining future financing was decided upon, several other decisions had to be made. As of December 31, 1987, the longest government coupon issue outstanding matured in the year 2017. Consequently, the 30-year period which runs from the end of 1987 to the end of 2017 was the period selected for

FIGURE III-19.1 Marketable Note and Bond Maturities—1988 Through 2017 (Billions of Dollars)

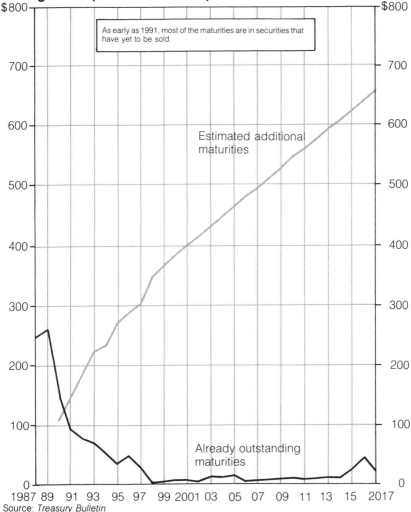

As early as 1991, most of the maturities are in securities that have yet to be sold.

Estimated additional maturities

Already outstanding maturities

1987 89   91   93   95   97   99 2001 03   05   07   09   11   13   15   2017

Source: *Treasury Bulletin*

analysis. The current pattern of note and bond auctions was retained as an assumption to simplify the analysis, especially since there is no indication the pattern will be revised in the near future. The analysis was limited to marketable coupon issues. Treasury bills were excluded because of the overwhelming number of auctions held during the course of a year, and nonmarketable obligations were omitted because they are issued on such an irregular basis.

The next decision was to determine a steady annual increase in note and bond offerings throughout the maturity spectrum which could hold the annual deficit at about the FY-87 level for close to 30 years. The objective was achieved by adding $500 million on average, compared with the previous year, to each note and bond maturity. Thus, if the average size of a 2-year note offering was $9 billion in CY-88, it would be $9.5 billion in CY-89, $10 billion in CY-90, and so on. The details of this approach are shown in Figure III-19.3.

By 2017, the amount of coupon issues maturing (using the little-changed-deficit approach) would be between 2 and 3 times the amount maturing in CY-88. The 1988 maturities should amount to about $245 billion, and would be almost $700 billion by 2017. That means, to cover the maturing amounts and to raise enough funds to finance the deficit, the Treasury would have to offer in 2017 over $800 billion of notes and bonds. That amount would be 2 to 3 times the $300 billion likely to be issued in CY-88. These numbers are graphically displayed in Figures III-19.1 and III-19.2.

While increases of 2 to 3 times in maturities and new offerings for 2017 versus 1988 may seem substantial, over a period of close to 30 years they are not all that large. They represent only a fraction of the rate of increase which took place from CY-74 to CY-87—although the base amount was much lower at that time. The amounts to be added to future note and bond issues seem relatively manageable, and should not be a great burden for the market. That would contrast with the CY-82-through-CY-87 period when annual increases of $1 billion to $2 billion over the previous year in each maturity were quite common. Finally, there would be no great need for the Treasury to alter significantly its present note and bond program.

Yet, it is optimistic to forecast annual budget deficits which average roughly $150 billion per year, since by the year 2017, the deficit as a percentage of GNP would be less than 1 percent. If the deficit moves to near 2 percent of GNP, it would add substantially to the amount of financing. The additional funding could be burdensome, especially if foreign demand for Treasury issues is on the disappointing side. The longest maturities would have the largest problems. Under these less optimistic circumstances, individual 30-year bond offerings could run $30 billion to $40 billion by the year 2017, rather than the $24 billion (a not-inconsequential amount) under a relatively optimistic deficit estimate of close to $150 billion.

FIGURE III-19.2 Estimated Offerings, Maturities, and Net Increases in Notes and Bonds—1988 Through 2017 (Billions of Dollars)

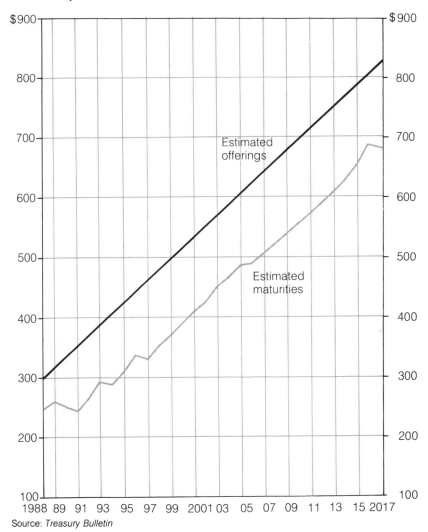

Source: *Treasury Bulletin*

FIGURE III-19.3 Estimated Marketable Note and Bond Maturities and Financings—1988 Through 2017 (Billions of Dollars)

Maturity Date	(a) Maturities as of 12/31/87			(b) Estimated Maturities of Future Offerings								(c) Total Maturities
	Notes	Bonds	Total	2 Yr.	3 Yr.	4 Yr.	5 Yr.	7 Yr.	10 Yr.	30 Yr.	Total	
1988	244.9	—	244.9	—	—	—	—	—	—	—	—	244.9
1989	259.3	—	259.3	—	—	—	—	—	—	—	—	259.3
1990	143.8	1.8	145.6	—	—	—	—	—	—	—	—	253.6
1991	94.4	—	94.4	108.0	—	—	—	—	—	—	108.0	244.4
1992	76.2	3.0	79.2	114.0	36.0	—	—	—	—	—	150.0	265.2
1993	64.4	7.3	71.7	120.0	38.0	28.0	—	—	—	—	186.0	295.7
1994	47.6	6.5	54.1	126.0	40.0	30.0	28.0	—	—	—	224.0	290.1
1995	29.3	6.1	35.4	132.0	42.0	32.0	30.0	—	—	—	236.0	311.4
1996	48.9	—	48.9	138.0	44.0	34.0	32.0	28.0	—	—	276.0	338.9
1997	29.1	—	29.1	144.0	46.0	36.0	34.0	30.0	—	—	290.0	333.1
1998	—	1.1	1.1	150.0	48.0	38.0	36.0	32.0	—	—	304.0	355.1
1999	—	2.4	2.4	156.0	50.0	40.0	38.0	34.0	36.0	—	354.0	372.4
2000	—	7.4	7.4	162.0	52.0	42.0	40.0	36.0	38.0	—	370.0	393.4
2001	—	8.2	8.2	168.0	54.0	44.0	42.0	38.0	40.0	—	386.0	410.2
2002	—	4.5	4.5	174.0	56.0	46.0	44.0	40.0	42.0	—	402.0	422.5
2003	—	17.0	17.0	180.0	58.0	48.0	46.0	42.0	44.0	—	418.0	451.0
2004	—	16.1	16.1	186.0	60.0	50.0	48.0	44.0	46.0	—	434.0	466.1
2005	—	17.8	17.8	192.0	62.0	52.0	50.0	46.0	48.0	—	450.0	483.8
2006	—	4.8	4.8	198.0	64.0	54.0	52.0	48.0	50.0	—	466.0	486.8
2007	—	5.7	5.7	204.0	66.0	56.0	54.0	50.0	52.0	—	482.0	503.7
2008	—	7.3	7.3	210.0	68.0	58.0	56.0	52.0	54.0	—	498.0	521.3
2009	—	8.8	8.8	216.0	70.0	60.0	58.0	54.0	56.0	—	514.0	538.8
2010	—	10.2	10.2	222.0	72.0	62.0	60.0	56.0	58.0	—	530.0	556.2
2011	—	9.5	9.5	228.0	74.0	64.0	62.0	58.0	60.0	—	546.0	571.5
2012	—	11.0	11.0	234.0	76.0	66.0	64.0	60.0	62.0	—	562.0	589.0
2013	—	14.8	14.8	240.0	78.0	68.0	66.0	62.0	64.0	—	578.0	608.8
2014	—	16.1	16.1	246.0	80.0	70.0	68.0	64.0	66.0	—	594.0	626.1
2015	—	26.7	26.7	252.0	82.0	72.0	70.0	66.0	68.0	—	610.0	652.7
2016	—	45.0	45.0	258.0	84.0	74.0	72.0	68.0	70.0	—	626.0	687.0
2017	—	23.4	23.4	264.0	86.0	76.0	74.0	70.0	72.0	—	642.0	681.4
201_				270.0	88.0	78.0	76.0	72.0	74.0	—	658.0	

Maturity Date	(d) Assumptions of Amounts Offered per Issue							(e) Assumptions of Amounts Offered Each Year							(f) Gross Money Raised	(g) Net Money Raised
	2 Yr.	3 Yr.	4 Yr.	5 Yr.	7 Yr.	10 Yr.	30 Yr.	2 Yr.	3 Yr.	4 Yr.	5 Yr.	7 Yr.	10 Yr.	30 Yr.		
1988	9.0	9.0	7.0	7.0	7.0	9.0	9.0	108.0	36.0	28.0	28.0	28.0	36.0	36.0	300.0	55.1
1989	9.5	9.5	7.5	7.5	7.5	9.5	9.5	114.0	38.0	30.0	30.0	30.0	38.0	38.0	318.0	58.7
1990	10.0	10.0	8.0	8.0	8.0	10.0	10.0	120.0	40.0	32.0	32.0	32.0	40.0	40.0	336.0	82.4
1991	10.5	10.5	8.5	8.5	8.5	10.5	10.5	126.0	42.0	34.0	34.0	34.0	42.0	42.0	354.0	109.6
1992	11.0	11.0	9.0	9.0	9.0	11.0	11.0	132.0	44.0	36.0	36.0	36.0	44.0	44.0	372.0	106.8
1993	11.5	11.5	9.5	9.5	9.5	11.5	11.5	138.0	46.0	38.0	38.0	38.0	46.0	46.0	390.0	94.3
1994	12.0	12.0	10.0	10.0	10.0	12.0	12.0	144.0	48.0	40.0	40.0	40.0	48.0	48.0	408.0	117.9
1995	12.5	12.5	10.5	10.5	10.5	12.5	12.5	150.0	50.0	42.0	42.0	42.0	50.0	50.0	426.0	114.6
1996	13.0	13.0	11.0	11.0	11.0	13.0	13.0	156.0	52.0	44.0	44.0	44.0	52.0	52.0	444.0	105.1
1997	13.5	13.5	11.5	11.5	11.5	13.5	13.5	162.0	54.0	46.0	46.0	46.0	54.0	54.0	462.0	128.9
1998	14.0	14.0	12.0	12.0	12.0	14.0	14.0	168.0	56.0	48.0	48.0	48.0	56.0	56.0	480.0	124.9
1999	14.5	14.5	12.5	12.5	12.5	14.5	14.5	174.0	58.0	50.0	50.0	50.0	58.0	58.0	498.0	125.6
2000	15.0	15.0	13.0	13.0	13.0	15.0	15.0	180.0	60.0	52.0	52.0	52.0	60.0	60.0	516.0	122.6
2001	15.5	15.5	13.5	13.5	13.5	15.5	15.5	186.0	62.0	54.0	54.0	54.0	62.0	62.0	534.0	123.8
2002	16.0	16.0	14.0	14.0	14.0	16.0	16.0	192.0	64.0	56.0	56.0	56.0	64.0	64.0	552.0	129.5
2003	16.5	16.5	14.5	14.5	14.5	16.5	16.5	198.0	66.0	58.0	58.0	58.0	66.0	66.0	570.0	119.0
2004	17.0	17.0	15.0	15.0	15.0	17.0	17.0	204.0	68.0	60.0	60.0	60.0	68.0	68.0	588.0	121.9
2005	17.5	17.5	15.5	15.5	15.5	17.5	17.5	210.0	70.0	62.0	62.0	62.0	70.0	70.0	606.0	122.2
2006	18.0	18.0	16.0	16.0	16.0	18.0	18.0	216.0	72.0	64.0	64.0	64.0	72.0	72.0	624.0	137.2
2007	18.5	18.5	16.5	16.5	16.5	18.5	18.5	222.0	74.0	66.0	66.0	66.0	74.0	74.0	642.0	138.3
2008	19.0	19.0	17.0	17.0	17.0	19.0	19.0	228.0	76.0	68.0	68.0	68.0	76.0	76.0	660.0	138.7

FIGURE III-19.3 (cont'd.) Estimated Marketable Note and Bond Maturities and Financings—1988 Through 2017 (Billions of Dollars)

Maturity Date	(d) Assumptions of Amounts Offered per Issue							(e) Assumptions of Amounts Offered Each Year							(f) Gross Money Raised	(g) Net Money Raised
	2 Yr.	3 Yr.	4 Yr.	5 Yr.	7 Yr.	10 Yr.	30 Yr.	2 Yr.	3 Yr.	4 Yr.	5 Yr.	7 Yr.	10 Yr.	30 Yr.		
2009	19.5	19.5	17.5	17.5	17.5	19.5	19.5	234.0	78.0	70.0	70.0	70.0	78.0	78.0	678.0	139.2
2010	20.0	20.0	18.0	18.0	18.0	20.0	20.0	240.0	80.0	72.0	72.0	72.0	80.0	80.0	696.0	139.8
2011	20.5	20.5	18.5	18.5	18.5	20.5	20.5	246.0	82.0	74.0	74.0	74.0	82.0	82.0	714.0	142.5
2012	21.0	21.0	19.0	19.0	19.0	21.0	21.0	252.0	84.0	76.0	76.0	76.0	84.0	84.0	732.0	143.0
2013	21.5	21.5	19.5	19.5	19.5	21.5	21.5	258.0	86.0	78.0	78.0	78.0	86.0	86.0	750.0	141.2
2014	22.0	22.0	20.0	20.0	20.0	22.0	22.0	264.0	88.0	80.0	80.0	80.0	88.0	88.0	768.0	141.9
2015	22.5	22.5	20.5	20.5	20.5	22.5	22.5	270.0	90.0	82.0	82.0	82.0	90.0	90.0	786.0	133.3
2016	23.0	23.0	21.0	21.0	21.0	23.0	23.0	276.0	92.0	84.0	84.0	84.0	92.0	92.0	804.0	117.0
2017	23.5	23.5	21.5	21.5	21.5	23.5	23.5	282.0	94.0	86.0	86.0	86.0	94.0	94.0	822.0	140.6

(a) Maturities as of 12/31/84: The marketable notes and bonds outstanding, broken out by maturity.

(b) Estimated Maturities of Future Offerings: The estimated amount added to annual maturities through the year 2017, broken out by issues (2 to 30 years).

(c) Total Maturities: Totals for sections (a) and (b) are combined for an estimate of total maturities by year, through 2017.

(d) Assumptions of Amounts Offered per Issue: Estimates of the average amounts offered, per issue, from 1988 through 2017, by maturity; $500 million per year is added to each maturity.

(e) Assumptions of Amounts Offered Each Year: The individual offerings in (d) are multiplied by the number of issues sold during the year. There are 36 offerings per year; 12 for the 2-year note, and 4 each for the remaining maturities.

(f) Gross Money Raised: Total of (e).

(g) Net Money Raised: Total maturities (c) are subtracted from gross money raised (f). These amounts should finance most of the estimated annual deficit.

20. Who were the primary domestic purchasers of Treasury debt from CY-74 to CY-87, and can they be counted on in the future?

At the end of CY-87, domestic investors (excluding the Federal Reserve) supposedly held $1.5 trillion of Treasury marketable debt outstanding, compared with about $200 billion at the end of CY-74. That increase in holdings by categories of investors is shown in Figure III-20.1.

A word of caution, however: the Treasury ownership survey is not one of the most complete or accurate of releases. It is therefore dangerous to make definitive statements based on these results. The "other" category is by far the largest and fastest growing of all the components. It includes savings and loan associations, nonprofit institutions, credit unions, mutual savings banks, corporate pension trust funds, dealers and brokers, certain U.S. government deposit accounts, and government-sponsored agencies. Of these holders, probably the largest and most meaningful is the corporate pension trust funds (most of their investments no doubt being in intermediate- and long-term maturities). Yet it also appears a major portion of this "other" component is simply unreported amounts in the remaining categories.

As for which categories, it can be presumed reports by financial or public institutions—such as banks, insurance companies, money market funds, and state and local governments—are probably quite accurate, as are reports by foreign central banks and international institutions. That means holdings by individuals and nonofficial foreign investors are the areas which are substantially understated. The book-entry recording system should gradually reduce these unreported amounts and, therefore, the size of the "other" category.

COMMERCIAL BANKS. In looking at the reported amounts, commercial banks are the largest domestic holders of marketable Treasury issues. However, it is evident the increases over the years were intermittent. For example, there were very large increases in CY-75 and CY-76, and again in CY-83, CY-86, and CY-87. The remaining years show declines, little change, or moderate growth. These large advances tended to occur when three factors were involved: the loan demand was on the soft side, debt instruments appeared to be relatively attractive investments, and the Treasury had a big increase in marketable offerings.

FIGURE III-20.1 Estimated Ownership of Marketable Securities (Billions of Dollars)

End of December	Commercial Banks	Individuals	Insurance Companies	Money Market Funds	Corporations	State and Local Governments	Foreign and International	Other	Total*
1974	55.6	20.8	6.2	—	12.4	28.5	36.0	21.5	181.0
1975	85.1	21.3	9.5	—	21.3	32.9	44.9	40.9	255.9
1976	103.5	29.6	16.2	1.1	23.5	35.3	55.8	42.8	307.8
1977	98.9	31.1	19.9	.9	18.2	44.1	87.4	42.5	343.0
1978	95.0	33.3	20.0	1.5	17.3	51.7	104.1	42.3	365.2
1979	88.1	38.1	21.4	5.6	17.0	57.1	90.2	84.7	402.2
1980	112.1	44.6	24.0	3.5	19.3	64.4	105.7	118.7	492.3
1981	111.4	42.7	29.0	21.5	17.9	73.8	117.6	166.8	580.7
1982	131.4	48.2	44.1	42.6	24.5	90.9	134.8	219.6	736.1
1983	188.8	61.9	65.3	22.8	39.7	113.8	153.9	248.7	894.0
1984	183.4	69.3	88.7	25.9	50.1	129.0	183.8	351.3	1081.5
1985	192.2	75.0	115.4	25.1	59.0	148.3	207.1	415.2	1237.3
1986	230.1	70.5	135.4	28.6	68.8	162.6	246.9	445.8	1388.7
1987	252.3	71.0	152.0	14.6	83.0	N.A.	283.6	N.A.	1483.6

*Excludes holdings of U.S. government investment accounts and the Federal Reserve.

The largest category of holders of marketable Treasury obligations is classified as "other." Part of this category should probably be in areas such as "individuals" and "foreign and international." Data from the Japanese confirm that "foreign and international" is understated. Commercial banks are reportedly the largest domestic holder of marketable Treasury issues (a considerable part of these holdings was acquired since 1981).

Source: Economic Report of the President, Treasury Bulletin

Based on this past performance, commercial banks can hardly be counted on in the future to be steady and larger buyers of Treasury issues.

STATE AND LOCAL GOVERNMENTS. State and local governments are reported to be the second largest domestic holders of marketable Treasury issues. Their two key components are pension and retirement accounts, and liquidity investments. Because both of these categories have shown sustained growth, it is no surprise their holdings have increased steadily over the years, representing an important and regular source of demand for Treasury issues.

INSURANCE COMPANIES. Insurance companies are the third largest domestic owners of marketable Treasury issues according to the questionable figures reported. From CY-74 to CY-81, their holdings were small and the annual increases were modest. Since that time, however, the growth of their Treasury investments has been substantial. The reasons are not hard to find. These investors are mainly interested in the longer end of the market and since the early 1980s, the Treasury has become an aggressive and regular issuer of long-term obligations. With life insurance companies aggressively seeking out pension fund money, part of these funds have been placed in government obligations.

Looking ahead, as long as life insurance companies continue to receive large amounts of pension fund money, the government market will continue to receive substantial investments from this source. That is likely even though these investors have become more yield conscious. Much will depend on the availability of other long-term investments, with new corporate obligations and the growth of the securitization process being very important factors. (The securitization process is the transformation of a loan into a marketable investment.) In the past, loans made by financial institutions often stayed with the lender until they matured. In recent years, however, similar-type loans have been packaged and sold to investors, typically in the mortgage area. These packages can be held by the new investors or resold.

INDIVIDUAL INVESTMENTS. The "individuals" category is reportedly the fourth in size, although in fact it probably rivals commercial banks as the largest domestic holder. A sizable portion of the huge CY-79 to CY-87 increase in the "other" category should no doubt be part of the "individuals" component. A reasonable guess is that a considerable part of these investments by individuals were for pension and retirement purposes. In any event, the numbers published for individuals are substantially understated and misleading. Irrespective of the accuracy of the data, the government will need to place considerable emphasis on longer-term individual investments if it is going to finance large deficits primarily from domestic sources.

CORPORATIONS. Corporations are next in order of size and show considerable fluctuations in their holdings of Treasury issues. A major reason for the variations is that most of the investments are in the money market area and are used for liquidity purposes. Liquidity increases can be due to a growth in corporate profits when firms have few acceptable long-term outlets for their funds; the selling off of companies or divisions; or the desire to accumulate a war chest for an acquisition or takeover.

Looking ahead, while purchases by corporations of Treasury issues in any one year can be helpful to the government, the increases are often too small and erratic to be heavily relied upon, especially since the investments are typically in the money market area.

The last domestic holder category, and the smallest, is money market funds. The amount invested here is relatively small because many investors want higher yields on short-term investments. Annual changes in holdings are highly erratic and depend upon competition from other outlets (primarily depository institutions) and the degree of concern about safety. When apprehension increases, investors look to short-term Treasury issues for safety and liquidity. That situation is not likely to change in the future, and money market funds are likely to remain a relatively small and sporadic investor in short-term Treasury obligations.

In summary, if domestic investors are going to carry a larger share of the debt financing burden for the Treasury, individuals will have to be the key factor. They clearly have the dollar resources to buy large amounts of Treasury issues on a regular basis, and Treasury issues fit many of their liquidity, investment, and retirement needs. Next in importance are the insurance companies (primarily life insurance firms) and corporate pension funds. They would be needed to help the Treasury place large amounts of intermediate and long-term obligations. As for the rest of the domestic categories, while there may be no one area of particular consequence, they are important as a group because of the large amounts of money they represent.

21. Have foreigners bought a large amount of Treasury debt issues since 1974?

Indeed they have, and the official figures are misleading. At the end of CY-87, it was officially reported foreign and international investors held about $284 billion of a total of $1.5 trillion of marketable debt outstanding. That amounts to only about 19 percent of the total. Figure III-21.3 provides a breakout of the types of holdings and the categories of holders. Figure III-21.1 illustrates the growth of these holdings and their proportion of Treasury debt outstanding.

Foreign holdings of marketables did not increase substantially until CY-84. But from December 31, 1983 to December 31, 1987, they grew $130 billion to a level of $284 billion. The increase in marketable holdings alone was even more impressive—$137 billion—as most of their nonmarketable holdings matured during this period.

In the 12-month period ended December 31, 1987, the increase in foreign and international holdings, as reported by the Treasury, was $37 billion versus a growth in total marketable debt of $95 billion (excluding Federal Reserve purchases). Thus, according to official U.S. data, foreigners acquired 39 percent of the increase in marketable Treasury debt.

As substantial as this percentage seems, it appears to be understated. Figure III-21.2 illustrates the problem. According to Japanese sources (Nomura Research Institute), their acquisitions of U.S. debt instruments (government as well as corporate) amounted to $73 billion in CY-87. Of this total, about $39 billion were government notes and bonds.

Yet, U.S. Treasury data for CY-87 show Japanese holdings of notes and bonds increased only $1 billion. Another $6 billion was added in short-term issues. Custody holdings at the Federal Reserve for all central banks and international institutions increased $36 billion—all of which was not the Japanese. Moreover, the Treasury should have included the custody data in its total.

The $39 billion Japanese figure is too high because it does not include redemptions and it is possible some liquidations in the secondary market were not captured in the data if the sales were made outside Japan with non-Japanese dealers. The U.S. Treasury figures, however, are substantially understated because there are probably substantial U.S. government securities held abroad in custody for foreigners.

Reenforcing this view is that in CY-87, Japanese dealers in the U.S. government securities market apparently took down about $25

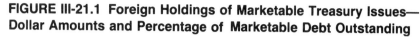

FIGURE III-21.1 Foreign Holdings of Marketable Treasury Issues—Dollar Amounts and Percentage of Marketable Debt Outstanding

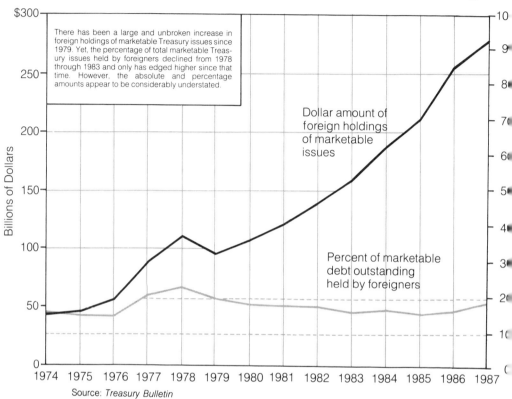

There has been a large and unbroken increase in foreign holdings of marketable Treasury issues since 1979. Yet, the percentage of total marketable Treasury issues held by foreigners declined from 1978 through 1983 and only has edged higher since that time. However, the absolute and percentage amounts appear to be considerably understated.

Dollar amount of foreign holdings of marketable issues

Percent of marketable debt outstanding held by foreigners

Source: *Treasury Bulletin*

billion in the four quarterly refundings. Orders from Japanese institutions made up a good part of the total, although they were considerably smaller than in CY-86. Investors were also more willing to trade out of past holdings.

Interest in the four refundings is only part of the story. Adding to the holdings were Japanese takedowns in other auctions, purchases in the secondary market, and purchases by the Bank of Japan. On the negative side were the liquidations in the secondary market. No one seems to know the exact amount of these operations.

The apparent underestimation of Japanese purchases by U.S. sources makes one wonder how much underreporting there is with respect to other countries' purchases of U.S. obligations. Even if other countries' purchases for CY-87 vary little from what is officially reported, it would still mean total foreign purchases would be somewhat over

FIGURE III-21.2 Annual Japanese Purchases of Treasury Coupon Issues—Japanese Data Compared with U.S. Data (Billions of Dollars)

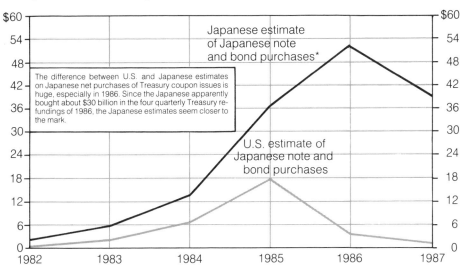

The difference between U.S. and Japanese estimates on Japanese net purchases of Treasury coupon issues is huge, especially in 1986. Since the Japanese apparently bought about $30 billion in the four quarterly Treasury refundings of 1986, the Japanese estimates seem closer to the mark.

Portfolio Investment by Japanese in the U.S. Market (Billions of Dollars)
(Japanese Statistical Sources)*

Year	Total	Equity	Fixed Income	Share of Fixed Income to Government Market	Japanese Estimate of Japanese Purchases†	U.S. Treasury Estimate of Japanese Purchases†
1982	$ 6.2	$ .2	$ 6.1	40%	$ 2.4	$ 0.8
1983	13.2	.7	12.5	47	5.9	2.3
1984	26.8	.1	26.8	52	13.8	6.3
1985	54.5	1.0	53.5	68	36.4	17.9
1986	100.2	7.1	93.2	57	53.1	4.0
1987	90.1	16.9	73.3	51	38.7	1.0

*Estimates based on Ministry of Finance and Japan Securities Dealers Association data. Includes a small amount of corporate data.
†U.S. notes and bonds.

Source: *Nomura Research Institute*

one-half of the increase in marketable issues. If this figure is in error, the percentage is probably larger, not smaller.

This analysis supports the conclusion much of the growth in the "other" category was the result of purchases by nonofficial foreigners. If the U.S. government were able to obtain more accurate foreign holdings figures, officials would be under increased pressure to reduce the trade and budget deficits.

Large foreign purchases of Treasury issues, and especially longer maturities, cannot be taken for granted year after year. Growing liquidations during much of CY-87 support this concern, and it seems unlikely that net foreign acquisitions, which appear to have been over $150 billion in the three years ended 1987, can be duplicated from 1988 through 1990.

As impressive as foreign purchases are, they do not fully reflect the growing importance of foreigners in the U.S. government market. Since the most recently offered issues are the ones most likely to be traded, foreigners are more involved in government market trading than their total holdings suggest. Foreign holders now seem more willing to trade the market and look at a wider range of maturities and investment outlets than they did in earlier years.

Foreigners have also become very substantial purchasers of intermediate and longer-term obligations, and their role in this important part of the market is of major consequence.

The Japanese have become an extremely important factor when 10- and 30-year issues are offered in the quarterly refundings. During CY-86 and CY-87, they were not only the dominant force in the auctions, but strongly affected the trading of issues with similar maturities in the secondary market. Most notable was their squeeze on other investors who tried to cover short positions during the May 1986 refunding; a scarcity which caused some issues to trade a half percent or more out of line with the yield curve. To avoid a recurrence, the Treasury now tends to reopen new 10- and 30-year issues three months later.

Nongovernment foreign investors have been very substantial purchasers of U.S. Treasury notes and bonds. At the end of CY-83, their holdings (according to U.S. statistics) amounted to only $15 billion, but by the end of December 1986, they were $59 billion. (In CY-87, there was virtually no change.) The numbers are shown in Figure III-21.3 and further illustrated in graphic form in Figure III-21.5.

Japanese private investors by far had the largest share of the increase in note and bond holdings. Figures III-21.6 and III-21.7 contain a table and a chart showing the breakout by country. Japan showed a $25 billion increase from the end of 1983 through December of 1987 (and it should be remembered this increase is understated). Since the Japanese government typically invested its foreign exchange reserves in Treasury bills and bank deposits, and only a modest amount in notes and bonds, it can be presumed the overwhelming majority of the increase in the latter came from the Japanese private sector. (The Japanese government recently has bought 3- to 5-year maturities.)

FIGURE III-21.3 Foreign Holdings of Treasury Bills, Certificates, Notes, and Bonds (Billions of Dollars)

End of Month	Holdings of Treasury Bills and Certificates				Holdings of Treasury Notes and Bonds			
	Total	Official Institutions	Banks and Other Foreigners	Nonmonetary International and Regional Organizations	Total†	Official Institutions	Banks and Other Foreigners	Nonmonetary International and Regional Organizations*
Dec. 1974	35.7	34.7	.5	.5	5.6	5.1	.5	N.A.
1975	37.4	34.2	.7	2.6	7.4	6.7	.7	N.A.
1976	40.7	37.7	.3	2.7	12.8	11.8	1.0	N.A.
1977	48.9	47.8	.4	.7	33.9	32.2	1.7	N.A.
1978	68.2	67.4	.6	.2	38.2	35.9	2.3	N.A.
1979	48.6	47.7	.8	.1	40.8	37.6	3.2	N.A.
1980	57.6	56.2	1.1	.3	46.6	41.5	5.1	N.A.
1981	55.3	52.4	2.4	.5	60.5	53.2	7.3	N.A.
1982	55.6	46.7	7.3	1.6	78.9	67.7	11.2	N.A.
1983	68.7	54.3	13.9	.5	83.8	68.5	15.3	N.A.
1984	76.4	60.0	15.5	.9	100.3	69.0	31.3	N.A.
1985	69.1	53.3	14.1	1.7	129.0	77.1	51.9	N.A.
1986	90.5	75.7	14.5	.3	150.3	91.4	58.9	N.A.
1987	101.8	88.8	12.7	.3	180.5	122.5	58.0	N.A.

*Not available.   †Excludes nonmonetary international and regional organizations.

A large majority of the Treasury bills held by foreigners are owned by official institutions. In the case of Treasury notes and bonds, after little change from 1978 through 1985, official institutions purchased large amounts in 1986 and 1987.

Sources: Federal Reserve Bulletin, Treasury Bulletin

FIGURE III-21.4 Foreign Holdings of Marketable Notes and Bonds Versus Holdings of Bills and Certificates (Billions of Dollars)

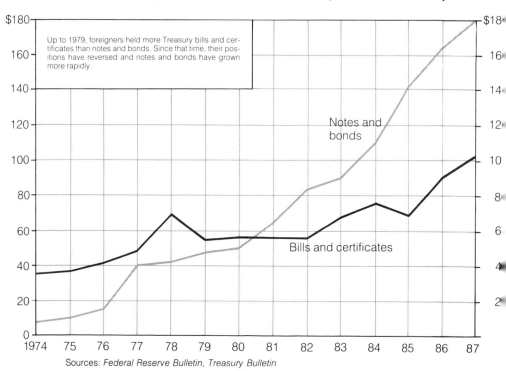

Sources: *Federal Reserve Bulletin, Treasury Bulletin*

While the overall figures do not give enough detail, much of the growth apparently came from large Japanese institutional investors, such as life insurance companies which were investing considerable amounts of pension plan money. Typically, their interest has been in the long end of the U.S. government market—from 10 years to 30 years. Recently there have been some signs of diversification both in terms of maturities and types of investments.

While private foreign investors showed considerable interest in the intermediate and long-term Treasury market, they showed very little interest in the bill area. At the end of December 1987, banks and other foreigners held only $13 billion of these issues (see Figure III-21.3). The primary reason for this lack of interest is most foreign investors appear to prefer commitments which are longer term than the money

FIGURE III-21.5 Breakout of Foreign Holdings of Treasury Securities (Percentage)

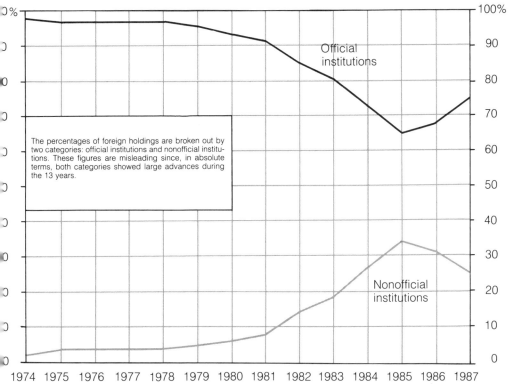

The percentages of foreign holdings are broken out by two categories: official institutions and nonofficial institutions. These figures are misleading since, in absolute terms, both categories showed large advances during the 13 years.

Sources: *Federal Reserve Bulletin, Treasury Bulletin*

market, and when they do invest in short-term instruments, they look for higher yielding obligations.

Foreign official holders showed a broader interest in the various types of Treasury issues than did private investors. Official holdings of Treasury bills moved up in CY-77 and CY-78, dropped off sharply in CY-79, and then showed little change through CY-82. Such holdings have moved up substantially since that time. By December 31, 1987, official holdings of bills amounted to $89 billion (see Figure III-21.3).

The largest official holders of Treasury bills are the Swiss, the Japanese, and the French—the three governments which probably take the most conservative approach with respect to the management of their

FIGURE III-21.6 Holdings of Notes and Bonds by Official and Nonofficial Institutions (Billions of Dollars)

End of Month	Total	France	Germany	Italy	Netherlands	Switzerland	U.K.	Other Europe	Total Europe	Japan	Korea
Dec. 74	5.7	—	—	—	—	—	.5	.4	.9	3.5	—
Dec. 75	7.7	—	.2	—	—	.1	.4	.4	1.1	3.3	—
Dec. 76	15.8	—	.8	—	.3	.3	.5	.4	2.3	2.7	—
Dec. 77	38.6	.1	3.2	—	.9	.5	8.9	.3	13.9	6.9	.4
Dec. 78	43.4	.1	7.1	—	1.4	1.0	5.4	.5	15.5	11.5	.4
Dec. 79	46.2	.2	10.0	—	1.5	.7	6.2	1.0	19.6	11.2	.3
Dec. 80	51.1	.3	7.1	—	1.9	.3	7.3	1.1	18.0	9.5	.3
Dec. 81	66.1	.6	8.2	—	2.0	.4	6.7	2.0	19.9	10.8	—
Dec. 82	83.5	1.0	13.6	—	2.7	1.1	6.5	2.6	27.5	11.6	—
Dec. 83	88.9	1.4	17.3	—	3.1	1.1	8.5	4.1	35.5	13.9	—
Dec. 84	110.4	1.3	20.2	.1	3.5	1.8	13.7	5.9	46.5	20.2	—
Dec. 85	139.5	1.0	22.1	.1	3.8	2.5	11.7	9.4	50.6	38.1	.2
Dec. 86	158.9	.3	29.8	.1	5.1	2.8	16.2	12.6	66.9	38.1	1.5
Dec. 87	184.8	.6	43.1	.1	4.2	4.7	20.3	17.3	90.5	39.0	1.6

The three most important changes in holdings by countries (or areas) of Treasury notes and bonds have been the very large increase in German and Japanese holdings since 1984 and the sharp decline in Middle East oil country holdings since 1983. If the Middle East oil countries are excluded from the Asian categories, then Europe becomes the largest holder of U.S. notes and bonds.
Sources: *Federal Reserve Bulletin, Treasury Bulletin*

countries' reserves. The exact amount of bill holdings by foreigners is not published by the Treasury, but it does publish the holdings of short-term Treasury obligations, which are mainly bills, but also include a few notes and bonds approaching maturity. The short-term holdings reported for Switzerland, as of December 31, 1987, were $21 billion; for Japan, $20 billion; and for France, $12 billion. The total investments of these three countries comprise over half of the short-term Treasury issues held by official institutions (see Figure III-21.8).

Many foreign governments have shown a more aggressive approach in managing their reserves during the past few years. That means not only trading more frequently and acquiring a broader group of investments, but also buying longer-term instruments. These governments are attempting to improve their rate of return, which means making judgments as to the direction of interest rates, the attractiveness of various points on the yield curve, what is likely to happen to their holdings of foreign exchange reserves, and where the dollar is heading.

The more aggressive approach is evident when different periods are studied. From the end of CY-74 through the end of CY-82, there

ingapore	Taiwan	Oil Exporting Nations Mid-East	Other Asian Countries	Total Asia	Other Govts.	International	Latin America Regional	Asia Regional	Total International and Regional
—	—	—	.2	3.7	.9	.1	.1	—	.2
—	—	1.8	.3	5.4	.9	.3	—	—	.3
.6	—	5.7	.2	9.2	1.3	2.9	—	.1	3.0
.7	—	10.1	.4	18.5	1.5	4.6	—	.1	4.7
.6	—	8.3	.7	21.5	1.3	5.1	—	—	5.1
.6	—	7.3	.4	19.8	1.4	5.4	—	—	5.4
.6	—	15.0	.7	26.1	2.4	4.5	—	—	4.6
.8	—	26.1	1.0	38.7	1.8	5.6	—	—	5.7
2.6	—	33.7	1.7	49.6	1.8	4.2	—	.4	4.6
1.4	—	28.3	2.4	46.0	2.3	4.4	—	.7	5.1
2.8	—	22.0	3.5	48.5	5.4	9.0	—	1.1	10.1
4.4	.1	20.5	5.1	68.4	9.9	8.6	—	1.9	10.6
5.0	.1	19.0	6.0	69.7	12.8	7.2	.2	2.1	9.5
1.2	9.9	15.9	6.8	74.4	15.5	3.0	.2	1.1	4.4

FIGURE III-21.7 Breakout by Countries of Major Holdings of Treasury Notes and Bonds (Billions of Dollars)

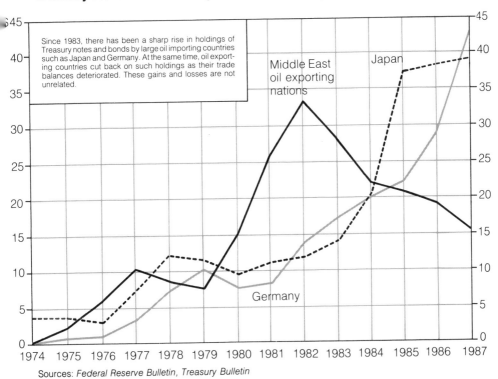

Since 1983, there has been a sharp rise in holdings of Treasury notes and bonds by large oil importing countries such as Japan and Germany. At the same time, oil exporting countries cut back on such holdings as their trade balances deteriorated. These gains and losses are not unrelated.

Middle East oil exporting nations

Japan

Germany

Sources: *Federal Reserve Bulletin, Treasury Bulletin*

FIGURE III-21.8 Short-Term Treasury Obligations Owned by Foreign Official Institutions and Unaffiliated Foreign Banks (Billions of Dollars)

End of Month	Total	France	Germany	Italy	Netherlands	Switzerland	U.K.	Other Europe	Total Europe	Japan	Korea	Singapore	Taiwan	Oil Exporting Nations Mid-East	Other Asian	Total Asia	Other
Dec. 1974	34.9	2.5	8.3	1.7	2.3	1.4	.9	2.9	20.0	6.1	.1	N.A.	.1	N.A.	N.A.	9.5	5.4
Dec. 1975	37.1	6.3	3.4	.1	2.4	2.0	.8	4.8	19.8	5.6	—	N.A.	.2	N.A.	N.A.	9.9	7.4
Dec. 1976	40.5	3.0	4.6	1.6	2.0	2.7	.6	3.4	17.9	9.7	.1	N.A.	.3	4.3	.7	15.1	7.5
Dec. 1977	48.7	3.4	5.4	4.8	1.6	5.1	3.2	4.9	28.4	11.2	.1	—	.2	3.2	1.1	15.8	4.5
Dec. 1978	68.2	6.4	14.9	4.0	.8	10.8	1.0	5.4	43.3	17.3	.1	—		2.4	1.1	20.9	4.0
Dec. 1979	48.2	6.5	8.9	4.6	.7	8.9	.8	3.0	33.4	4.5	.1	—	.5	5.9	.6	11.6	3.2
Dec. 1980	57.1	8.1	7.3	4.1	.8	6.9	.9	4.1	32.2	11.3	.2	—	.8	6.0	.9	19.2	5.7
Dec. 1981	54.6	4.4	5.1	3.3	.9	6.0	.8	3.3	23.8	13.9	.8	1.5	1.1	7.0	1.5	25.8	5.0
Dec. 1982	54.1	2.1	3.4	1.1	1.3	11.4	1.0	2.6	22.9	7.0	.8	3.7	1.3	7.1	1.1	20.6	10.6
Dec. 1983	65.0	3.4	.9	3.9	1.6	15.6	1.5	3.4	30.3	7.4	.4	5.8	2.3	6.4	1.6	23.8	10.9
Dec. 1984	71.8	4.4	.4	5.4	1.4	16.0	2.1	3.6	33.3	7.7	.3	6.5	2.9	8.5	3.3	29.3	9.2
Dec. 1985	64.5	4.7	2.0	2.1	1.1	15.4	1.8	3.6	30.7	5.2	.4	2.7	4.1	7.7	3.3	23.5	12.3
Dec. 1986	93.0	12.4	.6	3.4	1.5	17.9	2.7	2.4	40.9	17.2	.5	2.5	9.7	4.0	4.3	38.2	13.9
Dec. 1987	98.3	12.3	.9	3.6	1.2	20.9	5.1	2.8	46.8	20.2	.4	1.0	15.6	3.6	2.7	43.5	8.0

The three most conservative major central banks in investing their reserves are Switzerland, Japan, and France. Not surprisingly, they own the largest amount of bills—about half—held by foreign central banks.

Sources: Federal Reserve Bulletin, Treasury Bulletin

occurred a sharp increase in foreign official holdings of Treasury notes and bonds. After three years of little change, there was another good-size increase in CY-86 and CY-87. By the end of December 1987, the amount held was $123 billion. The amount exceeded bill holdings by about $34 billion (although some of the notes and bonds have a relatively short time span until maturity).

The Federal Reserve is not especially pleased with foreign official institutions actively trading in government securities because such participation tends to distort interest rates and the yield curve, and can have an undue influence on the pricing of Treasury financings as well. In addition, foreign central banks have access to information which places them in a more advantageous position than private investors. Yet from a political viewpoint, it is difficult to express displeasure, especially since these countries are helping to finance a meaningful part of the U.S. budget deficit. It appears part of the price the United States has to pay for attracting official foreign funds is to look the other way when countries aggressively trade the market for the purpose of making profits which will add to their official reserves.

The data suggest West Germany, the United Kingdom, Singapore, and Middle East oil exporting countries have been the nations most interested in buying Treasury notes and bonds. In the case of West Germany, it appears a decision was made in the late 1970s to move out of bills and into notes and bonds. (The United Kingdom never did have much of an interest in bills; as for Singapore, the increases seem fairly evenly split between bills and notes and bonds.)

Finally, the Middle East oil exporting countries put large amounts of their official reserves into notes and bonds, and by the end of CY-82 they held about $34 billion. Since that time, these OPEC countries have come under considerable financial pressure and there has been substantial liquidation, with their holdings down to $16 billion by the end of December 1987.

Foreigners have never shown great interest in acquiring nonmarketable Treasury issues. In the early 1970s, West Germany's Bundesbank bought a considerable amount of relatively long-term obligations, and from CY-78 through CY-80 several "Carter-bond"[1] offerings were made to the West Germans and the Swiss. Virtually all of

---

[1] This was a name given by market participants to nonmarketable bonds issued during the Carter administration specifically for sale to foreigners. Eight issues were sold abroad with 2-to-4-year maturities—six denominated in West German marks and two in Swiss francs.

these nonmarketable issues have matured.[2] Figure III-18.4 shows the annual changes in nonmarketable holdings.

There is a group of quasi-official holders of Treasury obligations classified as nonmonetary international. The World Bank has been an active, aggressive, and substantial investor in U.S. government obligations, especially in the intermediate market. Its impact on market prices and on the yield curve has been notable, particularly when it decides to make adjustments in its portfolio. The annual changes in the holdings of nonmonetary international organizations are not available in full; some details are presented in Figure III-21.3.

Foreign governments do not keep all of their foreign exchange reserves in U.S. Treasury obligations. At the end of CY-87, official foreign holdings of U.S. Treasury issues were over $200 billion. Yet, total foreign exchange reserves were roughly $600 billion. (See Figure III-21.9 and its caption.) That means many nations keep reserves in other currencies, in dollar-denominated instruments outside the Treasury securities area, or even in Treasury issues (held in custody outside the United States). Figure III-21.9 shows the foreign exchange reserves by country and how they have changed over the years.

A nation such as Taiwan, which has about the same amount of reserves as Japan and West Germany, does not hold a large portion of its reserves in U.S. government obligations. Even Japan, West Germany, and Singapore, which hold substantial U.S. government securities, have considerable investments elsewhere.

From the Treasury's perspective, this is a good-news-bad-news situation. A considerable amount of reserves held outside the U.S. government securities area represents buying potential for Treasury issues. But it also means foreign governments are quite willing to diversify away from the dollar and invest in other instruments besides Treasury obligations. The latter situation is one of great risk if the dollar shows extensive underlying weakness.

With foreigners having been responsible for acquiring about one-half of the growth in marketable Treasury financings in CY-86 and CY-87, these purchases obviously had a meaningful impact on U.S. interest rates. Without such purchases, interest rates would have been higher. A rough judgment as to how much higher can be made by analyzing market happenings.

[2]At the end of December 1987, there also were $4.0 billion of dollar-denominated nonmarketable issues outstanding. They all had maturities of less than one year and came about because of prepayments by foreign governments for defense items not yet received.

FIGURE III-21.9 Major Holders of Foreign Exchange Reserves (Billions of Dollars—End of Year)

Country	1974	1975	1976	1977	1978	1979	1980	1981	1982	1983	1984	1985	1986	1987
Japan	11.3	10.6	13.9	20.1	28.9	16.4	21.6	24.7	19.2	20.4	22.3	22.3	37.7	75.7
W. Germany	24.0	22.7	25.5	30.6	42.4	47.3	44.5	39.6	39.6	37.3	35.0	39.0	45.9	73.5
U.K.	4.9	3.4	2.7	19.5	15.5	18.5	18.8	12.8	9.7	8.7	7.0	9.7	14.9	38.6
France	3.8	7.4	4.4	4.7	8.3	16.1	25.3	20.0	14.6	18.1	19.1	24.3	28.4	29.6
Spain	5.6	5.4	4.6	5.9	9.8	12.8	11.3	10.2	7.2	7.0	11.4	10.5	13.8	28.3
Italy	3.2	1.2	3.1	8.0	10.5	17.3	21.6	18.6	12.6	18.5	19.1	14.1	18.1	27.8
Switzerland	5.4	6.9	9.3	9.8	17.4	16.2	15.3	13.5	14.9	14.4	14.7	17.5	21.3	27.2
China, People's Republic	—	—	—	2.3	1.6	2.2	2.3	4.8	11.1	14.5	16.7	11.9	10.5	15.2
Netherlands	3.5	3.4	3.5	3.9	3.9	6.5	10.4	8.1	8.7	8.7	7.8	9.2	9.6	14.2
Singapore	2.8	3.0	3.4	3.8	5.3	5.8	6.5	7.4	8.4	9.1	10.3	12.7	12.8	13.8*
Norway	1.7	2.0	1.8	1.8	2.5	3.8	5.6	5.8	6.3	5.9	8.6	13.1	11.5	13.3
Saudi Arabia	13.4	21.4	24.3	27.2	16.7	17.4	20.7	28.0	23.8	17.5	14.2	13.8	7.1	10.8
Total	79.6	87.4	96.5	137.6	162.8	180.3	203.9	193.5	176.1	180.1	186.2	198.1	231.6	368.0

*August.

At the end of 1987, foreign exchange reserves were about $600 billion. Of this total, $368 billion were held by those countries listed above. In addition, Taiwan held about $75 billion, with other IMF members holding the balance.

Source: International Financial Statistics, International Monetary Fund

121

One way of trying to measure the downward rate pressure is to observe what happened when foreign buying largely disappeared, which is what occurred from mid-March through mid-October of 1987.

In the money market area, higher rates due to a lack of foreign purchases were probably no more than about one-eighth percent. Bill rates were closely tied to the federal funds rate (which the monetary authorities target), and there was no shortage of domestic demand for such Treasury issues. However, in the 10-year maturity, the adverse impact was probably over one-half percent, and in the 30-year bond, the effect may have been over 1 percent. Of the 250 basis point increase in Treasury long bond rates from mid-March to mid-October 1987, the lack of foreign interest (and even some liquidations by the Japanese) may have accounted for roughly half the backup in rates.

Thus, when foreigners have been large buyers, they not only reduced the U.S. Treasury's borrowing costs in general, but they flattened out the yield curve by a fairly sizable amount. However, when they lost interest in the market, or liquidated securities, they have contributed in a meaningful way to increased borrowing costs and the upslope to the yield curve.

The impact of foreign purchases or sales of longer Treasury maturities is also important considering the amount of corporate and mortgage-type financing that is done in the United States. Higher Treasury bond rates can limit the amount of long-term financing done in the private sector.

22. Will foreigners continue to buy large amounts of Treasury obligations?

There are two ways to approach this question. One is to look at what caused some major countries to buy U.S. Treasury obligations, and whether these factors will continue to induce purchases. An alternative is to look at the more broadly based considerations which influence foreign acquisitions of government obligations. In the first approach, Japan and West Germany have been given special attention because they are the largest foreign holders of U.S. Treasury notes and bonds.

In studying the Japanese and West German situation, it is important to determine whether changes in note and bond holdings have been strongly influenced by foreign exchange rates, interest rates, and foreign trade considerations. Data pertinent to answering these questions are presented in charts (Figures III-23.1 and III-23.2) and in tables (Figures III-23.3 and III-23.4).

JAPANESE INVESTMENTS. Until late CY-86, there appeared to be little relationship between dollar-yen movements and Japanese purchases of notes and bonds. Japanese acquisitions of Treasury coupon issues began in earnest in CY-84 and continued in a major way into CY-86, while the yen during that period fluctuated sharply against the dollar. This suggests a lack of sensitivity on the part of private Japanese investors vis-à-vis foreign exchange movements. In CY-87, however, this situation changed substantially. There was even a period when long-term Treasury issues had a 6 percent rate advantage over similar Japanese obligations, and yet, because of the weakness of the dollar, the Japanese were not aggressive investors in U.S. debt instruments.

The earlier lack of responsiveness to dollar weakness appears to have come about in the following manner. When the dollar was rising, the Japanese investor in the U.S. debt market was gaining on all fronts—foreign exchange, capital gains, and interest rate differentials. Yet, when the dollar was falling, the situation was not viewed as especially adverse. The theory was that this was an investment averaging process and losses would not be very painful since the higher annual interest payments on United States versus Japanese securities would be sufficient to offset the foreign exchange loss.

In late CY-86, however, the Japanese began shying away from this reasoning because it contained some major fallacies. One is the presumption if investment averaging can work with interest rates, it can work with foreign exchange rates. Yet, there are major differences between the two. Interest rates, over a cycle, can have a central tendency and, therefore, investment averaging can be used. Rates do not stay at high or low levels indefinitely. In late CY-86, U.S. long-bond rates were not greatly different from what they were in CY-74, although the path during that period was far from smooth.

In the case of foreign exchange rates, however, there are underlying trends which seem to go on forever for many countries, with South American nations being a prime example. Even in the case of the West German mark and especially the yen, there has been an underlying trend. In CY-74, the yen traded around 300 to the dollar and the mark ran about 2.5 to the dollar. In CY-87, both were substantially higher against the dollar. Thus, it is unlikely that the yen and mark will return to their old dollar levels and a central tendency today is not likely to be present tomorrow. Thus, investment averaging, when buying currencies, does not have the same applicability as when buying debt instruments.

Changes in interest rate differentials between U.S. and Japanese bonds do not seem to be the key factor inducing investment, as indicated in Figure III-23.5. The most significant differential shown was in CY-84 and the largest purchases by the Japanese were in CY-85 and CY-86. At any given time, the Japanese seem to believe there are minimum interest rate differentials which make such investments worthwhile. These differentials are not constant but change, based on perceived risks involving foreign exchange and interest rate movements. There have been times when a rate advantage of less than 3 percent was sufficient to induce investments in long-term Treasury issues, and other times when a differential as large as 6 percent was not considered a sufficient attraction (as in the spring of 1987).

The Japanese are likely to continue to reassess (and probably downplay further) the importance they attach to interest rate advantages they receive on longer U.S. obligations versus similar Japanese instruments. (A history of the differentials is presented in Figure III-23.6.) Mark-to-market pricing on debt instruments and foreign exchange can result in embarrassingly large losses as price deterioration more than offsets interest rate advantages. The conviction that their outflow of funds to the United States will be large and regular and the money will not return home may also be questioned. The basic assumption of regular, substantial, one-way flows to the United States may not be true on an indefinite basis.

Surprisingly, the Japanese trade surplus with the United States has had a smaller effect on purchases of U.S. government securities than analysts seem to realize. From CY-74 through CY-84, Japanese exports to the United States and Japanese purchases of U.S. notes and bonds grew at about the same pace. However, both totals were fairly moderate in dollar terms. Then in CY-85, while Japanese exports moved sharply higher, their investments in U.S. notes and bonds literally exploded. The relationship is shown in Figure III-23.1.

The surge in investments was the result of a combination of factors which, to a large degree, were not directly related to trade. In addition to interest rate advantages, there was the internationalization of the yen, liberalization by both the United States and Japan in rules governing investments, a very high Japanese savings rate, long-term Japanese investors discovering the Japanese stock and real estate markets were highly priced, and a Japanese bond market that was not as well developed as that of the United States, particularly in the longer maturities. The growth of Japanese banks and securities houses in the United States, and the education of their Japanese clients about U.S. instruments and markets, also played a major role in the growth of Japanese interest in U.S. obligations.

Analysis indicates the key to future Japanese purchases of U.S. Treasury notes and bonds will not be the size of the Japanese trade surplus with the United States. Rather, it will depend on whether long-term Japanese investors continue to acquire sizable amounts of domestic funds, U.S. investments appear to be comparatively attractive, the Japanese government encourages an outflow of funds into such investments, and the Japanese investor believes the foreign exchange risks are tolerable.

Based on this analysis, a strong case can be made that when the United States reduces its trade deficit, which should be the case beginning in 1988, the adverse impact on Japanese purchases of U.S. government notes and bonds will be much smaller than common wisdom suggests. As a matter of fact, a smaller U.S. trade deficit could even induce greater Japanese interest because it would indicate the United States is coming to grips with one of its key problems.

The Japanese role in the U.S. money market area is quite different from its involvement in the bond market. While private Japanese investors prefer longer maturities, the Japanese government has a strong propensity to place funds in the shorter end of the market. Yet, beginning in 1988, the Japanese government is likely to add smaller amounts to their Treasury bill holdings as their trade surplus narrows, the need to acquire dollars in support operations moderates, and the Bank of Japan does some investment extension of its reserves.

From the United States' perspective, any reduction in Japanese holdings of Treasury bills would have little market impact. There is enough domestic interest in the U.S. bill market so that reduced Japanese interest (or any foreign interest for that matter) would hardly be noticed.

WEST GERMAN INVESTMENTS. The effect of dollar/mark fluctuations on West German purchases of U.S. notes and bonds does not appear to be especially strong. Figure III-23.2 shows three major changes in direction between the dollar and the mark since CY-74 with apparently little influence on such purchases. Part of the reason may be that officials, when investing reserves, are less concerned about foreign exchange losses than are private investors—although it would be a mistake to believe they are not concerned at all.

In addition, private West German investors have had a strong propensity to move intermediate and long-term funds abroad because of social, political, and cold war concerns, and because there are signs the post-World War II German economic miracle has ended. While a large part of these funds are aggressively invested, some apparently find their way into U.S. notes and bonds.

Interest rate differentials between the United States and West Germany do not seem to be an especially important factor determining West German purchases of Treasury coupon issues. Figure III-23.5 shows the yield differential favoring U.S. obligations started in CY-76 and reached a peak in CY-84. In CY-85 and CY-86, the differential narrowed. Yet, West German purchases of U.S. notes and bonds were fairly considerable in CY-85, and much more substantial in CY-86 and CY-87. Thus, the yield factor appears to be quite similar to the Japanese situation; yield differentials have to be sufficient to induce purchases, and what is viewed as sufficient changes over time.

In the trade area, the West Germans do not export a great deal of goods to the United States—compared with the Japanese—and, therefore, their trade surplus with the United States is of much smaller proportions. However, when West Germany's trade with other countries is considered, its trade surplus is very large and, therefore, so are its foreign exchange reserves. Thus, while there is little relationship between the United States/West German trade figures and the West Germans buying U.S. Treasury issues, there is a substantial relationship between their overall trade surplus and such purchases. The analysis suggests the foreign exchange rate relationships the West Germans have with their European Monetary System (EMS) partners may have more of an influence on the amount of U.S. Treasury securities purchased by the West Germans than does the dollar-mark relationship.

In the investment of funds, West German officials—in contrast to the Japanese—have been more aggressive in investing official reserves, and have shown considerable interest in buying Treasury notes and bonds. Therefore, a large part of the increase in holdings by the West Germans, as shown in Figure III-23.2, is made by the Bundesbank. The West Germans also tend to trade their investments in the secondary market. Thus, the Bundesbank is different from the Bank of Japan, not only because the former owns substantial notes and bonds, but also because it actively trades some of its investments.

Even if the Japanese continue to accumulate large amounts of reserves, they are not likely to try to match the Bundesbank in maturity extension or trading. That is so even though the Japanese have shown a growing interest in the intermediate Treasury market. A more conservative reserve management philosophy by the Japanese and a greater desire not to create additional friction between the countries are the reasons for the less aggressive approach.

In summary: as long as West Germany continues to run large trade surpluses with its trading partners, private investors want to move capital out of West Germany, and U.S. interest rates are viewed as relatively attractive, West German investors (both official and private) will continue to place funds in U.S. Treasury notes and bonds. As in the case of Japan, a reduction in the West German trade surplus with the United States is not likely to be the key factor determining West German investments in U.S. notes and bonds.

OTHER FOREIGN INVESTORS. In addition to Japan and Germany, there are other nations which have an important effect on future U.S. Treasury financing. In the case of Taiwan and Singapore, for example, a sharp reduction in their trade surpluses, especially with the United States, could strongly inhibit their purchases of U.S. Treasury obligations throughout the maturity spectrum. As for the Middle East OPEC countries, their sizable Treasury note and bond holdings are, to a considerable degree, a function of the price of oil and how it influences their balance of payments. A firming of oil prices is needed by these countries. Otherwise, the decline in their holdings of U.S. Treasury notes and bonds will continue in the years ahead. (See Figure III-21.6 and Figure III-21.7 for details.)

FACTORS THAT INFLUENCE FOREIGN INVESTORS. An analysis of foreign purchases of Treasury securities is far from complete without looking at broader factors which will influence foreigners when considering investments.

While the U.S. trade deficit appears to have peaked in CY-87, it will remain substantial for years to come, and the funds foreigners accumulate must be invested somewhere. Since the United States has by far the broadest money and capital markets in the world, a comparatively minimum amount of regulation, and a stable social and political structure, a sizable portion of these funds can be expected to be invested in the United States in some form. In addition, there are political inducements for foreigners with huge trade surpluses to keep or to recycle their funds in the United States. Fears of trade barriers and embargoes are at the top of their list of concerns.

Purchases of U.S. obligations can also be influenced by the penetration of foreign institutions in U.S. markets. For example, Japanese brokerage and dealer firms have become an integral part of the U.S. Treasury market. Of the five dealers owned by the Japanese, four are classified by the Federal Reserve as reporting dealers: Aubrey G. Lanston & Co., Daiwa Securities America Inc., The Nikko Securities Co. International, Inc., and Nomura Securities International Inc. The other seeking such classification—Yamaichi International—seems to have sufficient activity and capital and could well receive the reporting designation in 1988. In addition, in early 1988, there were two American-owned primary dealers negotiating to sell their firms to Japanese institutions, subject to U.S. regulatory approval.

In the case of four of the Japanese-owned dealers, much of their business comes from Japan, and the fifth (Aubrey G. Lanston & Co.) will undoubtedly strive for a greater share of Japanese business. As these Japanese-owned firms play a growing role in the U.S. government market, the inflow of funds from Japan should increase.

Yet there are some factors which could inhibit foreign purchases of Treasury issues. If inflation in the United States were to rise substantially, and real interest rates were to decline or turn negative, this would limit foreign investment, especially if other countries with growing money and capital markets offer higher real rates of interest and a more optimistic outlook for their currencies. If nominal interest rates in the United States should trend higher (and bond prices, therefore, lower), this could also inhibit purchases, especially by investors trying to maximize total rate of return.

A look at the recent past can help highlight some of these concerns. From mid-CY-84 to early CY-85, a number of key factors moved in favor of foreign holders buying Treasury obligations. The dollar improved, the Treasury note and bond market rallied, and U.S. interest rates were especially attractive from both a real and nominal standpoint. From early CY-85 to early CY-86, while the dollar deteriorated (from levels which many viewed as excessively high from a trade perspective), the debt markets improved considerably and real and nominal interest rates were still relatively attractive.

From early CY-86 to early CY-87, however, the investment picture turned noticeably less favorable. The dollar continued its deterioration, and in late CY-86 and early CY-87, its fluctuations were not always orderly. Greater concern developed as to whether the dollar decline could be contained. The debt market improved early in the period, but despite several tries, long bonds could not move down to the 7 percent level. The upside risk seemed greater than the downside rate potential.

From the spring of 1987 to early 1988, private foreign investors found the U.S. debt markets unattractive due to increased concerns regarding the U.S. trade picture, the dollar, the economic and budget outlook, and inflation. The overwhelming majority of foreign investments in the U.S. debt markets were from foreign governments that had substantial dollars to invest. Interest rate differentials favoring the United States had little pulling power.

Looking ahead, the United States will have to come to grips with its economic problems in order to entice private foreign investors back to the U.S. debt market. Of particular importance are reductions in the budget and trade deficits, and perhaps most important of all, a better performance by the dollar. No one wants to invest in a depreciating asset.

23. Does it make sense for a nation, such as Japan, with huge official dollar reserves, to invest mainly in U.S. Treasury bills?

There is no reason for the Bank of Japan (BOJ) to hold a large amount of bills (maturities of one year or less). As a matter of fact, there is no reason for the BOJ to hold any bills at all. Officially reported Japanese reserves are huge (over $75 billion at the end of 1987), and the country is running very large current account surpluses year after year. This means no liquidity concerns. Moreover, investing very short-term causes an undue amount of portfolio reinvestment.

A far better approach for a country such as Japan is to use a planned program for investing in intermediate-term U.S. obligations. The program suggested here is to have an investor such as the BOJ invest in all outstanding 2-, 3-, 4-, and 5-year Treasury issues. There are 72 maturities involved—twenty-four 2-year issues, twelve 3-year obligations, sixteen 4-year issues, and twenty 5-year obligations. Figure III-23.8 shows the schedule of maturities for these 72 issues.

The 2-year note is the shortest maturity in the portfolio. A major advantage of this issue is that it typically yields between one-half percent and 1 percent more than 1-year bills, and between 1 percent and 1½ percent more than 3-month bills. Of course, if the Japanese were to aggressively buy the 2-year obligation and gradually eliminate all its bill holdings, the yield spreads would shrink considerably.

Another important attraction of the 2-year note is that since it is offered at the end of each month, there is only one month between maturities. No other coupon issue is offered, or matures, that frequently. In addition, the issue runs about $9 billion, which means an active and liquid market.

The next maturity in the portfolio would be the 3-year note. It is auctioned, and matures four times a year in the middle of each quarter. The size of a typical auction is about $9 billion, which makes it similar in magnitude and in advantages to the 2-year note. The 3-year obligation typically yields about one-quarter percent more than the rate on the 2-year note.

The 4-year note would be included in the portfolio. It is offered and comes due at the end of the last month of each quarter. The auctions are typically not as large as the 2- and 3-year issues, running about $7 billion, but this is still a good size and offers considerable liquidity. The

FIGURE III-23.1 Dollar Versus Yen, Japanese Exports to United States, and Japanese Purchases of U.S. Treasury Notes and Bonds

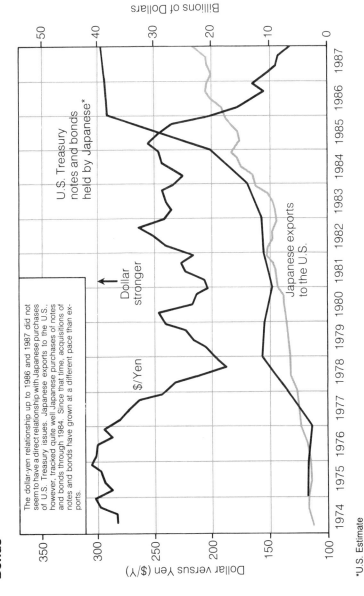

The dollar-yen relationship up to 1986 and 1987 did not seem to have a direct relationship with Japanese purchases of U.S. Treasury issues. Japanese exports to the U.S., however, tracked quite well Japanese purchases of notes and bonds through 1984. Since that time, acquisitions of notes and bonds have grown at a different pace than exports.

Billions of Dollars

U.S. Treasury notes and bonds held by Japanese*

Dollar stronger

$/Yen

Japanese exports to the U.S.

Dollar versus Yen ($/¥)

*U.S. Estimate

Sources: *Treasury Bulletin, Federal Reserve Bulletin, Survey of Current Business*

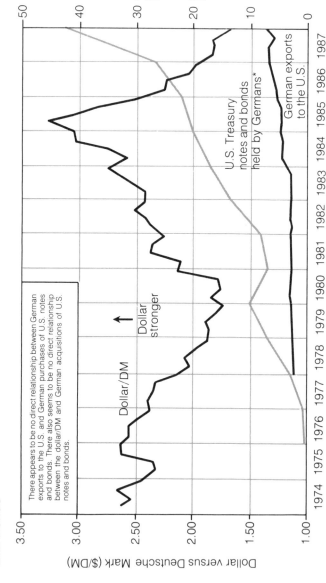

FIGURE III-23.2 Dollar Versus Deutsche Mark, German Exports to United States, and German Purchases of U.S. Treasury Notes and Bonds

Billions of Dollars

Dollar versus Deutsche Mark ($/DM)

There appears to be no direct relationship between German exports to the U.S. and German purchases of U.S. notes and bonds. There also seems to be no direct relationship between the dollar/DM and German acquisitions of U.S. notes and bonds.

Dollar stronger

Dollar/DM

U.S. Treasury notes and bonds held by Germans*

German exports to the U.S.

*U.S. Estimate

Sources: *Treasury Bulletin, Federal Reserve Bulletin, Survey of Current Business*

132

FIGURE III-23.3 Deutsche Mark (DM) and Yen Versus the Dollar

	1974		1975		1976		1977		1978		1979		1980	
	DM	Yen	DM	Yen	DM	Yen	DM	Yen	DM	Yen	DM	Yen	DM	Yen
Mar	2.6170	282.06	2.3191	287.93	2.5595	300.52	2.3917	280.21	2.0333	231.76	1.8603	206.31	1.8505	248.47
Jun	2.5251	282.97	2.3405	293.45	2.5775	299.19	2.3555	272.84	2.0840	213.93	1.8838	218.58	1.7673	217.89
Sep	2.6610	299.05	2.6184	299.90	2.4895	287.36	2.3237	266.77	1.9694	189.91	1.7935	222.41	1.7895	214.39
Dec	2.4500	300.41	2.6216	305.67	2.3829	294.70	2.1506	241.02	1.8791	195.43	1.7340	240.31	2.1387	205.70

	1981		1982		1983		1984		1985		1986		1987	
	DM	Yen	DM	Yen	DM	Yen	DM	Yen	DM	Yen	DM	Yen	DM	Yen
Mar	2.1054	208.78	2.3800	241.23	2.4110	238.25	2.5973	225.27	3.2982	257.92	2.2752	178.69	1.8355	151.43
Jun	2.3779	224.11	2.4292	251.20	2.5490	240.03	2.7397	233.57	3.0636	248.84	2.2337	167.54	1.8189	144.55
Sep	2.3522	229.48	2.5055	263.29	2.6679	242.35	3.0314	245.46	2.8381	236.53	2.0415	154.73	1.8134	143.29
Dec	2.2579	218.95	2.4193	241.94	2.7500	234.46	3.1044	247.96	2.5122	202.79	1.9880	162.05	1.6337p	128.70p

From late 1979 to early 1985, the Deutsche mark (DM) substantially underperformed against the yen. Since that time, the DM has held its own versus the yen. However, both currencies during the 13 years substantially improved against the dollar.

Source: Federal Reserve Bulletin

FIGURE III-23.4 German and Japanese Exports to the United States (Billions of Dollars)

	1974		1975		1976		1977		1978		1979		1980	
	Germany	Japan	Germany	Japan	Germany	Japan	Germany	Japan	Germany	Japan	Germany	Japan	Germany	Japan
1Q	N.A.	2.6	N.A.	3.2	N.A.	3.6	N.A.	4.2	2.4	5.8	2.4	6.3	3.1	7.4
2Q	N.A.	3.0	N.A.	2.6	N.A.	3.8	N.A.	4.6	2.4	6.2	2.8	6.5	3.0	7.7
3Q	N.A.	3.3	N.A.	2.6	N.A.	4.0	N.A.	5.0	2.5	6.3	2.8	6.5	2.9	7.8
4Q	N.A.	3.5	N.A.	2.9	N.A.	4.2	N.A.	5.1	2.6	6.2	2.9	7.0	2.7	8.2

	1981		1982		1983		1984		1985		1986		1987	
	Germany	Japan	Germany	Japan	Germany	Japan	Germany	Japan	Germany	Japan	Germany	Japan	Germany	Japan
1Q	2.7	8.7	2.9	10.1	3.0	9.3	4.4	12.9	4.7	15.3	5.7	18.1	6.6	20.0
2Q	2.8	9.1	3.1	9.4	3.1	9.6	4.2	15.1	4.7	15.8	6.0	20.1	6.8	20.8
3Q	2.8	9.5	3.0	9.5	3.1	10.2	4.1	15.9	4.6	16.6	6.2	21.3	6.2	21.4
4Q	3.1	10.3	2.9	8.7	3.5	12.2	4.8	16.3	5.5	17.9	6.6	21.1	7.3p	23.2p

From 1983 through 1987, Japanese exports to the United States grew very rapidly, much more than in the case of the Germans. The latter's exports to the United States were quite modest during the 13-year period studied.

Source: *Survey of Current Business*

134

FIGURE III-23.5 Important Interest Rate Relationships—U.S. Treasury Bonds Compared with Japanese and German Treasury Bonds (Foreign Yields Higher Plotted as a Plus)

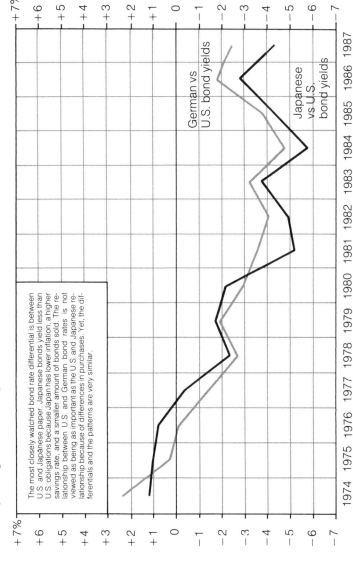

The most closely watched bond rate differential is between U.S. and Japanese paper. Japanese bonds yield less than U.S. obligations because Japan has lower inflation, a higher savings rate, and a smaller amount of bonds sold. The relationship between U.S. and German bond rates is not viewed as being as important as the U.S. and Japanese relationship because of differences in purchases. Yet, the differentials and the patterns are very similar.

German vs
U.S. bond yields

Japanese
vs U.S.
bond yields

Sources: International Financial Statistics, International Monetary Fund

135

FIGURE III-23.6 Treasury Bill and Bond Yields—United States Compared with Other Countries

Treasury Bill Yields (Average During Period)

	1974	1975	1976	1977	1978	1979	1980	1981	1982	1983	1984	1985	1986	1987p
U.S.	7.87	5.82	4.99	5.27	7.22	10.04	11.62	14.08	10.72	8.62	9.57	7.49	5.97	5.82
Germany	—	5.40	4.93	4.00	4.00	7.87	7.41	9.77	6.16	5.99	5.25	4.20	3.90	3.28
		(−.42)	(−.06)	(−1.27)	(−3.22)	(−2.17)	(−4.21)	(−4.31)	(−4.56)	(−2.63)	(−4.32)	(−3.29)	(−2.07)	(−2.54)
Switzerland	—	—	—	—	—	—	5.15	7.82	3.87	3.04	3.58	4.15	3.54	3.18
							(−6.47)	(−6.26)	(−6.85)	(−5.58)	(−5.99)	(−3.34)	(−2.43)	(−2.64)
U.K.	11.37	10.18	11.12	7.68	8.51	12.98	15.11	13.03	11.47	9.59	9.30	11.56	10.37	9.24
	(+3.50)	(+4.36)	(+6.13)	(+2.41)	(+1.29)	(+2.94)	(+3.49)	(−1.05)	(+.75)	(+.97)	(−.27)	(+4.07)	(+4.40)	(+3.42)

Government Bond Yields (Average During Period)

	1974	1975	1976	1977	1978	1979	1980	1981	1982	1983	1984	1985	1986	1987p
U.S.	8.06	8.19	7.87	7.67	8.49	9.33	11.39	13.91	13.00	11.11	12.52	10.62	7.68	8.38
Japan	9.26	9.20	8.72	7.33	6.09	7.69	9.22	8.66	8.06	7.42	6.81	6.34	4.94	4.20
	(+1.20)	(+1.01)	(+.85)	(−.34)	(−2.40)	(−1.64)	(−2.17)	(−5.25)	(−4.94)	(−3.69)	(−5.71)	(−4.28)	(−2.74)	(−4.18)
Germany	10.40	8.50	7.80	6.20	5.80	7.40	8.50	10.38	8.95	7.89	7.78	6.87	5.92	5.80
	(+2.34)	(+.31)	(−.07)	(−1.47)	(−2.69)	(−1.93)	(−2.89)	(−3.53)	(−4.05)	(−3.22)	(−4.74)	(−3.75)	(−1.76)	(−2.58)
U.K.	14.77	14.39	14.43	12.73	12.47	12.99	13.79	19.74	12.88	10.81	10.69	10.62	9.87	9.44
	(+6.71)	(+6.20)	(+6.56)	(+5.06)	(+3.98)	(+3.66)	(+2.40)	(+.83)	(−.12)	(−.30)	(−1.83)	(—)	(+2.19)	(+1.06)

U.S. interest rates during the period tended to be higher than rate levels in Germany, Japan, and Switzerland. The U.K., however, generally had higher interest rates than the U.S. The lower interest rate countries tended to have the stronger currencies.

Source: International Financial Statistics, International Monetary Fund

FIGURE III-23.7 Japanese Foreign Debt Market Investments by Country (Purchases Minus Sales)

Year	U.S		Euro-Market		U.K.		Canada		Australia		Other		Total
1983	+$ 4.7b	47.0%	+$ 1.9b	19.4%	+$ .8	7.8%	+$1.5b	14.8%	+$ .5b	5.3%	+$ .6b	5.8%	+$10.0b
1984	+ 10.0	51.6	+ 4.3	22.4	+ 1.1	5.6	+ 1.7	8.7	+ 1.1	5.5	+ 1.2	6.2	+ 19.3
1985	+ 28.3	67.5	+ 8.0	19.0	+ 2.1	4.9	+ 1.7	4.2	+ .7	1.8	+ 1.1	2.6	+ 41.9
1986	+ 37.1	56.9	+ 17.1	26.1	+ 4.2	6.5	+ 4.8	7.4	+ .2	0.3	+ 1.8	2.7	+ 65.3
1987	+ 39.6	52.8	+ 22.0	29.4	+ 4.6	6.1	+ 1.5	2.0	+ 2.0	2.6	+ 5.3	7.1	+ 75.1

In 1986-87, while the Japanese purchased a huge amount of U.S. securities, there was an attempt to diversify investments. The Euro-market picked up a growing proportion.

Source: *Nomura Research Institute* (Estimates Based on Ministry of Finance and Japan Securities Dealer Association Data)

yield is typically one-eighth percent to one-quarter percent more than on a 3-year offering.

The final maturity in the portfolio would be the 5-year notes. These obligations which are auctioned quarterly are actually offered about 5 years and 2 months before maturity. They mature in the middle of each quarter. Thus, while the 2- and 4-year issues mature at the end of a month, the 3- and 5-year obligations mature in the middle of a month. The amount sold is similar to the 4-year (about $7 billion), and typically yields about one-eighth percent to one-quarter percent more than a 4-year note.

With investments spread over 72 different issues, 1 percent to 2 percent of the portfolio should probably be held in each obligation. The exact amount to be acquired in an issue would depend upon such factors as the size of the country's reserves and its expected changes, yield curve consideration, and liquidity needs.

To institute this portfolio approach, the central bank would invest in every new 2-, 3-, 4-, and 5-year issue. Also, over a fairly substantial period, maybe as much as one year, outstanding issues would be bought to fill in the open maturities. Once the portfolio is established, most of the acquisitions would be made in auctions, with the Federal Reserve handling the bids and holding the issues in custody accounts. Because of the large amounts involved, the purchases at auction would probably be in the form of "add ons," that is, an amount above the size of the auction announced by the Treasury.

This portfolio approach has advantages for an investor such as the BOJ, and for the Federal Reserve and Treasury as well. The BOJ would be able to substantially increase its rate of return and reduce investment frequency without causing any meaningful liquidity or market risk problems. Moreover, the approach should be viewed favorably by the Federal Reserve and Treasury since it would not create undue fluctuations in the government market, would cause little in the way of distortions in the yield curve, can be accomplished with minimum operations in the secondary market, and would raise a large amount of money for the United States outside the short-term market.

FIGURE III-23.8 Hypothetical Central Bank Portfolio of 2-, 3-, 4-, and 5-Year Maturities (as of 12/31/87)

Maturity	Original	Maturity	Original	Maturity	Original
1/31/88	2 years	1/31/89	2 years	2/15/90	3 years
2/15/88	3 years	2/15/89	3 years	2/15/90	5 years
2/15/88	5 years	2/15/89	5 years	3/31/90	4 years
2/28/88	2 years	2/28/89	2 years	5/15/90	3 years
3/31/88	2 years	3/31/89	2 years	5/15/90	5 years
3/31/88	4 years	3/31/89	4 years	6/30/90	4 years
4/30/88	2 years	4/30/89	2 years	8/15/90	3 years
5/15/88	3 years	5/15/89	3 years	8/15/90	5 years
5/15/88	5 years	5/15/89	5 years	9/30/90	4 years
5/31/88	2 years	5/31/89	2 years	11/15/90	3 years
6/30/88	2 years	6/30/89	2 years	11/15/90	5 years
6/30/88	4 years	6/30/89	4 years	11/15/90	4 years
7/31/88	2 years	7/31/89	2 years	2/15/91	5 years
8/15/88	3 years	8/15/89	3 years	3/31/91	4 years
8/15/88	5 years	8/15/89	5 years	5/15/91	5 years
8/31/88	2 years	8/31/89	2 years	6/30/91	4 years
9/30/88	2 years	9/30/89	2 years	8/15/91	5 years
9/30/88	4 years	9/30/89	4 years	9/30/91	4 years
10/31/88	2 years	10/31/89	2 years	11/15/91	5 years
11/15/88	3 years	11/15/89	3 years	12/31/91	4 years
11/15/88	5 years	11/15/89	5 years	2/15/92	5 years
11/30/88	2 years	11/30/89	2 years	5/15/92	5 years
12/31/88	2 years	12/31/89	2 years	8/15/92	5 years
12/31/88	4 years	12/31/89	4 years	11/15/92	5 years

24. Whatever happened to the argument that private borrowers would be crowded out by Treasury borrowings?

"Crowding out" is supposed to occur when Treasury borrowing needs are so great that the ability of some private borrowers to raise money in the domestic capital markets are severely limited. This crowding out never really materialized, which is the good news; the reasons why constitute the bad news.

Budget deficits were very large from FY-84 through FY-87, but during the same period, the private sector of the economy was far from robust. In particular, plant and equipment expenditures surged in CY-83 and CY-84, creating excess capacity in the economy which sharply reduced the justification for greater spending from CY-85 through CY-87. Moreover, economic activity in general remained disappointing beginning in mid-1984, with the advance a lackluster 3 percent real growth through the end of CY-87. Thus, the private sector was not strong enough to create a crowding out problem.

In addition, a substantial portion of the United States' budget was financed from abroad. Crowding out assumes, to a large degree, that the deficit is financed domestically and there is a relatively fixed amount of funds available for all domestic needs. Thus, the more the Treasury borrows, the less there is available for the private sector. The reasoning proved to be misleading because of the large inflow of foreign funds from CY-84 through much of CY-87, not only to the public sector, but to the private as well.

Finally, in mid-1984, the Federal Reserve moved toward a more accommodative monetary policy. The large budget deficit did not dissuade the monetary authorities in any noticeable way from easing policy. This factor, along with further moves toward deregulation, reduced any financial strains which might result from a lack of available funds.

This analysis does not mean to suggest crowding out could not occur in the future. The demand for funds by the business sector will not always be modest, the Treasury cannot always expect to have such a large portion of its deficit financed from abroad, and monetary policy will not always be highly accommodative. The considerable improvement in the FY-87 budget, where the deficit declined about $71 billion, will be impossible to sustain in the years ahead. The only area where an underlying change would be difficult to reverse is deregulation. The greater the deregulation, the less severe a crowding-out problem is likely to be.

In terms of timing, crowding out does not appear imminent. The budget deficit is not likely to return to the $221 billion level of FY-86, at least in this decade; a surge in plant and equipment spending financed by debt obligations does not seem to be in the offing; foreign investment in U.S. government issues is still likely to grow (although not as much as in recent years); and the newer members of the Board of Governors of the Federal Reserve seem to have an accommodative leaning. Thus, if some crowding out does occur, it will not be during the remainder of the 1980s. A positive aspect of this analysis is it gives government officials more time and flexibility to reduce the deficit. Of course, it takes several years of sustained effort to reduce the deficit by a significant amount.

25. Should individual investors play a much larger role in financing the deficit?

An obvious shortcoming of current financing methods is the Treasury's inability to attract large amounts of funds from domestic individual savers.

A very large portion of the $150 billion deficit in FY-87 was financed from abroad or by domestic institutional investors. Only a negligible portion of the debt increase was financed by individuals, part of the reason being the sharp drop in interest rates from mid-1984 through CY-86 caused them to look elsewhere to invest their funds. The lack of interest is unfortunate, since foreign investors are not a reliable source of funds, and domestic institutional investors show varying degrees of interest depending upon availability of funds, alternative uses, and rate attractiveness. Under these circumstances, a large and sustained program to sell government securities to individuals would make a great deal of sense.

Possibly standing in the way of such a program is that some depository institutions have argued against the government directly tapping large amounts of funds from individuals. These institutions view themselves as indispensable intermediaries between the individual's money and how the funds are invested in the money and capital markets. In the past it was argued they had a competitive disadvantage compared with the government; they had to contend with large reserve requirements, Regulation Q limitations, and other restrictions which limited their ability to pay attractive and competitive rates, especially during periods of tight money or disintermediation.

However, times have changed.

With so much deregulation having taken place, and with reserve requirements and other restrictions having been reduced, this argument has lost much of its strength. Moreover, the size of the budget deficit is so large and the reliance on foreign financing so great, the need to attract domestic individual savings is much more compelling.

To regularly borrow money directly from individuals, the government must tap into savings on a continuing basis. (Money market funds and deposit accounts already do this to some degree.) It is insufficient to draw upon individual funds only when interest rates are temporarily attractive versus competing investments. Thus, opportunities must exist for individuals to buy government securities easily, inexpensively, with an attractive rate of return, and with little or no market risk. These necessary considerations argue for a new nonmarketable government savings bond program.

As a starting point, new nonmarketable obligations could be offered to individuals which would enable them to invest funds regularly in retirement-type accounts such as IRAs, 401(k)s, or Keoghs. The obligations could have a 10-year maturity with the yield based on a floating rate, such as the average daily yield on the 10-year marketable issues as computed by the Treasury on a constant maturity basis. Since the Federal Reserve publishes daily Treasury yields, and since the Treasury has available the daily rates on 10-year maturities on a constant maturity basis, this approach seems feasible. An important consideration is to make sure individuals understand how the yields are determined. Book entry, rather than physical delivery of the securities, would be used.

There are advantages to this program from the individual's viewpoint: the minimum investment can be quite small, and there is an attractive rate of return, accompanied by complete safety and no market risk. Investment timing would be of minimum importance because of the way the return is computed, and the individual would not have to be very knowledgeable about economics or investments.

From the Treasury's viewpoint, it would be able to tap a major source of funds at going market rates. Yet, since this program would be more expensive for the Treasury to operate than the usual means of financing, it is important for it to become a significant method of raising money. Although depository institutions would experience some siphoning of funds, the damage should be minimal since a 10-year maturity is longer than these institutions usually try to attract. Finally, in terms of the overall state of the economy, such an approach would induce a savings rate higher than the abysmal levels at which it has been running, and would help finance the deficit in a noninflationary manner.

26. Should the Treasury consider offering new maturities in its marketable debt obligations?

The Treasury should offer a new 18-month note and reinstate the 20-year bond. An 18-month maturity is viewed by many investors as still being in the money market area, and except for some occasional agency offerings, there are few maturities against which such an issue would compete. Since there is enough space between the 1-year bill and the 2-year note, there would be no maturity crowding. The sharp upslope to the yield curve which traditionally exists between the 1- and 2-year maturities should give an 18-month issue enough of a yield advantage over the 1-year to make it attractive. Perhaps the most important point is that it fills a significant maturity void.

The financing pattern for the 18-month note could be the same as for the 1-year bill—an auction every four weeks offered at a point midway between the 1-year bill auctions. That would add 13 auctions annually. While it would make the financing schedule more crowded, once the market becomes accustomed to the routine, the additional financings hardly would be noticed. For the first 18 auctions, there would be no offsetting maturities. Thus, even if issues are as small as $5 billion, $90 billion would be raised in 18 months.

The Treasury did away with the 20-year maturity offering primarily because it appeared to be costly. Typically, it not only yielded substantially more than the 10-year maturity, but also more than the 30-year issue. It was the highest yielding obligation on the curve. However, after the Treasury stopped issuing the 20-year bond, market results seemed to indicate it was not only because the 20-year bond yield was high, but rather the 30-year rate was low. For a considerable period after the cancellation of the 20-year offering, the 30-year issue actually traded at a lower yield than the 10-year obligation.

There are other arguments which support the use of a 20-year maturity. The 10-to-30-year gap which currently exists between Treasury maturities does not offer investors a full complement of choices, especially for those investing pension or retirement funds. It is a maturity which is likely to have considerable appeal to the Japanese; when it was discontinued they were just starting to show a much greater appetite for longer maturities. The 20-year issue is also a method of raising a meaningful amount of money over a considerable number of years. If there is some concern about the issue having too high a yield versus other issues on the curve, the Treasury could offer a 20-year maturity semiannually. If each offering were about the same size as the 30-year issues (about $9 billion), it would still raise $18 billion annually—a not inconsequential amount of money. Similar to the 30-year maturity, there probably should be one reopening to improve tradeability.

The combination of the 18-month note and the 20-year bond, if started simultaneously, would probably raise $110 billion to $120 billion of net new money in the first 18 months. Thereafter, while the amount raised would drop sharply (18-month issues would be maturing), it would not be inconsequential. If such offerings were used, it would require readjusting the other Treasury offerings to smaller amounts—which is not all that bad from a potential "market-indigestion" viewpoint.

27. Should bill financing as a portion of the total financing be expanded?

The primary case for selling a larger portion of debt in bills is to limit interest costs. Traditionally, there is an upslope to the yield curve with bills costing the Treasury less than notes and bonds. Another argument favoring additional bills is the bill market has a greater absorptive capacity than either the note or bond areas. Since bill offerings are much more frequent, large amounts of money can be raised by moderate additions to each auction. Excessive amounts of note and bond offerings might crowd out other issuers, but this is not likely to happen with bills. Shorter maturities also attract a more substantial and sustained investor demand than the longer issues.

Yet, when debt management is viewed from a broader perspective, note and bond offerings should not be reduced in importance. They spread maturities further into the future. Since the deficit is not likely to decline appreciably in coming years, large amounts of securities will need to be offered to raise new money and to refund maturing issues (see Question 19). Under these circumstances, too much of a reliance on bills, with their short-term maturities, could put a burden on this sector of the market.

Finally, the conservative approach to financing suggests if there are long-term needs, financing should be with long-term sources. Few would question the applicability of this approach in the private sector where financial difficulty and bankruptcy may lurk. Governments do not experience the same risks, because of their ability to tax. But poor financial management can lead to market indigestion, higher interest costs, and an economy which has its performance dampened—a substantial price to pay for poor debt management.

28. How can the Treasury improve the steadiness of its cash flow?

To determine whether improvements are needed in cash flow, it is necessary to look at the types of liquid balances the Treasury maintains, and what causes these accounts to fluctuate.

The Treasury keeps its funds in two types of accounts—one at commercial banks in the form of tax and loan accounts, and the other at Federal Reserve Banks. (Figures III-28.4 through III-28.6 show the balances.) The accounts at commercial banks receive most of the Treasury's tax receipts. Thus, they are typically larger than those at the Federal Reserve and tend to fluctuate more sharply. Yet, the fluctuations tend to follow a rather predictable pattern during the year.

When the Treasury spends money, checks are typically drawn on its account at the Federal Reserve. For this account to have sufficient funds, money is transferred (i.e., ''called'') from the Treasury's balances at the commercial banks. The size of the Treasury's balance at the Federal Reserve also is affected by Treasury borrowings and debt repayment.

For example, if the total cash balance is a very modest $5 billion, about $2 billion typically would be at the commercial banks and the remainder would be at the Federal Reserve. If the total balance moves to about $30 billion, almost the entire increase would typically take place at the commercial banks. The goal is to keep the balance at the Federal Reserve relatively stable (about $3 billion to $4 billion in CY-87) because changes in this balance add or drain reserves from the banking system.

Once the Treasury cash balance moves above $30 billion, almost the entire increase takes place at the Federal Reserve. This is because commercial banks cannot take on any more funds due to a shortage of collateral.

At first glance, very large cash balances might seem favorable from the Treasury's perspective. Not so.

Large balances mean borrowings could have been less, and interest costs could have been smaller. Large balances also create reserve management problems for the Federal Reserve. When the balance at the Federal Reserve rises sharply, it drains reserves from the banking system, which the Federal Reserve then needs to offset with open market operations. Such cash balance and reserve moves can create undue volatility in short-term interest rates (especially Federal funds) and also can send confusing signals to investors concerning Federal Reserve intentions.

Typically, there are a few times during the year when the Treasury's cash balance falls to levels which are difficult to manage because they are too low. This often happens when there is a debt ceiling problem and the Treasury cannot borrow (which was the case in the latter part of July 1987). A total balance of about $5 billion is roughly the minimum amount the Treasury can maintain and still easily meet daily outflows. If the total balance moves below that level, the portion held at the Federal Reserve will fall, which creates a cash squeeze and pushes reserves into the banking system, which need to be offset.

Probably the most disturbing combination of circumstances is when the cash balance is unduly low, the Treasury has reached its debt ceiling, and Congress drags its feet on raising the ceiling. The Treasury plays no part in creating the problem, but must suffer the consequences.

To understand why there is such variability in the cash balance, consider the following.

RECEIPTS.

1. Withheld individual taxes are the largest single revenue component and tend to be spread evenly over the year. Yet, monthly Treasury receipts as a whole tend to fluctuate substantially because other receipts categories experience large monthly variations.
2. Nonwithheld individual income taxes and corporate income taxes are concentrated during several months of the year. (See Figure III-28.1.) Payments for nonwithheld taxes occur primarily in January, April, June, and September, while the largest payments by corporations take place in March, April, June, September, and December. In months where these two types of payments coincide (April, June, and September), the Treasury's cash inflows are very large. There also is a large cash balance in late January because the Treasury receives substantial mid-month estimated individual tax payments.
3. Income tax refunds are a form of negative tax receipts. They are very large in March, April, and May, and quite small in all other months. The situation can create a cash lowpoint in the first half of March. However, in April and May it poses no problem because of all the months, April experiences the largest inflow of tax receipts.
4. The timing of tax inflows within a month depends upon the type of tax. Withheld individual taxes are spread out, while nonwithheld individual taxes and corporate income taxes are due at mid-month.

FIGURE III-28.1 Current System—Nonwithheld Income Tax Payment Pattern

Month	Type	Date Due
Jan	Estimated individual income tax payment	15th
Feb	—	—
Mar	Corporate income tax makeup payment for previous year	15th
Apr	Estimated individual income tax payment	15th
	Individual final payment for previous year	15th
	Estimated corporate income tax payment	15th
May	—	—
Jun	Estimated individual income tax payment	15th
	Estimated corporate income tax payment	15th
Jul	—	—
Aug	—	—
Sep	Estimated individual income tax payment	15th
	Estimated corporate income tax payment	15th
Oct	—	—
Nov	—	—
Dec	Estimated corporate income tax payment	15th

Summary

Corporate	Individual	Largest Spreads Between Major Payments	
Mar 15	Jan 15	Jan 15	
Apr 15	Apr 15	Mar 15	—Two Months
Jun 15	Jun 15		
Sep 15	Sep 15	Apr 15	
Dec 15		Jun 15	—Two Months
		Jun 15	
		Sep 15	—Three Months
		Sep 15	
		Dec 15	—Three Months

There is a heavy concentration of tax payments between mid-March and mid-June. All of the above payments take place at mid-month.

FIGURE III-28.2 Proposed System—Nonwithheld Income Tax Payment Pattern

Month	Type of Payment	Business Day of Month When Due
Jan	Estimated individual income tax	Third
Feb	First corporate income tax makeup for previous year	First
Mar	Estimated corporate income tax	First
Apr	Estimated individual income tax	First
May	Final individual income tax for previous year	First
Jun	Estimated corporate income tax	First
Jul	Estimated individual income tax	First
Aug	Final corporate income tax makeup for previous year	First
Sep	Estimated corporate income tax	First
Oct	Estimated individual income tax	First
Nov	—	—
Dec	Estimated corporate income tax	First

Summary		
Corporate	Individual	Largest Spreads Between Major Payments
Feb 1	Jan 3	Oct 1
Mar 1	Apr 1	Dec 1 —Two Months
Jun 1	May 1	
Aug 1	Jul 1	
Sep 1	Oct 1	
Dec 1		

The tax payments are spread throughout the year. All nonwithheld payments are made at the beginning of a month.

FIGURE III-28.3 Approximate Monthly Receipts/Expenditures if the FY-87 Budget Were in Balance* (Billions of Dollars)

	Receipts	Expenditures	Deficit
Oct '86	65	77	− 12
Nov	63	75	− 12
Dec	75	73	+ 2
Quarter	203	215	− 22
Jan '87	85	75	+ 10
Feb	63	73	− 10
Mar	67	75	− 8
Quarter	215	223	− 8
Apr	104	76	+ 28
May	61	78	− 17
Jun	100	78	+ 21
Quarter	261	229	+ 32
Jul	69	77	− 8
Aug	67	79	− 12
Sep	94	76	+ 18
Quarter	230	232	− 2
FY-87 Hypothetical	909	909	—0—
FY-87 Actual	854	1004	− 150

*The $908 billion receipts and outlay level was determined by splitting the difference between actual receipts and outlays for FY-87 (excluding one-time receipts estimated at $40 billion).

Thus, in the six months of the year when withheld taxes dominate receipts (February, May, July, August, October, and November), the tax inflows are spread during the month. In January, March, April, June, September, and December, however, there is a receipts bulge right after mid-month. (March is included in the latter grouping because there is a large mid-month corporate income tax payment representing tax obligations for the previous year.) Figure III-28.1 summarizes these details.

EXPENDITURES.

1. Spending is spread out by months on a relatively even basis. Yet there are a few months where outlays are often larger than usual. For example, October—the first month of the fiscal year—often shows a large advance. Also, Commodity Credit Corp. (CCC) payments are substantial and are usually heaviest in the fall and winter months.
2. Within a typical month, the expenditure pattern is not smooth. The largest outlays are usually made in the first week, which incidentally is typical for individuals and businesses in the private sector. A considera-

ble amount of government outlays at the beginning of the month are related to social security and retirement payments.

3. There is generally an expenditure increase at month-end caused by large interest payments. There also are very large Treasury interest outlays four times a year—February 15, May 15, August 15, and November 15; these are associated with the four major Treasury refunding dates.

EXPENDITURES AND RECEIPTS—COMBINED IMPACT.

1. As demonstrated, the deficit is not spread evenly over the course of the year; the fluctuations result primarily from receipts. The worst period for the budget is when there is an absence of both corporate and nonwithheld individual taxes; this usually occurs during the October–December period. The most favorable time of the year occurs when these two payments are large, such as in the April–June quarter. If a balanced budget condition exists, there would be a huge surplus from April through June, with deficits in the other three quarters. Figure III-28.3 shows what the numbers might have looked like in FY-87 if there were no deficit.

2. Since expenditures are greater early in any given month, while receipts are either spread out or at their heaviest after mid-month, the cash balance typically drops sharply early in the period and then flattens or rises sharply in the second half of the month.

3. If the current receipts-and-outlay pattern persists, swings in the budget and cash balance will become larger, not only between quarters and months, but also within months. For example, in a month such as April, with a balanced-budget, the deficit in the first half of the month could be about $30 billion and the surplus in the second half about twice that amount. As both receipts and outlays grow, so will the size of these intra-monthly swings.

CASH FLOW SUGGESTIONS. The cash balance fluctuations need to be smoothed. Yet, changes should be acceptable to individuals, equitable to all parties, and reduce the filing burden for the IRS.

Since the timing and pattern of expenditures are difficult, if not impossible, to change (many recipients need payments early in the month to meet their own obligations), most of the adjustments would have to be made on the receipts side. The withheld tax approach does not require any major changes since it is working quite well. Therefore, major changes would have to occur in nonwithheld individual taxes and in corporate taxes. Figure III-28.1 shows the current approach to nonwithheld taxes and Figure III-28.2 shows the suggested changes. In summary:

1. Nonwithheld income tax payments could be made on the first of the month rather than on the fifteenth. Payments also could be spread more evenly during the year than currently. The new approach would result in a much better match between the inflow of funds and the current expenditure pattern. Starting with the corporate tax area, estimated taxes could be due at the beginning of March, June, September, and December. Although somewhat earlier in the year than the way the law now stands, it should be no great burden for corporations. Corporate makeup taxes would be in two installments during the following year, with the first half due at the beginning of February, and the remainder at the beginning of August. The makeup payments on balance would come at a later time.

2. Nonwithheld individual income taxes would be paid at the beginning of January, April, July, and October, again, in an effort to better match the timing of expenditures. The payment of estimated taxes on the first business day of January may create a problem for taxpayers since it is difficult to find the time to work on taxes during the holiday season. It may make sense, therefore, to delay the payment for a few days. As in the case of corporations, the tax burden would be spread more evenly throughout the year. Then, in the following year, the final tax settlement would be filed at the beginning of May. It would be a welcome relief for many middle and upper income taxpayers to have 15 additional days. Computing taxes (despite the Tax Reform Act of 1986) is still a complicated process for many.

3. When these individual and corporate tax payment suggestions are looked at in total (see Figure III-28.2), there is no month with an overlap. In 11 out of 12 months, payments are made at the beginning of the month. In contrast, under the current law, substantial nonwithheld payments occur at mid-month, and only during six months of the year. Not only is this proposed system more consistent with the heavy Treasury outflows at the beginning of each month, it also spreads the workload for the IRS.

These proposals are not meant to change the overall tax-take. While there initially would be some changes in revenue in the first year or two of the program, it would be modest; and after the initial phase, there should be negligible revenue effect. Even if the government is unwilling to make all of these changes, moving some tax dates to the beginning of a month would still reduce undue cash fluctuations and excessive balances, and the problems they create.

FIGURE III-28.4 1987 Treasury Cash Balance (Billions of Dollars)

Day	Jan	Feb	Mar	Apr	May	Jun	Jul	Aug	Sep	Oct	Nov	Dec	Day
1	H	—	20.7	11.1	48.2	25.8	34.7	—	18.0	35.6	—	23.4	1
2	19.6	38.0	20.8	10.3	—	23.6	21.4	—	17.9	23.5	32.4	25.1	2
3	—	30.4	18.3	8.9	—	22.0	25.0	20.1	17.5	—	23.2	16.4	3
4	—	29.0	17.8	—	47.7	22.7	—	18.0	19.0	—	21.5	16.4	4
5	24.1	30.2	16.3	—	46.0	19.4	—	16.3	—	29.5	24.9	—	5
6	21.7	29.1	—	9.2	49.5	—	32.7	20.0	—	28.8	25.5	—	6
7	25.7	—	—	16.4	49.2	—	32.7	19.3	H	27.8	—	12.3	7
8	28.1	—	14.5	14.9	48.2	17.0	32.8	—	14.9	28.2	—	10.8	8
9	27.4	27.6	12.7	15.4	—	16.3	33.2	—	14.0	27.6	27.4	12.3	9
10	—	26.6	11.6	15.0	—	17.1	32.4	17.9	15.4	—	28.9	12.6	10
11	—	27.5	10.7	—	46.9	17.2	—	16.8	16.4	—	H	12.7	11
12	27.2	29.3	9.8	—	45.9	16.8	—	17.0	—	H	29.4	—	12
13	27.7	28.2	—	15.3	46.4	—	31.7	18.5	—	26.6	30.2	—	13
14	29.4	—	—	16.4	44.7	—	31.4	17.3	16.8	27.3	—	12.0	14
15	29.3	—	10.2	13.8	42.2	16.5	27.5	—	18.7	38.1	—	10.8	15
16	32.9	H	20.0	15.8	—	29.2	31.4	—	36.7	41.2	22.4	24.1	16

154

17		28.3	20.2	19.5	—	33.5	31.2	20.8	44.6	—	23.8	28.1	17
18		30.8	21.4	—	42.3	35.4	—	21.4	47.4	—	24.1	28.4	18
19	H	28.7	20.3	23.4	40.7	40.5	30.8	22.2	—	40.1	27.9	—	19
20	36.3	29.9	—	31.5	39.8	—	32.6	26.7	51.8	40.1	26.9	—	20
21	40.7	—	18.8	34.4	41.1	42.0	32.6	25.8	53.3	43.4	—	30.5	21
22	40.6	29.9	16.0	31.4	40.1	42.6	20.6	—	53.5	42.2	25.3	29.9	22
23	42.7	28.5	16.2	34.6	—	42.7	19.6	25.0	44.2	43.3	24.5	30.3	23
24	—	29.3	13.3	—	—	44.4	—	25.0	44.0	—	24.2	30.7	24
25	—	26.7	12.1	—	H	43.6	19.2	24.8	—	43.0	H	H	25
26	42.1	24.8	—	40.1	38.7	—	18.7	25.7	42.9	42.6	23.9	—	26
27	43.2	—	10.5	45.8	37.7	43.0	19.0	24.7	42.9	43.6	—	—	27
28	43.7		9.0	51.7	33.8	40.1	21.8	—	36.4	42.8	—	31.9	28
29	41.3			55.7	33.1		19.4	22.6		38.3	21.2	31.9	29
30										—		33.0	30
31												22.4	31

The balance was as high as $55.7 billion and as low as $8.9 billion. The balance through much of the year was excessively large.

Source: Treasury Daily Statement

155

FIGURE III-28.5 1987 Treasury Tax and Loan Balance at Commercial Banks (Billions of Dollars)

Day	Jan	Feb	Mar	Apr	May	Jun	Jul	Aug	Sep	Oct	Nov	Dec	Day
1	H	—	—	6.5	26.2	24.3	24.7	—	13.3	25.6	—	18.9	1
2	13.0	25.7	16.4	6.5	—	20.2	25.5	—	12.4	17.3	27.0	20.3	2
3	—	23.0	17.7	5.0	—	17.6	21.2	15.3	10.8	—	20.3	10.8	3
4	—	23.7	14.4	—	26.3	17.6	—	12.6	15.4	—	18.3	13.0	4
5	16.9	24.8	14.4	—	26.4	15.0	—	11.7	—	25.3	20.1	—	5
6	18.6	25.0	12.5	5.0	26.5	—	26.4	15.8	—	26.6	20.7	—	6
7	21.6	—	—	12.1	26.5	—	26.8	16.4	H	25.0	—	9.6	7
8	23.3	—	—	11.3	26.6	14.4	26.6	—	12.5	24.3	—	7.4	8
9	23.4	24.6	11.4	11.9	—	13.9	26.0	—	11.6	24.6	25.3	7.8	9
10	—	24.0	9.8	11.6	—	14.3	26.2	15.6	12.5	—	25.6	7.8	10
11	—	24.0	8.9	—	26.6	14.0	—	13.8	13.4	—	—	8.2	11
12	23.5	24.3	7.6	—	19.5	14.5	—	13.4	—	H	25.6	—	12
13	23.7	24.4	6.2	11.5	26.5	—	26.3	14.7	—	22.9	25.8	—	13
14	23.8	—	—	11.2	26.8	—	26.4	14.1	13.4	23.6	—	8.9	14
15	24.4	—	—	9.7	27.1	14.5	24.2	—	14.1	28.1	—	7.8	15
16	24.7	H	6.6	13.0	—	22.2	25.2	—	27.2	28.4	19.0	15.0	16
17	H	24.1	17.0	16.0	—	25.4	26.3	17.9	27.6	—	20.5	23.1	17

Day													Day
18	—	25.4	17.8	—	27.2	25.4	—	18.5	27.6	—	21.2	23.6	18
19	—	25.6	19.5	—	27.1	26.0	—	19.1	—	28.6	23.5	—	19
20	24.9	25.9	17.3	19.8	27.2	—	26.4	23.1	—	29.0	23.7	—	20
21	25.0	—	—	24.5	27.1	—	26.5	23.3	27.7	29.1	—	26.4	21
22	25.1	—	—	25.0	27.0	26.0	26.6	—	27.8	29.2	—	27.0	22
23	25.3	25.9	15.5	25.2	—	26.3	17.3	—	27.8	29.2	21.8	27.3	23
24	—	25.8	13.3	25.6	—	26.4	16.0	21.7	28.1	—	21.5	27.6	24
25	—	25.1	13.2	—	H	26.6	—	21.4	28.6	—	21.4	H	25
26	—	25.2	10.8	—	27.0	26.6	—	20.8	—	29.3	H	—	26
27	25.3	21.3	9.7	25.8	26.8	—	15.1	22.2	—	29.3	21.2	—	27
28	25.4	—	—	25.8	26.7	—	14.5	22.4	28.4	29.3	—	26.8	28
29	25.5		—	25.9	26.7	26.4	14.3	—	28.4	29.4	—	28.2	29
30	25.6		7.3	26.1	—	26.3	16.0	—	27.3	29.4	17.6	28.2	30
31	—		5.4	—	—		14.1	18.9		—		17.1	31

When Treasury balances approach $30 billion, the banks run short of sufficient collateral.

Source: Treasury Daily Statement

157

FIGURE III-28.6 1987 Treasury Balance at the Federal Reserve (Billions of Dollars)

Day	Jan	Feb	Mar	Apr	May	Jun	Jul	Aug	Sep	Oct	Nov	Dec	Day
1	H	—	—	4.6	22.0	1.5	10.0	—	4.7	9.9	—	4.5	1
2	6.6	12.3	4.3	3.8	—	3.3	4.2	—	5.5	6.1	5.4	4.9	2
3	—	7.4	3.1	3.9	—	4.4	3.9	4.9	6.7	—	2.9	5.6	3
4	—	5.3	3.9	—	21.4	5.1	—	5.5	3.6	—	3.1	3.4	4
5	7.2	5.4	3.5	—	19.6	4.4	—	4.6	—	4.2	4.8	—	5
6	3.1	4.1	3.9	4.3	23.0	—	6.3	4.2	—	2.1	4.8	—	6
7	4.1	—	—	4.2	22.7	—	5.9	2.9	H	2.8	—	2.7	7
8	4.8	—	3.1	3.5	21.6	2.6	6.1	—	2.3	3.9	—	3.4	8
9	4.0	3.1	2.8	3.5	—	2.4	7.2	2.3	2.4	2.9	2.1	4.6	9
10	—	2.6	2.7	3.4	—	2.8	6.3	3.0	2.9	—	3.3	4.8	10
11	—	3.5	3.0	—	20.2	3.2	—	3.5	3.0	—	H	4.5	11
12	3.7	5.0	3.6	—	26.4	2.3	5.4	3.8	—	H	3.9	—	12
13	4.0	3.8	—	3.8	19.9	—	5.0	3.2	—	3.7	4.5	—	13
14	5.5	—	—	5.2	17.9	—	3.4	—	3.4	3.7	—	3.2	14
15	4.9	—	—	4.1	15.1	2.0	6.1	—	4.6	10.0	—	3.1	15
16	8.3	H	3.6	2.8	—	6.9	—	2.9	9.5	12.8	3.4	9.0	16
17	—	4.3	3.0	3.5	—	8.1	4.9	2.9	17.0	—	3.3	5.0	17
18	—	5.4	2.4	—	15.1	10.0	—	—	19.8	—	2.9	4.8	18

19	H	3.1	1.9	—	13.6	14.5	—	3.1	—	11.4	4.4	—	19
20	11.4	4.0	3.1	3.6	12.6	—	4.4	3.5	—	11.2	3.2	—	20
21	15.7	—	—	6.9	14.0	—	6.1	2.5	24.1	14.3	—	4.1	21
22	15.5	4.0	3.3	9.4	13.1	16.0	6.0	—	25.5	13.0	3.5	2.9	22
23	17.4	2.7	2.7	6.2	—	16.3	3.3	—	25.7	14.1	3.0	3.0	23
24	—	4.2	3.0	9.0	H	16.4	3.6	3.3	16.1	—	2.8	3.1	24
25	—	1.5	2.5	—	11.7	17.7	—	3.5	15.4	—	H	H	25
26	16.7	3.5	2.4	—	10.8	16.9	4.1	4.0	—	13.7	2.7	—	26
27	17.7	—	—	14.3	7.1	—	4.2	3.5	—	13.3	—	5.1	27
28	18.1	—	—	20.0	6.4	—	4.7	2.4	14.5	14.3	—	3.8	28
29	15.7	3.3	3.3	25.8	—	16.6	5.8	—	14.5	13.4	3.6	4.8	29
30	—	3.6	3.6	29.7	—	13.8	5.4	3.8	9.1	8.9	—	5.3	30
31	—				—					—			31

A balance of $3 billion to $4 billion is considered normal. An increase drains bank reserves and a decline adds reserves.

Source: Treasury Daily Statement

29. Can the Treasury's financing pattern be changed so as to improve cash management?

A strong case can be made that it is politically easier and more practical to change financings than to change rules governing receipts and outlays. Changes in bill financings are likely to be easier than adjustments in note and bond offerings because of less resistance from market participants.

One suggestion is that the Treasury in the first week of every month would auction bills with a 6-week maturity. Thus, the bills would mature in the third week of the following month. At the same time, the Treasury would cut back on the size of its regular 3-month, 6-month, and 1-year bill auctions.

For example, the Treasury could sell on average $8 billion of 6-week bills. This would mean that about half the time there would be $16 billion outstanding. At the same time, the Treasury would cut back its regular 3-month, 6-month, and 1-year bill auctions by an average of $300 million each. Over 3 months, the cutback would be $8.7 billion (13 auctions of 3-month and 6-month bills, and 3 auctions of 1-year bills). In the next 3 months the reduction would be $4.8 billion (13 auctions of 6-month bills, and 3 auctions of 1-year bills), and in the following 6 months the cutback would be $2.1 billion (7 auctions of 1-year bills). Over the full year, the regular bill reductions would be $15.6 billion.

The Treasury could use this technique to limit excessive cash balances (which was the case through much of CY-87). With the 6-week bill, the money comes in early in the month when spending is heavy and it matures after the middle of the month when receipts are often rising. Thus, these financings would help smooth cash balances, which is not the case with current bill offerings.

A 6-week bill would also have other advantages. It is a maturity which currently is not tapped by the Treasury and should be of interest to short-term investors. The maturing amounts could be accepted on the fifteenth of the month to meet tax payments. The size of the 6-week issues could be changed, depending on the size of the taxes when the issues mature. The use of this bill would add to the liquidity of the short bill market and could limit any supply overhang in other bill maturities.

Some changes could also be made in the note and bond area to help smooth the cash flow and reduce market indigestion, which might result from a bunching of offerings.

Under the present approach, note and bond financing is at its heaviest from the seventh through the tenth week of the quarter, while at other times it is rather light. The situation could be rectified by moving the 30-year bond payment date ahead by two weeks (to the fifth week of the quarter). Thus, the middle-of-the-quarter refunding would offer only 3- and 10-year issues, which would still be more than the amount of maturing issues. Rescheduling this issue earlier in the month would offset the usual heavy outflow of funds and would raise a substantial amount for the Treasury two weeks earlier than at present.

The primary argument likely to be made against this suggestion is that a three-offering financing, which includes a long bond, is given high visibility by the media; this attention can mean greater investor interest. Yet, one also wonders whether it also means greater market volatility, and overall, a higher cost to the Treasury.

Figure III-29.1 shows an approximation of the current quarterly Treasury financing pattern, and Figure III-29.2 shows the specific recommendations.

FIGURE III-29.1 Marketable Treasury Financing—July Through September 1987 (Billions of Dollars)

GROSS AMOUNTS ANNOUNCED

Weeks in Quarter	Bills				Notes						Bonds	Total	Weeks in Quarter
	3-Month	6-Month	1-Year	Cash Mgmt	2-Year	3-Year	4-Year	5-Year	7-Year	10-Year	30-Year		
1	6.6	6.6										13.2	1
2	6.6	6.6	9.8						7.0			30.0	2
3	6.6	6.6										13.2	3
4	(a)	(a)										—	4
5	6.6	6.6			9.8							36.2	5
6	6.6	6.6	9.5									22.7	6
7	6.6	6.6				9.8				9.3	9.0	41.3	7
8	6.6	6.6										13.2	8
9	6.6	6.6			9.8							23.0	9
10	6.6	6.6	9.5					7.8				30.5	10
11	6.6	6.6										13.2	11
12	6.4	6.4										12.8	12
13	(b)	(b)			9.3		(c)					9.3	13
Total	79.0	79.0	28.8	—	28.9	9.8	—	7.8	7.0	9.3	9.0	258.6	**Total**

162

NET AMOUNT RAISED

									Total
1	– 1.0								– 1.0
2	– 1.1	+ .1					+ 7.0		+ 6.0
3	– .5								– .5
4	– 13.7								– 13.7
5	+ 13.2								+ 12.9
6	– .5	– .7		+ .2					– 1.0
7	– .3					+ 7.8		(d)	+ 17.0
8	– .3								+ .1
9	+ .1	—							+ .1
10	+ .1								+ 7.7
11	– .1		—						– .1
12	– .1								– .3
13	– 13.1			– .8	– 6.5				– 20.4
Total	– 17.6(e)	– .6	—	– .6 (d)	– 6.5	+ 7.8	+ 7.0	(d)	+ 6.8

(a) Three- and six-month bills ($13.2 billion) were delayed due to a debt ceiling problem.

(b) Three- and six-month bills ($12.8 billion) were delayed due to a debt ceiling problem.

(c) Four-year notes ($7.3 billion) were delayed due to a debt ceiling problem.

(d) There were three new issues and two maturing issues. A net amount of $17.3 billion was raised.

(e) Three- and six-month bills combined.

The majority of new money raised by the Treasury is in 5-year and longer maturities. This is the case, although there is only one offering each quarter of 5-year, 7-year, 10-year, and 30-year obligations.

Source: *Treasury Bulletin*

FIGURE III-29.2 Recommendations as to Timing of Note and Bond Offerings (Billions of Dollars)

Weeks in Quarter	Present Maturity	Present Net Amount	Proposed Maturity	Proposed Net Amount	Weeks in Quarter
1	—	—	—	—	1
2	—	—	—	—	2
3	7 yr	+ 4	7 yr	+ 4	3
4	—	—	—	—	4
5	2 yr	+ 1	2 yr & 30 yr	+10	5
6	—	—	—	—	6
7	3 yr, 10 yr, 30 yr	+14	3 yr & 10 yr	+ 5	7
8	—	—	—	—	8
9	2 yr	+ 1	2 yr	+ 1	9
10	5 yr	+ 8	5 yr	+ 8	10
11	—	—	—	—	11
12	—	—	—	—	12
13	2 yr & 4 yr	+ 2	2 yr & 4 yr	+ 2	13
Total		+30		+30	**Total**

30. Has the growth of the government securities market kept pace with the growth of Treasury debt financing?

At the end of 1960, there were 18 firms classified by the Federal Reserve as reporting dealers[1] in government securities. A decade later the number moved to 24, by 1975 reached 30, and by 1980 had grown to 37. It dipped to 36 by the end of 1985 but, by early 1988, had reached 42 firms. The number is likely to increase during the next several years. (A list of reporting dealers is given on pages 170 and 171.)

The recent increase in the number of firms seeking reporting dealer status has been strongly influenced by three factors: the CY-84–86 bull market in bonds, domestic and international institutions deciding to broaden their financial products and services, and the prestige of having such a designation. That is in contrast to the period from late CY-79 through mid-1984, which was generally bearish for bonds. Although there were some trading opportunities during this period, the overall lack of major profit incentives acted as a deterrent to new firms seeking reporting dealer status.

From the middle of CY-84 to late CY-86, however, the picture brightened considerably for bond dealers. It was the greatest bull market in the history of U.S. government securities, and it was almost impossible not to make a great deal of money. Moreover, during this period, many foreign and domestic firms were of the opinion that every major financial institution had to have a U.S. government dealer operation as one of its primary businesses. Since there was a time lag before some firms were ready to act, it was CY-86 before much of this increased interest reached fruition. The increase in the number of dealers and changes in interest rates since CY-80 is shown in Figure III-30.1.

Along with the growth in the number of dealers was a substantial increase in Treasury debt outstanding and in the number of transactions. (Figure III-30.2 gives dealer position and transaction details from CY-74 through CY-87.) Marketable Treasury debt amounted to $283 billion at the end of CY-74, of which only $27 billion were in 5-year-and-over maturities held by private investors. Dealer transactions on an average daily basis amounted to only about $3.6 billion during CY-74, with

---

[1] "Reporting dealer" is a designation given by the Federal Reserve based on such factors as capital, trading activity, and support of Treasury auctions. Firms seeking such a classification report daily trading activity and positions to the Federal Reserve Bank of New York. There is neither a specified trial period nor a guarantee such a designation will be given. Once a firm has the designation, it then has the opportunity to engage in transactions with the Federal Reserve trading desk.

FIGURE III-30.1 Number of Reporting Dealers Compared with 30-Year Bond Performance

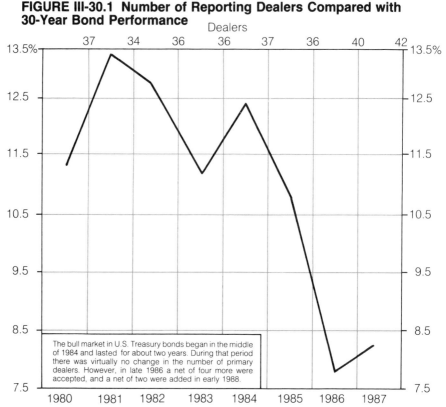

The bull market in U.S. Treasury bonds began in the middle of 1984 and lasted for about two years. During that period there was virtually no change in the number of primary dealers. However, in late 1986 a net of four more were accepted, and a net of two were added in early 1988.

Source: *Federal Reserve Bank of New York*

$400 million in five-year-and-over maturities. The market primarily was domestic. Foreigners owned only $36 billion of marketable Treasury obligations.

By the end of CY-87, total marketable debt outstanding amounted to $1.73 trillion, with about $460 billion in 5-year-and-over maturities held by private investors. Thus, in 13 years, marketable debt outstanding had grown over 500 percent and privately held securities of 5 years and over had increased more than 1600 percent.

Daily dealer transaction increases were even more astounding. In CY-87, dealer transactions in Treasury obligations averaged $110 billion, of which $41 billion were in maturities of 5 or more years. The $110 billion of total transactions was over 30 times greater than in CY-74, and transactions in the 5-year-and-over category were about 100 times their CY-74 level.

FIGURE III-30.2 Dealer Positions and Transactions (Billions of Dollars; Averages of Daily Figures)

	Positions						Transactions					
CY	Bills	Other Issues Within 1 Yr	1–5 Yrs	5–10 Yrs	Over 10 Yrs	Total	Bills	Other Issues Within 1 Yr	1–5 Yrs	5–10 Yrs	Over 10 Yrs	Total
1974	1.9	—	.3	.3	.1	2.6	2.6	.3	.5	.3	.1	3.6
1975	4.3	.3	.9	.3	.1	5.9	3.9	.2	1.4	.4	.1	6.0
1976	6.3	.2	.5	.4	.2	7.6	6.7	.2	2.3	1.0	.2	10.4
1977	4.8	.1	.1	.1	.1	5.2	6.7	.2	2.3	1.1	.4	10.8
1978	2.5	.3	– .1	—		2.7	6.2	.4	1.9	1.0	.9	10.3
1979	3.8	– .3	– .5	.2	—	3.2	7.9	.5	2.4	1.2	1.3	13.2
1980	4.1	– 1.1	.4	.2	.7	4.3	11.4	.4	3.3	1.5	1.7	18.3
1981	6.5	– 1.5	1.5	.3	2.3	9.0	14.8	.6	4.4	2.5	2.5	24.7
1982	4.8	– .2	2.9	.3	2.0	9.3	18.4	.8	6.3	3.6	3.2	32.3
1983	10.8	.9	1.9	– .1	.5	14.1	22.4	.7	8.8	5.3	5.0	42.1
1984	5.5	.1	2.2	– 1.1	– 1.2	5.4	26.0	1.3	11.7	7.6	6.1	52.8
1985	10.1	1.1	5.2	– 6.2	– 2.7	7.4	32.9	1.8	18.4	12.7	9.6	75.3
1986	12.7	3.7	9.3	– 9.5	– 3.2	13.1	34.2	2.1	24.7	20.5	14.0	95.4
1987p	3.8	1.4	.5	– 6.5	– 6.2	– 7.0	37.9	3.3	27.9	24.0	16.9	109.9

Dealer transactions during the 13 years grew much more rapidly than dealer positions. Yet, the dealer positions do not include forward or futures positions, or mort-gaged-back or agency holdings.

Source: Federal Reserve Bank of New York

WHY GROWTH IN TRADING EXCEEDED GROWTH IN DEBT. The growth in trading substantially outpaced the growth in outstanding Treasury debt for several reasons.

The Treasury now offers a much broader group of maturities to attract greater numbers of investors at home and abroad, and to appeal to a broader cross-section of investors. Further, the growth of the mortgage-backed and futures markets facilitates a substantial amount of arbitrage and hedging operations with Treasury notes and bonds. The marketability of Treasury issues has been enhanced through technological improvements such as book-entry recordkeeping and dealer innovations such as stripping of coupons.

Finally, the government market is worldwide, with active trading taking place in Tokyo and London. Foreign holdings of government securities are reported by the Treasury to be close to $300 billion, or about eight times the amount foreigners held at the end of CY-74. Moreover, this figure appears to be grossly understated, which may also help explain the large amount of trading in London and Tokyo.

The growth of the government market was significantly understated in another respect. The dealer community is larger than the growth in the number of firms would suggest. Many of the dealers have been taken over by large and well-capitalized corporations with worldwide operations. Most of the firms which have not been taken over have amassed large amounts of capital. In addition to the 42 reporting dealers, about a dozen or so firms had expressed a desire to be classified as such, and there are several dozen more who have been seriously considering the possibility. Therefore, many firms not classified as reporting dealers have been trading government securities, although without the benefits of status such a designation entails.

The very rapid growth in dealers and their operations have not seemed to affect the safety or efficiency of the government market. There have been only a few cases where dealers failed and none of these were major firms. The amounts lost by investors have been infinitesimal compared with the volume of transactions. The efficiency of the market actually appears to have improved as measured by the relatively small spreads between bid-and-offered prices and the ability of the market to distribute large amounts of Treasury securities during and after auctions.

Looking ahead, the dealer community is likely to continue to expand during the next several years, and the few remaining independent dealers are likely to be purchased by large business and financial institutions. The number of primary dealers will increase, in part, because of the dozen or so firms waiting in the wings, pressing for reporting status. However, the number may not advance to much more than 50. Foreign-owned firms are not likely to increase anywhere near as rapidly as in the past since there are fewer firms to buy, their countries would have to allow relatively easy access of American firms into their markets, and Congress probably would not be happy if foreigners controlled a major portion of the dealer business in U.S. government securities. Entrance into the dealer business may be further discouraged by increased regulation of the industry (reporting dealers may be less seriously affected than others). Increased capital requirements may also limit the entrance of new dealers.

Irrespective of the exact increase in dealers, there will be no shortage of securities for government dealers to trade in the 1990s. In this period, and beyond, the refunding of Treasury issues will be enormous and the gross offerings will continue to expand. Moreover, budget deficits will not disappear, although it is possible they may become more controllable. While the deficit, as a percentage of GNP, is likely to move lower in the years ahead, the Gramm-Rudman-Hollings forecasts represent an exercise in wishful thinking.

Maybe the most interesting question with respect to dealers and their profit opportunities is how the new firms, or those under new management, will react when their first major bear market develops. The sharp deterioration in the bond market in the spring, and again in the fall of 1987, were the first tests. The recent wave of expansion in the dealer community was induced largely by the greatest bull market in the history of U.S. Treasury obligations. Many of these firms are not accustomed to huge unexpected losses of a highly leveraged business in a short period.

Number of Reporting Dealers (End of Calendar Year)

1960	18
1970	24
1975	30
1980	37
1981	34
1982	36
1983	36
1984	37
1985	36
1986	40
1987	42*

*Excludes E.F. Hutton, which no longer reports to the Federal Reserve as of January 6, 1988.

The growth in the number of dealers has not been all that large. However, during this period, many of the independent dealers have been acquired by large and well-capitalized firms.

Reporting Dealers on January 1, 1974

Bank of America NT & SA
Bankers Trust Company
A.G. Becker Paribas
Chase Manhattan Government Securities
Chemical Bank
Citibank
Continental Illinois National Bank
Discount Corporation of New York
Drexel Burnham Lambert
First Boston Corporation
First Interstate Capital Markets Inc.
First National Bank of Chicago
Harris Trust & Savings Bank
Irving Securities Inc.
Aubrey G. Lanston & Co., Inc.
Lehman Government Securities
Merrill Lynch Government Securities
J.P. Morgan Securities
The Northern Trust Company
Nuveen Government Securities
Wm. E. Pollock Government Securities
Salomon Brothers
Second District Securities
Stuart Brothers—NY Hanseatic Division
Total—24

Reporting Dealers on January 6, 1988

Bank of America NT & SA
Bankers Trust Company
Bear, Stearns & Co., Inc.
Brophy, Gestal, Knight & Co., L.P.
Carroll McEntee & McGinley
  Incorporated
Chase Manhattan Government
  Securities, Inc.
Chemical Bank
Citibank, N.A.
Continental Illinois National Bank
  and Trust Company of Chicago
CRT Government Securities, Ltd.
Daiwa Securities America Inc.
Dean Witter Reynolds Inc.
Discount Corporation of New York
Donaldson, Lufkin & Jenrette
  Securities Corporation
Drexel Burnham Lambert
  Government Securities Inc.
The First Boston Corporation
First Interstate Capital Markets, Inc.
First National Bank of Chicago
Goldman, Sachs & Co.
Greenwich Capital Markets, Inc.
Harris Trust and Savings Bank
Irving Securities, Inc.
Kidder, Peabody & Co.,
  Incorporated

Kleinwort Benson Government
  Securities, Inc.
Aubrey G. Lanston & Co., Inc.
Lloyds Government Securities
  Corporation
Manufacturers Hanover Trust
  Company
Merrill Lynch Government Securities,
  Inc.
Midland-Montagu Government
  Securities Inc.
J.P. Morgan Securities, Inc.
Morgan Stanley & Co. Incorporated
The Nikko Securities Co.
  International, Inc.
Nomura Securities International, Inc.
Paine Webber Incorporated
Prudential-Bache Securities, Inc.
L.F. Rothschild & Co.
Salomon Brothers Inc.
Security Pacific National Bank
Shearson Lehman Government
  Securities, Inc.
Smith Barney, Harris Upham & Co.,
  Inc.
Thomson McKinnon Securities Inc.
Westpac Pollock Government
  Securities, Inc.

Total—42

31. How useful is the debt ceiling from a public policy perspective?

Those who support a ceiling on debt do so on the basis that it draws public attention to the budget shortfall, which, in turn, leads to limiting the size of that deficit. Yet, from FY-74 through FY-87, there were 35 debt ceiling changes (see Figures III-31.1 and III-31.2) and the deficit exploded to $150 billion from $6 billion (the deficit having been as high as $221 billion in FY-86). So much for that argument.

Members of Congress want a debt ceiling for many reasons—virtually none of which has anything to do with containing the deficit. The most obvious reason is it provides them with a visible target at which to direct verbal broadsides to convince constituents they are on the side of frugality and other fiscal virtues. Nevertheless, the same congressmen often have voted for the very expenditures and tax bills which contributed to these huge deficits.

There are others who use a debt ceiling bill as a convenient vehicle for passing a piece of legislation which cannot stand on its own merit. The legislation can be incorporated as part of the debt ceiling bill even though it has absolutely nothing to do with debt levels. Also, prolonged wrangling over the debt ceiling is a convenient ploy which can be used when there is a desire to avoid, or delay, other legislation developing in the near term. A long, drawn-out fight over the debt ceiling is an easy way to achieve this result.

The price to be paid for debt ceiling legislation can be considerable. Congress spends an inordinate amount of time arguing about it, expending energy which could be put to better use on more pressing matters. Debt ceiling delays change the timing of Treasury financings, which often results in bunching of new offerings and creates unnecessary price volatility in the debt market. Usually the greater the price volatility, the higher the interest cost to the Treasury. Finally, the debt ceiling problems can complicate life for the Federal Reserve in its open market operations and can lead to investor confusion concerning monetary policy.

As illogical as the debt ceiling approach may be, the chances of it being abolished are remote. Congress as a body jealously guards its powers, especially a power which is viewed as a check and balance against the executive branch. The events surrounding Vietnam, Watergate and most recently, Iranscam, have caused Congress to be even more protective of its powers.

FIGURE III-31.1 Debt Ceiling Changes (Billions of Dollars)

Dates	Ceiling	Dates	Ceiling
11/30/73 — 6/30/74	475.7	2/7/81 — 9/30/81	985.0
6/30/74 — 2/19/75	495.0	9/30/81 — 6/28/82	1079.8
2/19/75 — 6/30/75	531.0	6/28/82 — 9/30/82	1143.1
6/30/75 — 11/14/75	577.0	9/30/82 — 5/26/83	1290.2
11/14/75 — 3/15/76	595.0	5/26/83 — 11/21/83	1389.0
3/15/76 — 6/30/76	627.0	11/21/83 — 5/25/84	1490.0
6/30/76 — 9/30/76	636.0	5/25/84 — 7/6/84	1520.0
6/30/76 — 3/31/77	682.0	7/6/84 — 10/13/84	1573.0
6/30/76 — 9/30/77	700.0	10/13/84 — 11/14/85	1823.8
10/4/77 — 3/27/78	752.0	11/14/85 — 12/6/85	1903.8
3/27/78 — 7/31/78	752.0	12/12/85 — 8/21/86	2078.7
8/3/78 — 3/31/79	798.0	8/21/86 — 10/21/86	2111.0
4/2/79 — 9/29/79	830.0	10/21/86 — 5/15/87	2300.0
9/29/79 — 5/30/80	879.0	5/15/87 — 7/17/87	2320.0
5/30/80 — 6/5/80	879.0	7/30/87 — 8/6/87	2320.0
6/6/80 — 6/28/80	879.0	8/10/87 — 9/23/87	2352.0
6/28/80 — 12/19/80	925.0	9/29/87 — xxx*	2800.0
12/19/80 — 2/7/81	935.1		

*xxx = open-ended

Every year during the period analyzed, there was at least one increase in the debt ceiling. In most years there were two or three changes.

Source: *Daily Treasury Statement*

If the Treasury and the American people are to be burdened with this debt ceiling anachronism, an attempt should be made to improve its applicability. The ceiling should be raised annually and at the same time of the year. It should not revert to any lower and meaningless level, and it should relate to deficit numbers.

For example, late in the fiscal year, the ceiling should be raised to a level which would reflect a hoped-for (but plausible) deficit in the coming year. If the new ceiling is reached well before the end of the fiscal year, it would send a signal the deficit is approaching unacceptable levels. The next annual increase in the ceiling could be used to express dissatisfaction with this state of affair.

The ceiling should exclude all nonmarketable debt obligations issued to trust funds managed by the government, since this does not contribute to the deficit problem. It should be proposed and passed on its own merits with no riders or amendments. If these improvements are adopted, there would be no need for the Treasury to look for loopholes (such as financing through the Federal Financing Bank) to circumvent a debt ceiling limit.

FIGURE III-31.2 Debt Ceiling—End of Each Fiscal Year—1974 Through 1987 (Billions of Dollars)

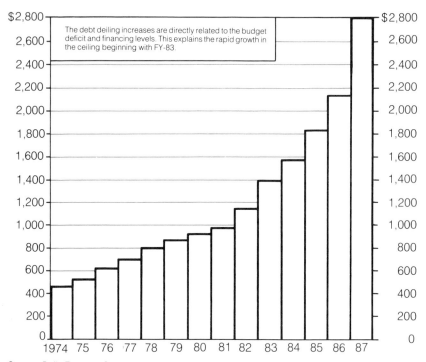

The debt deiling increases are directly related to the budget deficit and financing levels. This explains the rapid growth in the ceiling beginning with FY-83.

Source: *Daily Treasury Statement*

PART FOUR

THE BUDGET DOCUMENT AND PROCESS— PRACTICALITY COUNTS

32. Should budget outlays be subdivided—one for capital goods and one for operations—with only operations used in computing the deficit?

The distinction here is between spending money on assets which have a fairly extensive useful life (capital goods), and spending money on services and programs that are used or consumed rather quickly (operations). The idea of subdividing the budget sounds attractive but abuses would probably outweigh potential advantages.

On the plus side, it can be argued that purchases of capital assets should be separated form other outlays because they are for the long term and should not be viewed as one-time expenses. Only the annual writedown of assets would be included in the operations budget. That approach, which is much closer to the method used in private-sector accounting, would allow the deficit to be computed on the operations budget alone. If this were done, most, if not all, of the deficit would disappear. The approach also would support the view that since much of the public debt outstanding was used to finance capital outlays, which are not part of the deficit, the huge amount of outstanding debt is not especially adverse. Finally, the separation of outlays would make it easier to analyze the impact of specific budgetary areas on the economy.

The biggest disadvantage of this budget-division system is it would no doubt result in a sizable increase in total government spending and, therefore, an even larger deficit as currently measured. Since capital spending would not be included in the deficit numbers, there would be less political pressure to suppress such outlays. Moreover, when a difference of opinion exists as to whether an outlay should be in either the capital or operations area, there would be a strong inclination to place it in the capital sector because of its exclusion from the deficit. That situation could arise frequently because many government outlays are difficult to categorize, even if the decisions are made objectively.

Another area of concern is trying to measure the useful life of an asset so annual writeoffs can be determined. An additional problem in many cases is that cost may have to be the sole determinant of value since there is no resale market for many government assets. That could be an especially difficult problem in the defense area.

Another argument against splitting expenditures results from government being different from a corporation. It can be argued that it is the total funds or resources a government uses (compared with the size of the economy), which should be considered of paramount importance, not the mechanics of how the spending is divided. Finally, and not inconsequentially, there is a question as to motivation on the part of the proponents of the expenditure-division concept.

It is much easier to reclassify numbers to reduce the deficit than it is to make hard decisions relative to slicing expenditures or raising taxes. If this proposal had been actively supported when the total budget was close to balance, the motivation for such a change would not have been as suspect.

33. *Should a two-year rather than a one-year budget be used?*

The advantages of having a two-year budget are obvious. A one-year period is very short considering the number of items Congress must deal with and the number of days it is in session.

A two-year period may better reflect underlying budget movements since, in any given year, special factors can strongly influence the results. A two-year period can lead to a smoother flow of funding and can add to the outcome certainty for various undertakings. Complex projects typically take years to conceive and to implement, with the defense area being a prime example. Finally, even under the best of circumstances, it is difficult for Congress to consider adequately all items in a critical way, in a time span as short as one year.

Despite these reasons supporting a two-year budget, it probably would have little positive impact, and surely much less than its proponents espouse. If budgets were submitted, and deficits released at two-year intervals, the public's attention with respect to the deficit problem would wane. The lessening of public interest in a two-year budget would be even more pronounced if the data were released and the new budgets presented in off-election years. If the budget deficit moves to unacceptably high levels, it will take more time for this to become apparent. Consequently, it will take more time to rectify the problem. When changes in the budget do occur, they would probably be larger, more abrupt, and more disruptive.

It can also be argued if Congress is under less of a time constraint, procrastination and excessive debate would become commonplace. Part of the current problem may not be how much time Congress has to work on the budget, but how well it uses the time. In addition, a new administration, or a new Congress, should have the opportunity to affect the budget as quickly as possible. A two-year budget would not allow them to do so.

The fact that the two-year proposal has become more popular as the deficit has skyrocketed should cause some skepticism as to the motives of its advocates. The purpose of a two-year budget should not be to find a way to allow larger and less controllable deficits. Finally, it is simply a delusion to believe that changing from a one-year to a two-year budget will have a positive effect on the most important of issues—the size of the budget deficit.

Many who support a two-year budget have a fallback position:

placing a portion of the budget on a two-year cycle. Defense spending is the area most often suggested. It is also proposed if outlays should ultimately be broken into operating and capital segments, the former could be on a one-year and the latter on a two-year basis. While these alternatives appear to be reasonable compromises, they still have the previously mentioned problems of a full two-year budget. Moreover, they add to the possibility Congress might reorder its timing priorities and procrastinate on the two-year items, creating an even larger degree of uncertainty, especially for big-ticket items.

34. Is the submission of the budget approximately eight months before the start of the fiscal year the most logical time to do so?

The period between the submission of the budget in January or February, and the start of the fiscal year October 1, is an excessively long time; a span of some 8 months between the presentation of the budget and the beginning of the fiscal year, and 20 months between the presentation and end of the fiscal year. The longer the time span, the greater the room for error. (Figure IV-34.1 shows the historical information with respect to the submission of past budgets.)

As the table shows, the time lags were not always as long as at present. Prior to FY-77, the fiscal year ran from July 1 through June 30, resulting in a period of about five months from the submission of the budget in late January to the beginning of the fiscal year.

It would make sense to revert to a shorter time span with the budget being submitted around June 1 for the fiscal year beginning October 1.

As a benefit, when a new president is elected, the extra time would enable the new administration to present its own budget. It would require the staffs of both candidates to work on budget proposals even before the election, but this makes sense even under current conditions. A new administration submitting its budget is certainly preferable to having a lame-duck administration submit a meaningless wish list. In the FY-74-through-FY-86 period, a new president was elected in CY-76 and CY-80. The budget submitted in January 1977 for FY-78 (the Ford administration) was not very wide of a mark, but the estimates submitted in January 1981 for FY-82 (the Carter administration) were disgraceful.

By delaying the budget submission date from February 1 to June 1, an administration would gain additional time to discuss with Congress what is feasible and what is out of the question.

The way things stand now, the new Congress convenes in mid-January and the budget is submitted only a few weeks later. By allowing an extra four months, an administration could arrive at more realistic assumptions for the new fiscal year.

At the same time an administration submits its budget on June 1, it would also review and revise the information for the current fiscal year. By that time, more than half of the fiscal year would be history and the numbers should reflect a reasonably accurate portrayal of the likely numbers for the year as a whole. As things now stand, by February 1, only four months of the fiscal year have elapsed, and there is solid data

FIGURE IV-34.1 Budget Submission Information

Budget Year	Submitted By	Date Submitted	Date FY Began	Difference—Submission vs. Beginning of FY (in months)
FY-74	Nixon	1/29/73	7/1/73	5
FY-75	Nixon	2/4/74	7/1/74	5
FY-76	Ford	2/3/75	7/1/75	5
FY-77	Ford	1/21/76	10/1/76	8½
FY-78	Ford	1/17/77	10/1/77	8½
FY-79	Carter	1/20/78	10/1/78	8½
FY-80	Carter	1/22/79	10/1/79	8½
FY-81	Carter	1/22/80	10/1/80	8½
FY-82	Carter	1/15/81	10/1/81	8½
FY-83	Reagan	2/8/82	10/1/82	8
FY-84	Reagan	1/31/83	10/1/83	8
FY-85	Reagan	2/1/84	10/1/84	8
FY-86	Reagan	2/4/85	10/1/85	8
FY-87	Reagan	2/5/86	10/1/86	8
FY-88	Reagan	1/5/87	10/1/87	9
FY-89	Reagan	2/18/88	10/1/88	7½

When the fiscal year began in July, the budget was submitted five months before the year started. Beginning with FY-77, the fiscal year started in October and the budget has generally been presented eight months before the year began.

for just three of those months. The room for error in estimating results for the future nine months is considerable. If there is a major estimating error for the current year, it adds to the possibility of a larger error in the coming fiscal year. Unforeseen weakness in the economy is probably the greatest risk.

Despite this analysis, it will no doubt be argued the June 1 presentation date does not give Congress enough time to react, and then act, on the budget before the fiscal year begins. The argument loses considerable force, however, when one asks how Congress has used the extra months it currently has with respect to the new budget—the answer typically being, not very profitably. As a rule, very little is resolved and no appropriations bills are passed before the start of a new fiscal year.

A June 1 submission date would allow Congress slightly more than a month to examine the budget before the summer recess, and then most of September to actually work on the proposals. Moreover, the February 1 through June 1 period does not have to be lost time from a congressional perspective since Congress could be working with the administration on what is achievable in budget proposals. Finally, prior to FY-77, when the fiscal year began on July 1, no great problems were encountered by having only five months between the budget submission date and the beginning of the new fiscal year.

35. Should the president have the power to use a line-item veto to delete segments of legislation?

The line-item veto[1] is a product of frustration—frustration at being unable to control either budget expenditures or resulting deficits. Its genesis is similar to Gramm-Rudman-Hollings and the balanced-budget amendment, two other well-intentioned but misguided approaches. The line-item veto presupposes much of the legislation sent to the president by Congress is flawed and the chief executive has a higher degree of wisdom, or is less politically motivated, than Congress.

That is a difficult argument to justify.

In addition, a line-item veto cannot only substantially revise legislation, but the final product can prove contradictory to congressional intentions. Thus, the power of the line-item veto could well be the power to legislate.

The argument is made that the line-item veto is needed because Congress is the primary culprit in the deficit explosion. The facts, however, do not bear this out. In the FY-75/FY-76 period, both the legislative and executive branches were equally responsible for the large deficit increase: Congress spent, but the White House displayed little in the way of fiscal leadership. In the FY-82/FY-83 period—the "worst of the worst" from a deficit perspective—the executive branch bears most of the responsibility for instigating the collapse of tax receipts.

All of this is not to say the current situation is satisfactory. Ill-advised amendments or riders are often attached to legislation by members of Congress who know that the individual items cannot pass on their own merits. The president, either because of a time constraint, or because most of the legislation is worthwhile, may reluctantly sign such a bill. Yet, the proper solution to this problem is for Congress to place limitations on riders and amendments, especially in areas of legislation such as debt ceiling increases, and to limit the use of omnibus bills.

---

[1] A "line-item" veto would allow the president to delete unacceptable portions of a proposed piece of legislation. Presently, he either accepts or vetoes the legislation in its entirety.

36. Should a nongovernment/nonpartisan body be established whose specific task is estimating budget deficits?

The establishment of an independent organization to make budget estimates could perform a considerable public service. It would mean improved objectivity and would put pressure on public officials to come up with reasonable estimates. The group would have to be financed and chosen by nonofficial sources. It would have to concentrate entirely on making budget forecasts, and must not show any preference as to whether taxes or expenditure should be raised or lowered. Objective assessments would be made as to what is likely to occur with regard to economic activity, inflation, interest rates, and what legislation is likely to be passed by Congress.

New budget projections could be released every six months and the group would concentrate its attention on both the current and upcoming fiscal year. Such budget enlightenment would induce appropriate decisions and policies on the part of the government at a much earlier date. For example, in FY-82 and FY-83, a group such as this might have been very helpful in pointing out the receipts shortfall. Such an analysis might have induced Congress to suppress spending at an earlier date.

The need for a nonpartisan budget-estimating group is strictly a function of objectivity. If the budget remains primarily a political document, the need for such an organization is considerable. Objectivity is difficult to measure, but one way of assessing it is to ask the question: did the administration, in its projections, start with a desired budget deficit and then work its way back to the receipts and expenditures levels which would achieve that objective? If the answer is yes, then the nonpartisan estimating group could serve a very useful purpose since it would start with the most likely levels of receipts and expenditures, adjust for likely policy changes, and arrive at a deficit which may not be to an administration's liking.

It should be noted the scope of this proposed independent body is extremely limited. There is no attempt to determine a ''proper'' level of receipts and expenditures, or what constitutes a reasonable deficit. Nor is there an attempt to assess whether, or how, expenditures or taxes should be changed. The reason for this is that it is impossible to form a politically neutral group able to formulate concrete and practical recommendations which could be legislated without political tampering.

37. Is there a price to be paid for using the current Gramm-Rudman-Hollings (GRH) approach?

There are numerous shortcomings in the GRH legislation passed in September 1987, which requires across-the-board spending reductions if budget deficits are above targeted levels. Most of these failings were inherited from previous legislation that was unconstitutional. Nevertheless, a price ultimately will be paid for the shortcomings.

GRH lacks a systematic approach as to how deficit targets should be set; it lacks flexibility when economic performance is substantially different from expectations; its long-term targets are no more than wishful thinking; and it adds to the relative power of the Office of Management and Budget (OMB) at the expense of the Congressional Budget Office (CBO). Moreover, GRH ultimately will require spending reductions in areas that should not be reduced, and will penalize areas that were the most frugal in the past. The following discussion addresses several of these problems starting with the lack of flexibility.

If the economy should move into a recession, the combination of a huge budget deficit and the GRH legislation could cause the government to follow policies which would result in a weaker economy and a worsening budget deficit. As the economy softens, tax receipts decline and government spending tied to economic activity (such as unemployment payments) expands. However, GRH requires expenditure cutbacks as the deficit increases.

Supporters of GRH would contend this analysis is unfair since GRH contains a fail-safe mechanism—it would not apply if there are two quarters of less than 1 percent real GNP growth. Yet, this offers little in the way of real protection since the time lag between when a recession begins and when it is realized can be considerable. There is no guarantee a recession will start at the beginning of a quarter, and if there is enough strength early in the period, real growth could remain above 1 percent for the quarter as a whole. The preliminary GNP results are not published for about one month after a quarter ends—not exactly real-time information. And, there are a number of revisions in the GNP numbers, with the second revision coming almost three months after the end of any given quarter.

As an example, a recession could begin in the middle of the second quarter, but not show in that quarter's GNP numbers. Third-quarter data could indicate less than 1 percent real growth, but the preliminary number for the fourth quarter could turn out to be above 1 percent.

However, late in the first quarter of the following year, real GNP for the fourth quarter might well be revised below 1 percent. Thus, the two quarters showing below 1 percent real growth would have finally materialized. In this case, the fail-safe mechanism would not have taken hold until almost one year after the recession began. So much for this method of protection.

If such a mechanism is to be used, a much more timely indicator is necessary. Industrial production, for example, is published monthly and is not subject to major revisions. However, it, too, is not without some important limitations. It does not include services, it can be influenced by strikes, and it does not directly reflect consumer spending or income.

A problem in using any economic indicator is determining how much weakness is needed, and for how long, before the fail-safe mechanism is triggered. There is also the question of what would be needed in the way of economic improvement for the GRH targets to again be operative. Finally, if the economy is barely moving ahead and is in a growth recession, it is possible the fail-safe mechanism could be turned on and off excessively.

A better approach would be to make GRH targets more reasonable and to forget about a flawed fail-safe system which offers little real protection. A more realistic procedure would be to base deficit-reduction targets on the CBO's real GNP forecast for the new fiscal year, made several months before the period begins. That target would then be adjusted near the middle of the fiscal year, based on changes in the CBO's real GNP forecast. Once the deficit declines to a point where it is at a moderate percentage of nominal GNP—1 percent or less—the formula would no longer be operative.

The size of the deficit reduction could be based on a predetermined formula related to real GNP growth. If the executive branch is the one to propose the formula, this might limit any constitutional problems. The table on page 187 presents one possibility.

Thus, if annual real growth is estimated at 3 percent, the deficit-reduction target for the year would be 10 percent. If the estimate is 1 percent for real GNP growth, the target would be to hold the deficit unchanged, and if the GNP estimate is minus 3 percent, the deficit deterioration would be held to 16 percent.

Such an approach should work reasonably well. Since underlying GNP growth is about 3 percent (based on the likely growth in the labor force and productivity) and not 1 percent, the formula over time would lower the deficit. The fact that percentage changes targeted in the deficit move up more rapidly when the economy is rising than when it is falling

CBO Real GNP Estimate		Targeted Change in Budget Deficit
+ 6%	=	− 25%
+ 5	=	− 20
+ 4	=	− 15
+ 3	=	− 10
+ 2	=	− 5
+ 1	=	0
0	=	+ 4
− 1	=	+ 8
− 2	=	+ 12
− 3	=	+ 16
− 4	=	+ 20

should also help bring down the deficit. Yet the decline targeted for the deficit in any one year would not be so precipitous as to cause the economy to slip into a recession. The approach would explicitly recognize a deterioration in the budget should be expected in a recession, and this includes a period of unchanged real GNP growth.

This technique would add to the power of the CBO and reduce the power of other congressional committees, which is a good idea when the objective is to reduce the deficit. The system also puts considerable pressure on the CBO to make its GNP forecast as accurate and nonpolitical as possible since the deficit target will be based on this number. The targeting authority should be given to the CBO rather than the OMB because an agency in the executive branch is likely to be slower and more reluctant to forecast either economic or budget adversity.

The suggested targeting technique is based on the premise there is no inherent reason to have a precisely balanced budget. This is a logical assumption since the accounting approach used does not give an exact measurement of the deficit. Moreover, the purpose of fiscal control should be to create an environment whereby if deficits do occur, they are contained at manageable levels with no major economic or financial problems as a result.

As a matter of fact, one could argue there is an important plus in having regular but moderate-size deficits: it allows the government securities market to expand and to be viable and highly liquid as well, which is a plus for those seeking outlets for their funds. A deficit of 1 percent of nominal GNP would mean less than a $50 billion addition to Treasury debt outstanding (excluding the trust accounts)—a quite manageable amount.

38. Is there a better way, under Gramm-Rudman-Hollings, to improve mandated expenditure reductions?

The current legislation lacks flexibility and equity, and can be improved. The Office of Management and Budget (OMB) determines the size of the deficit reduction, and if Congress and the president cannot agree on tax increases and/or spending reductions, an across-the-board percentage cut in outlays is mandated. There is an inflation adjustment before the spending reduction, and some areas, such as social security, are excluded from reductions entirely. Across-the-board reductions occur even though some areas should have larger cuts, while others should have little or none.

If Congress and the president cannot agree in stage one, a better approach would be to allow each side to "protect" 25 percent of total spending (excluding interest costs). The protection, however, would not be complete. Spending increases would be limited to the estimated advance in the CPI for the fiscal year, but not exceeding 6 percent. Both Congress and the president could take full advantage of this protection, use it partially, or not use it at all. If both decide to protect 25 percent, spending reductions will center in the remaining 50 percent.

Nonprotected areas will also have a spending ceiling; half the estimated advance in the CPI for the fiscal year, but no more than 3 percent.

Once maximum spending levels are determined for the protected and nonprotected areas, any additional reductions would come from the nonprotected areas. Congress and the president would separately determine how each wants to divide the nonprotected cutbacks, and where differences exist, an average would be used.

If this approach had been used in FY-88, Congress would probably have protected HHS items, while President Reagan would have protected military areas.

Under the current system, the second or mandatory phase is viewed as so onerous it puts pressure on Congress and the president to arrive at a tax increase/expenditure reduction agreement. Yet, the proposal presented here is not without its pressures. No spending area would be excluded from the system (except interest costs), and the cutback in some nonprotected areas could be so large as to be even more painful than a tax increase. Individual programs would be studied more closely for possible savings, which is not the case when an across-the-board percentage reduction is imposed. Finally, the suggested system puts additional pressure on the OMB to come up with realistic budget deficit targets. Otherwise, it could mean large and politically painful reductions for some areas.

39. Would a balanced-budget amendment be an improvement over Gramm-Rudman-Hollings (GRH)?

The current balanced-budget amendment proposal has many shortcomings, considerably more than GRH.

The FY-87 deficit (of $150 billion) is so large it would be impossible to move quickly to a balanced-budget position. Moreover, if the attempt was made to do so, a far-from-robust economy would probably move into a recession, which would cause the deficit to rise, not decline. At least in the case of GRH, there is a plan to move the budget into balance over a number of years.

In the area of flexibility, while neither proposal distinguishes itself, the balanced-budget amendment is much less flexible. There are many instances when the economic situation dictates that a balanced budget is inappropriate, and perhaps not even possible. At least GRH has some provisions which allow exceptions to its rules. Moreover, Congress can change both the deficit targets and their timing.

GRH also is more than just budget targets. It tries to achieve its objectives by forcing Congress to make cuts in spending. The balanced-budget proposal, however, does not have a game plan for achieving its objective. Thus, not only is its goal unachievable under current budget definition, but there is no designated method for reaching this goal. The result would be an open invitation to chaos.

The balanced budget proposal clearly runs a distant second to GRH. To be a distant second is bad enough, but especially so since GRH has more than its own share of shortcomings—its deficit targets are unrealistically low, quite rigid, and likely to result in spending cutbacks in the wrong areas, for the wrong amounts, and at the wrong time.

40. Is it possible to devise a budget amendment that makes sense?

On November 18, 1987, this author presented a proposal to a subcommittee of the House Committee on the Judiciary. Following is the proposal and text of the statement:

PROPOSAL. If the unified budget in the previous fiscal year was in deficit, then passage by Congress of spending bills would require a 60 percent approval by each house and a 70 percent approval to override a presidential veto.

This spending-control amendment (SCA) would be a substitute for the balanced-budget amendment (BBA). An explanation of the advantages of SCA indicates the shortcomings of the BBA.

The SCA is based on actual budget numbers, not controversial estimates for the new fiscal year. It is not necessary, for example, to make highly tentative receipts estimates which is the case under the BBA.

The SCA attacks excessive spending in a preventive manner since spending bills will be more difficult to pass. Congress will be able to pass only those spending increases they feel the strongest about. Under the BBA, the spending process itself is not addressed. Moreover, major problems are likely on what areas should be cut, by how much, who should make the decisions, and what are the penalties if the reductions are not made. The best decisions are not likely to be made under the BBA.

The SCA would have no major transition problems. Spending growth would be contained, and assuming reasonable economic growth, the deficit problem would disappear over several years. There would be no $150 billion or $200 billion deficit reduction shock, which is apparently what would happen under the BBA.

After the transition adjustment, the SCA would still allow flexibility in the budget. If the economy is soft, moderate deficits could occur, and if economic growth is too strong to be sustainable, surpluses would be possible. In a recession, for example, if Congress felt strongly about increasing spending, it would do so in order to induce economic growth. Incidentally, weak economic growth will make it virtually impossible to balance the budget because of a receipts shortfall.

There is no need under the SCA to look for loopholes or changes in the current accounting system. Under the BBA, that may not be the case, since it could require creative accounting to reach a balanced budget level.

The SCA has two reenforcing proposals. Not only will it be more difficult for Congress to increase spending, but it will be more difficult for Congress to override the president's veto on spending bills. It also reduces any need, or justification, for a line-item veto as it achieves the same objective. The BBA does not incorporate techniques for holding down government spending.

One of the most important advantages of the SCA over the BBA is utilization of time. When Congress is bogged down in one area, it has less time for other items. The decision making and implementation of the BBA would be a very time-consuming process.

CONCLUSIONS. The objective of budgetary policy should not be to have a balanced budget every year, irrespective of the economic consequences. The objective should be to have strong and sustainable economic growth over an extended period and to have a budget policy that leads to that end. Such a budget policy would involve moderate surpluses in some years, and moderate deficits in other years. The spending control amendment would indicate the seriousness that pragmatic economists place on controlling spending and budget deficits, without the inflexibilities and administrative nightmares that the balanced-budget amendment would involve. Because one is against the current balanced-budget amendment proposal does not mean one is against balancing the budget.

41. Have official forecasts of appropriations and outlays accurately predicted turning points in spending?

For an extended period, official spending estimates were not reliable indicators. As illustrated in Figure IV-41.1, these estimates failed to predict the large spending growth in FY-75, the sharp increase in FY-80, and initially the major slowing from FY-81 through FY-84. That should come as no surprise, even setting aside political considerations, inasmuch as the estimates are published about 8 months before the fiscal year begins and 20 months before it ends. Yet, from FY-83 through FY-87 these estimates were a respectable predictor of outlays. If this relationship is valid for FY-88, the spending increase would be about 3 to 4 percent.

Since estimates of appropriations and outlays have not been consistently successful forecasters of outlays over the FY-74 to FY-87 period, the question arises as to whether actual appropriations may be a better forecaster.

The answer is no.

New appropriations often are not passed before the actual spending occurs, and there are nuances to contend with such as continuing and supplemental appropriations. Often a fiscal year starts with few if any budget appropriations in place. Moreover, when funds may be appropriated does not indicate when they will be spent.

The best approach for private forecasters to use in estimating spending is still judgmental. It involves looking at recent changes in inflation and interest rates, the trend of government contract awards, especially in the military area, changes in outlays mandated by current or probable changes in the law, and then analyzing what appear to be underlying trends in various spending areas. Official estimates add one more item to these forecasting tools.

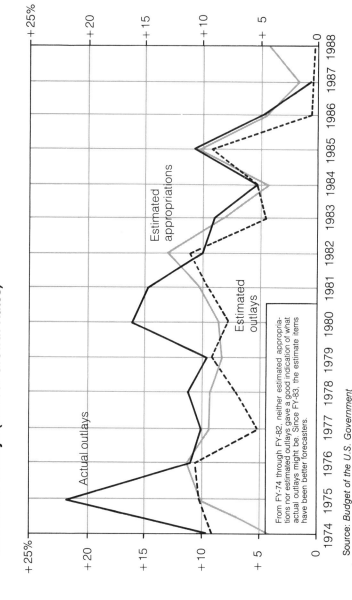

FIGURE IV-41.1 Estimated Appropriations and Outlays Compared with Actual Outlays (Annual Growth Rates)

From FY-74 through FY-82, neither estimated appropriations nor estimated outlays gave a good indication of what actual outlays might be. Since FY-83, the estimate items have been better forecasters.

Actual outlays

Estimated appropriations

Estimated outlays

Source: *Budget of the U.S. Government*

194

42. How can the budget deficit be so large when both Congress and the administration claim they are "saving" so much money?

When any politician talks in terms of "saving"—beware! There is a good chance the figures presented are misleading. The so-called savings are often based on unrealistic spending estimates or are accomplished in ways which do not represent true savings, such as selling assets, which are booked as negative outlays. Also, what may be saved can, and often is, quietly added back later.

Talking about savings in specific areas also gives the appearance of more broadly based savings than actually exists, and diverts attention from those areas where cost overruns do exist. These areas, of course, receive little publicity.

The only way to analyze outlays properly is to start with the most detailed spending items and work to the broader totals. It is what is spent that counts, not what is purportedly saved. As evidence of this apparent semantics game, look at how much expenditures have grown since FY-74, despite all the money that has been "saved."

The events of November 1987, resulting from Gramm-Rudman-Hollings, are another illustration of how the savings concept can be misused. The Act requires a deficit reduction of at least $23 billion for FY-88 and the president and Congress promise even more. Yet, this savings is not from the $150 billion actual shortfall for FY-87, but from the estimated deficit for FY-88. Without the savings, the FY-88 deficit would probably be $180 billion or $190 billion. Thus, even after the savings, the deficit for FY-88 will increase.

This is not the end of this savings story. Budget deficit targets drop sharply during the first half of the coming decade. However, the underlying improvement in the budget will not keep pace. Thus, the requested savings will grow each year to a point where they are grossly unrealistic. GRH deficit targets will then have to be rewritten.

43. Can government accounting remove expenditures merely by placing them off budget?

The government has used a unified budget concept since FY-69 and, therefore, virtually all fiscal transactions with the public are presented.

The unified budget separates receipts and outlays into on-budget and off-budget categories and the result of the two are then combined. Official budget estimates and actual outcomes emphasize the combined figures as do the monthly receipts and expenditures data published by the Treasury. Therefore, there is no attempt to exclude categories from the overall budget totals. (The Federal Savings and Loan Corp. [FSLIC] may be one of the few exceptions.)

Although items are included in the budget, they may not be presented in the most straightforward manner. The separation between on- and off-budget items often seems arbitrary, and quite a few changes have been made over the years. That makes it difficult to analyze the components of the budget and how they affect the overall picture.

Off-budget items do not usually go through the same rigors of the budget process as on-budget items, with the result that the former are more difficult to control. To better understand these distinctions and problems, a history of the most important changes since the early 1970s is presented.

Since the adoption of the unified concept approach in 1969, items have been moved in and out of the on-budget category. In 1971, various laws were enacted which removed several items from the on-budget section. The first was the Export-Import Bank, followed by the Postal Service Fund, the Rural Telephone Bank, the Rural Electrification and Telephone Revolving Fund, and the Housing for the Elderly or Handicapped Fund.

Several organizations were established off budget. They were the Federal Financing Bank, the U.S. Railway Association, and the Pension Benefit Guaranty Corp. The Exchange Stabilization Fund at that time was outside the budget and was initially classified as a deposit fund rather than an off-budget entity.

The trend toward a steady expansion of off-budget items subsequently changed. The Export-Import Bank, the Housing for the Elderly and Handicapped Fund, and the Pension Benefit Guaranty Corp. were put on budget by statute. The operations of the Exchange Stabilization Fund were also put on budget, as were most of the transactions of the U.S. Railway Association.

An exception to this trend occurred in the early 1980s when two new off-budget entities were established to implement certain energy programs: the Synthetic Fuels Corp. and the cost of purchasing oil for the strategic petroleum reserve.

Although entities may have been classified as off budget, some outlays relating to their operations have been included in the on-budget totals. These include funding for the previously mentioned Synthetic Fuels Corp. and certain expenses of the strategic petroleum reserve, federal payment to the Postal Service Fund, administrative expenses of the U.S. Railway Association, and administrative expenses and appropriations to reimburse losses sustained by the Rural Electrification Administration.

Moreover, portions of some off-budget entities have been subject to other methods of presidential and congressional review. Most notable is the credit budget which includes direct-loan obligations and guaranteed loan commitments for both on- and off-budget agencies. Since1981, budget resolutions have contained credit targets, including obligations for new direct loans made by the off-budget federal entities.

Those entities which were off budget before 1986 primarily made direct loans to the public, with the Federal Financing Bank (FFB) accounting for most of the off-budget outlays. The FFB did not operate programs itself; rather, it financed other programs within the government. In December 1985, the Gramm-Rudman-Hollings (GRH) Act placed the FFB, along with all other off-budget entities, on budget.

The Act required the outlays of the FFB be charged to the agencies which used the FFB to finance their programs. Previously this spending was treated as an outlay of the FFB itself. Therefore, such spending is now reflected in both outlays and the on-budget deficit, and the authority for programs is now included in the budgetary authority totals.

While the trend in the early and mid-1980s was to switch entities from off budget to on budget, that was not the case for social security. The Social Security Amendments of 1983 provided, beginning in 1993, old age and survivors insurance (OASI), disability, and hospital insurance trust accounts would be excluded from the budget. Then in late 1985, the GRH legislation accelerated the off-budget status of OASI and disability to 1986. However, GRH did provide that the receipts and disbursements of these two funds be included in calculating both the excess deficit and the maximum deficit allowed under this Act.

As of mid-1987, by law, the off-budget deficit must be included when calculating the maximum deficit amounts set by GRH. The surplus or deficit of off-budget entities is added to the on-budget deficit to derive the total deficit. Off-budget entities may hold a significant amount of debt securities, but almost all are subject to the statutory debt limitation. However, appropriations for off-budget programs and other sources of authority are not included in the totals of budgetary authority. Moreover, their outlays, receipts, and surpluses or deficits ordinarily are not subject to targets as established by the congressional budget resolution.

If the last several pages seem confusing and complicated, they have achieved their objective. These are the problems analysts have had to contend with in studying the budget numbers and process. For those who want additional historical detail, the information can be obtained in the *Budget of the U.S. Government*, fiscal year 1987, Section 6a, page 6.

44. Besides off-budget items, are there other ways the government can be less than straightforward in its budget reporting?

There are several approaches the government uses which make the interpretation of its data more difficult. For example, total government outlays are reduced by a category called undistributed offsetting receipts. In FY-87, this totaled $73 billion, a not inconsequential amount. The category is composed primarily of interest received by trust funds, the employer share of employee retirement accounts, rents and royalties on the outer continental shelf, and sale of major assets. Interest and the retirement areas account for the major portion, although in FY-81 and again in FY-83, rents and royalties contributed over $10 billion. As of FY-87 the sale of major assets amounted to only $2 billion. If it had been up to the Reagan administration, asset sales would have been much larger.

UNDISTRIBUTED OFFSETTING RECEIPTS. Despite the philosophical and accounting benefits, the current treatment of undistributed offsetting receipts isn't necessarily logical or proper. A better approach would be to add the undistributed offsetting receipts to the revenue side. The reported deficit would remain the same, but the budget would show higher receipts and expenditures than under the current system. More significantly, the numbers would better reflect expenditure levels and their annual growth rates and patterns.

ASSET SALES. Asset sales fit in well with the Reagan administration's idea of a greater privatization of the budget. They enable the administration to move the production of goods and services from the government to the private sector, which is one of its major philosophical objectives. At the same time, asset sales reduce government spending—another administration objective. Major privatization initiatives late in the Reagan era included the sale of Conrail, Amtrak, Naval Petroleum Reserves, Power Marketing Administration, Helium Operations, and real property considered as excess.

Negative outlays were important to the Reagan administration in another respect. It was unwilling to make substantial reductions in military outlays. And with Congress controlled by the Democrats, it was difficult to attain large reductions in nondefense outlays. With government spending having slowed considerably in recent years, there are a reduced number of areas where substantial cuts can be made. That makes negative outlays attractive because they allow large-scale expenditure reductions over a relatively short time.

LOANS AND LOAN GUARANTEES. Loans and loan guarantees are a second area which makes interpretation of the budget results more difficult. These items are placed in "the Credit Budget."

By the end of FY-87, the amount outstanding for these items was $741 billion. Despite $187 billion in new loans and guarantees made in FY-87, the amount outstanding declined. The Reagan administration hopes that by FY-92, the gross annual increases can be held to $150 billion. This may be wishful thinking.

The key question with respect to loans and loan guarantees is one of potential adversity. When loans are made, there is an outflow of funds similar to what happens with expenditures. However, there is an assumption all the loans will be repaid, which is not a sure thing. Loan guarantees are different because there is no initial outlay of funds, and it is impossible to predict if any of these guarantees will ever be implemented.

In the case of both loans and guarantees, they are included in the credit budget, which is the proper place. It would be misleading to consider either as expenditures. What is questionable, however, is the lack of prominence given to the credit budget totals. If credit budget numbers were inserted immediately following the expenditure figures in the annual budget book and the monthly Treasury statement of receipts and outlays, analysts would have an overall perception of the amounts outstanding and how they are changing.

THE DEFENSE BUDGET. The defense budget is another area where there is room for improvement in data presentation. At this point, the major categories of defense spending are (1) personnel, (2) procurement, (3) operations and maintenance, and (4) research and development. The problem with this approach is it emphasizes how funds are spent generically—how much for people, equipment, daily operations, and development of future weapons systems. Even the accuracy of this breakout is questionable since there are personnel costs in other areas which are not classified as such.

Therefore, not only is the classification faulty, but it does not inform analysts of the types of defense items which are being purchased. Large increases in these generic categories do not automatically translate into a commensurate improvement in defense capability.

What is needed is to divide the defense budget into categories based on various missions, and to present the monthly results on that basis. This should pose no great problems inasmuch as the government already divides budget authority by missions. If it can be done in terms of authority, it can also be done in terms of expenditures. There are ten mission categories listed by the government: (1) strategic forces; (2) general purpose forces; (3) intelligence and communications; (4) airlift and sealift; (5) guard and reserve; (6) research and development; (7) central supply and maintenance; (8) training, medical, and other general personnel activities; (9) administration and support activities; and (10) support of other nations.

The breakout by mission allows an analyst to make a better qualitative judgment as to how money is being spent. Much of the nondefense budget is already presented on a similar basis. For example, the largest area in the budget—health and human services (HHS)—is broken out by the type of service rendered, not by the type of input which went into the spending.

The current defense budget is misleading in two other respects. Military pensions have been moved from the Department of Defense (Military) to the Department of Defense (Civil). Thus, while the total remains the same, the classification is somewhat less than straightforward. Veterans Benefits and Services are listed under a separate category outside the defense area, which understates military costs. If one wants to carry this analysis even further, there are also some military costs included in International Affairs, and General Science, Space, and Technology.

It is not the intention of this analysis to imply excessive amounts are being spent on defense, or that the government is trying to hide something. What it does suggest, however, is that more money is being spent on the military than a cursory glance would suggest, and that data can be presented in such a way as to allow analysts to make better judgments as to whether funds are being spent in the most effective and efficient manner.

PART FIVE

BUDGET CONCEPTS QUESTIONED, BUDGET RELATIONSHIPS ANALYZED

45. Is fiscal "policy" truly a policy?

The word policy in the term fiscal policy is a misnomer. There is no highly orchestrated single policy, but rather what may best be described as a broad array of fiscal forces, often moving in different directions, where the results and their timing are unknown.

Fiscal forces are ongoing, but policy decisions are framed and implemented in a rather sporadic manner.

Both the executive and legislative branches share fiscal responsibility. Yet while an administration has the power to propose, it does not have the power to implement. Congress has the power to review, revise and implement, but seldom has the capability to act with unity of purpose. Therefore, when Congress finally does act, original budget proposals are often unrecognizable and the timing of their passage inappropriate.

Government outlays are uncontrollable—at least in the short run. Lack of control often is due to past commitments or current laws, as well as to outside forces such as interest rate changes, unexpected international occurrences, and domestic political shocks. The three largest expenditure categories in the budget—health and human services, defense, and interest—are among the least controllable. In FY-87, they accounted for roughly two-thirds of $1 trillion in total outlays, which helps explain why it has been so difficult to contain spending.

While the budget does not lend itself to control on the outlay side, it is even less controllable on the receipts side. Tax inflows are primarily a function of the strength of the economy rather than specific government policies. Tax law changes often take years to implement and the receipts impact is quite uncertain and difficult to predict.

The disastrous revenue results of the 1981 tax law change are a good example of unexpected problems encountered; the economy was not stimulated anywhere near the degree expected and the hemorrhaging of tax receipts was massive. Moreover, persistent unrealistic expectations as to what the legislation might have achieved caused policies to remain in place. Thus, an opportunity was lost to change receipts and expenditure policies in an enlightened manner. Unfortunately, it took several years for those with vested economic and political interests to admit the 1981 tax package had done more harm than good—and there are still those who refuse to admit its failure. Therefore, it should come as no surprise in the period from FY-74 to FY-86, while economic performance was respectable, the tax system was a drag on receipts, especially in the 1980s.

The results of the Tax Reform Act of 1986 will not be known for several years. Preliminary evidence indicates the errors of commission seem less in this legislation than in the 1981 act, plus the tax system now seems more equitable. However, the errors of omission in the 1986 legislation may be considerable, which is unfortunate because the budget is still far from under control. By attempting to make the legislation revenue neutral, the government may have made it revenue negative (for FY-88 and beyond). There is no indication the revenue loss will stimulate the savings and investment components of the economy, and could well retard them. It will probably take until CY-89 or CY-90 before these shortcomings are realized, and in the meantime, opportunities to address the budget deficit problem realistically will have been lost.

Possibly the best way to point up the inherent problems of orchestrating fiscal forces is to compare the fiscal process with monetary policy. The latter is designed, implemented, and fine-tuned by one organization—the Federal Reserve. Substantial and sufficient power is placed in the hands of the Federal Open Market Committee (FOMC) and its chairman, so the system can act quickly and decisively. The chairman typically has been able to dominate policy, and inaction is seldom a problem. There is a general understanding that policy is an ongoing process, even if no overt changes take place.

Since the Federal Reserve does both the planning and implementing of policy, it is solely responsible for the results. If necessary, adjustments to policy can be made in a matter of hours, and the overall breadth of policies, and the types of decisions made, are relatively limited. The Federal Reserve is more insulated from political pressure than almost any other government-type organization and can more easily make decisions which are politically unpopular in the short run to achieve positive results in the long run.

The public is not fully aware of modest policy changes as they occur, which allows the monetary authorities to change gears quietly and easily, and without public embarrassment. The Federal Reserve benefits from a strong research staff, and its employees often stay for decades. That same type of longevity is also true with respect to FOMC members. The monetary authorities do not take time off for recesses or electioneering, and can devote almost full-time attention to monetary policy.

Fiscal policy lacks in varying degrees all of the positive characteristics of monetary policy. Such fiscal policy shortcomings make it obvious why the Federal Reserve should have greater authority and responsibility for the shorter-term performance of the economy—in particular fine-tuning and cyclical adjustments. The government, in trying to orchestrate its fiscal forces, should have the responsibility for longer-term economic growth, budget performance, and equitability of the fiscal system. Except for automatic stabilizers inherent in some budget areas, it should stay out of the fine-tuning and countercyclical business.

46. Is the federal budget document and process similar to those in the corporate world?

Federal and corporate budget approaches are worlds apart. Yet, many who study the federal budget do not fully appreciate the difference. A corporate budget document is an internal operating plan where there is no need for outside public relations—although there is plenty inside. The chief executive officer (CEO) normally has the final word on the document and its implementation. If conditions change drastically, the CEO can usually—by a command—either change the budget, or the way it is carried out. In well-run corporations, budget assumptions used for estimates tend to be realistic. Often, more than one set of assumptions is used, and more than one plan is developed.

In some companies, the CEO tends to hold his leadership position for a substantial number of years and has the opportunity to develop a budget staff and procedures which suit a particular style of management. Those who work on the specifics of the budget are typically senior members of management with considerable longevity in their firms, who have had a chance to prove themselves over time to the CEO. They are often involved in carrying out the budget, and are held directly responsible for errors in their estimates and judgments.

The federal budget situation is different in virtually every one of these aspects. The government document is submitted to the public and, therefore, has a strong public relations aspect. Many of the assumptions and forecasts are developed in the light of such public relations. With the document usually presented about eight months before the fiscal year begins, many of the forecasts are out of date by the time the budget goes into effect. Once the budget and its philosophies are presented, an administration usually finds it politically awkward to reverse course. Fine-tuning becomes very difficult because once the budget is released, the administration lobbies for its acceptance by Congress.

The actual procedures for carrying out the federal budget also make the ultimate results far less certain than in the business sector. The government is a labyrinth of checks and balances, while most corporations are run on a dictatorial basis. Proposals have to go through numerous committees in both houses of Congress before being approved, and then, when each house accepts the proposals, their differences have to be reconciled. Not only are there opposing political parties involved in this process, but members of the president's own party are often not supportive. The final result is that many proposals are either buried in Congress, or are so drastically altered, they become almost unrecognizable. Those proposals that do get through are often implemented at such a distant date, they can even prove to be counterproductive.

As for the quality of estimates and projections, the government sector generally lacks the objectivity of the private sector. Federal estimates and projections always have a bullish bias; recessions are never anticipated, interest rates are always expected to move down and stay down, and spending is always expected to remain under control. Only one scenario and one set of assumptions are used.

The massive and all-encompassing nature of the federal budget makes it difficult to coordinate its various areas. The problems of familiarity and coordination are considerable, especially for a new administration, as there is not much time to put its people into place. The large number of so-called uncontrollable outlays seems to be more of a problem in the public sector, and a new administration is again at a considerable disadvantage. External forces often affect the government budget in major and surprising ways, probably more so than in the private sector.

Then there is the difference with regard to responsibility for the accuracy of estimates. In the corporate world, department heads bear much of the responsibility, not only for budget estimates, but for the results as well. In the case of government, it is staff members who are primarily involved in the forecasts, and if their projections prove faulty, penalties are nowhere near as severe as in the private sector (or there are no penalties at all). Procedures in the public sector often demand that many individuals within the bureaucratic chain of command have to be involved in the budget process, which makes accountability almost impossible.

The experiences from FY-74 through FY-87 make it abundantly clear both the government budget and its process are in dire need of some major improvements. At present, the cost of making errors is too great and the penalties for being wrong are too modest.

The thrust of the suggestions made throughout this book is to improve the budget and its process, not to denigrate those public servants engaged in making estimates. Yet it is not unreasonable to require at least some minimal amount of accountability with respect to the accuracy of these estimates.

A simple way to apply a reasonable amount of pressure would be to present, as part of the annual budget document, all of the preceding year's assumptions and forecasts. The actual results would be compared with those forecasts and detailed explanations given as to what went wrong. If this had been done at the beginning of the FY-83 budget document, some of the horrendous estimating errors might have been avoided.

47. Should fiscal policy be used for countercyclical purposes such as stimulating the economy?

The use of fiscal policy to achieve countercyclical[1] goals is a bad idea. (The thought was touched upon previously in answering the question: Is fiscal policy truly a policy?) There are two general and a number of specific arguments which can be made against such a proposal. One of the general arguments is there are more important budget priorities, and they are likely to conflict with countercyclical measures. The second general argument is a countercyclical approach is neither practical nor workable.

As for the first argument, there are three priorities for fiscal policy which should take precedence over a countercyclical approach. The number one priority, from both an economic and political standpoint, is to reduce the budget deficit. From an economic perspective, a huge budget deficit puts upward pressure on interest rates, limits the degree of accommodativeness of monetary policy, creates greater potential for higher inflation, and because of a low domestic savings rate, requires substantial investment funds be attracted from abroad. The more the United States finances its budget deficit abroad, the larger the current account deficit, and the greater the possibility of downward pressure on the dollar. From a political perspective, a large budget deficit is one of the most disturbing areas to the American voter. Excessive deficits do not indicate a sound government, and no politician wants to be considered a part of, or contributing to, an unsound government.

The second priority of fiscal policy should be to help maximize economic growth over the long run. Tax laws should induce well-conceived, long-term investments and government outlays should be directed, whenever possible, to their most productive uses. The better the job fiscal policy does in stimulating long-term economic growth, the easier it will be to achieve the first objective of reducing the budget deficit.

The third priority should be to improve the equitability of fiscal policy. That involves not only how the tax burden is divided, but also who gets what on the spending side. Many of the political battles over the Tax Reform Act of 1986 had to do with who would win and who would lose. The initial conflicts centered on individuals versus corporations, and then on the division of burdens (and benefits) among upper-,

[1]Countercyclical policies are those that attempt to prevent the economy from becoming either too weak or too strong. They will be stimulative if the economy is faltering and restrictive if it is becoming overheated.

middle-, and lower-income individuals. There was considerable redressing of the tax burden and the result was a much more equitable system after the legislation was passed.

Equity in expenditures is an especially important issue because the Reagan administration tried to do the impossible—eliminate the deficit almost entirely by cutbacks in outlays. Considerable conflicts have developed as to where the cutbacks should be made. While much of the conflict is between defense and nondefense outlays, there are considerable differences of opinion as to which nondefense programs should be cut. Thus, if the main objectives of fiscal policy should be to reduce the deficit, cultivate long-term economic growth, and manage receipts and expenditures in a fair and equitable manner, there is little room to think in terms of countercyclical measures, especially when they are in conflict with other objectives.

Further arguments against a countercyclical emphasis for fiscal policy are not hard to find. It is difficult for the government to develop countercyclical policies that are well conceived, well orchestrated, and timely. Specifically, there is a time lag between when budget proposals are presented and when they are implemented; there is the problem of original proposals bearing little, if any, resemblance to what is finally put in place; and once a policy becomes law, it is very hard to fine-tune or reverse course based on realities. Another problem is that countercyclical proposals are often chosen on the basis of their political and public relations appeal, rather than on their economic merit.

If fiscal policies are to be countercyclical, then the government must be willing—in unsustainably strong economic times, when fear of inflation is a problem—to lower spending, raise taxes, or do both. History suggests, however, such awkward political decisions are seldom, if ever, made. Thus, if the government stimulates with politically attractive measures, but is unwilling to restrict through politically unpalatable measures, an out-of-control deficit is the ultimate outcome.

Finally, the administration and Congress carrying out fiscal policies may be different from the preceding administration and Congress which proposed and inaugurated the policies. That can lead to inconsistency and confusion.

This analysis strongly suggests the government should avoid a countercyclical approach in its fiscal policies, even if the budget is close to balance, the long-term economic outlook is favorable, and the American people are relatively satisfied with the equity of the tax burden and government outlays. These three objectives are not one-time propositions; they need to be met on a continual basis. If these guidelines are followed, fiscal policy would then make its maximum long-run contribution to economic well-being.

If the government is not to be held accountable for fine-tuning and other countercyclical policies, the responsibility must be placed in other hands. A logical choice for much of the responsibility would be the Federal Reserve.

If this is done, it would need to be emphasized monetary policy cannot be a cure-all because its scope and powers are limited. But at least the monetary authorities would not have to concern themselves with trying to counterbalance fiscal policies which lead to excessive budget stimulation or restraint, especially the former.

Choosing the Federal Reserve as the primary agent for cyclical responsibility and fine-tuning is nothing more than using the law of comparative advantage. All monetary authorities have the ability to decide quickly, act quickly, and adjust quickly—usually without direct political interference. These are important prerequisites for countercyclical policies, and designating the Federal Reserve with much of this task makes it clear who has the responsibility.

Looking back, one suspects that the Federal Reserve, if it had primary cyclical responsibility, would not have allowed inflation to get out of control to the degree that it did in the late 1970s. Therefore, the restrictive nature of monetary policy from late 1979 to mid-1984 could have been more subdued.

48. Can it be proven a relationship exists between large budget deficits and high interest rates?

From both a logical and conceptual viewpoint, a relationship should exist between large budget deficits and high interest rates.

First, larger government borrowing needs require a rise in interest rates. As the demand for funds increases, an additional supply must be attracted, and higher interest rates attract funds.

Second, monetary policy in nonrecession periods is typically less accommodative when budget deficits are rising than when they are falling. Much of the reason is associated with fears of rising inflation. FOMC minutes, Humphrey-Hawkins testimony by Federal Reserve chairmen, and statements by FOMC members all have indicated monetary policy would be more accommodative (and interest rates lower) if it were not for large budget deficits.

Third, the more deficit financing which exists, the greater the upward pressure on inflation, especially if it is in a period of near full employment, and if the deficit is financed through the banking system, since this process does not absorb individual purchasing power.

Finally, interest rates (especially those on longer maturities) are influenced by expectations, particularly with respect to the budget, inflation, and monetary policy. It is this last point which receives special attention in this analysis.

The best way to determine the impact of the budget deficit on interest rates is to look at the circumstances in a specific period. The 12 years from FY-74 through FY-86 is ideal for this purpose; in FY-74 the deficit was only $6 billion, in FY-83 it was $208 billion, and in FY-86 it was $221 billion.

In CY-74, the economy had slipped into a recession as real gross national product (GNP) declined 0.5 percent. Monetary aggregate growth was rather docile with two measurements of the money supply, the relatively narrow M-1 and the more broadly based M-2, increasing 4.4 and 5.5 percent respectively. The $6 billion budget deficit in FY-74 (July 1, 1973 through June 30, 1974) was very small, less than half of what had been officially estimated. The GNP deflator, a measure of inflation, grew at a very rapid 9.1 percent, but the average yield on Treasury bonds with 20 years to maturity was only 8.05 percent. Thus, the inflation rate was about 1 percent above interest rates on long-term Treasury bonds, which strongly suggests the bond market did not expect inflation to stay at this high level. Otherwise, bond yields would have been noticeably higher. The modest budget deficit and moderate growth in the monetary aggregates appear to have played a considerable role in the expectation inflation would slow.

Turning to FY-83, it was the second consecutive year when the budget deficit rose sharply, to nearly double what had been officially estimated. In CY-83, real GNP grew at 3.6 percent, inflation as measured by the deflator was 3.9 percent, and the yield on 20-year Treasury maturities averaged 11.34 percent. Thus, the yield was more than 7 percent greater than the deflator, while in FY-74 it was 1 percent less. The difference of more than 8 percent is huge by any standard.

The very wide spread between 20-year Treasury yields and inflation in CY-83 seems to indicate the market did not believe inflation could be contained between 3 and 4 percent on a long-term basis. The budget deficit in FY-83 came in at $208 billion, over $100 billion more than estimated in the original official document. Moreover, there was considerable talk that deficits of $300 billion to $400 billion were not far off. The picture was also bleak for the monetary aggregates; M-1 and M-2 advanced at unacceptably high rates of about 10 and 12 percent respectively in CY-83.

This analysis indicates that when both the budget deficit and the monetary aggregates are viewed as growing at excessively rapid rates, investors build in a substantial risk premium when contemplating purchases of long-term debt instruments. In CY-74, the budget deficit was negligible, the growth in the monetary aggregates was moderate, and fears regarding these areas were marginal. Thus, the 20-year bond yielded less than the going rate of inflation. In CY-83, the deficit and the monetary aggregates appeared out of control, and investors demanded a very large additional yield over the rate of inflation.

The last period to be analyzed is CY-86. Real GNP growth and the deflator advanced between 2 and 3 percent—a very modest amount in both cases. However, in the case of the monetary aggregates, the picture was much different as M-1 increased about 15 percent and M-2 moved up roughly 9 percent. The budget deficit for FY-86 turned out to be a very sizable $221 billion. The average yield on 20-year Treasury issues was close to 8 percent, which meant more than a 5 percent risk premium over inflation.

While the spread in CY-86 is substantial, especially when compared with the CY-74 negative differential, it is moderate when viewed against the over 8 percent spread which occurred in CY-83. The change from FY-83 to FY-86 suggests long-term investors were still nervous about the inflation outlook, but their fears had subsided noticeably from CY-83.

It is worthwhile to look at the budget and monetary aggregate picture from CY-83 through CY-86 to see which item bore most of the responsibility for the reduced inflation premium demanded by investors.

From FY-83 through FY-86, the budget deficit edged slightly higher ($208 billion to $221 billion). Yet the fears about the deficit diminished because the general expectation was that the shortfall had peaked. Private deficit forecasts for FY-87 were in the $160 billion to $200 billion range. While this dashed any hopes of reaching the Gramm-Rudman-Hollings target, fears that the deficit would be heading toward $300 billion or $400 billion disappeared.

In the case of the monetary aggregates, there was still considerable nervousness concerning excessive growth. M-1 experienced a remarkably large advance of about 15 percent in CY-86. Most of this increase was due to special factors, among them a move by investors to financial assets and away from real assets. (Investors showed reduced interest in real estate, oil ventures , and similar tax-sheltered outlets, placing large amounts of funds in equities, debt instruments, and deposits.) Also playing a role was reduced interest rate attractiveness of non-M-1 outlets, and an increased desire for safety and liquidity. Nevertheless, the underlying growth in M-1 still seemed excessive.

Even the growth in the more narrowly defined M-1A (which excludes interest-sensitive NOW accounts) appeared too large; this aggregate should have been much less influenced by special factors since its components are noninterest bearing. The fact that in CY-86 the Federal Reserve downgraded M-1's importance from a policy perspective did not reduce the market's concern. In fact, the downgrading may have added a degree of risk with respect to excessive ease and potential inflation.

The broader monetary aggregates and reserves also gave investors reason for concern, although not to the same degree as M-1. In CY-86, both M-2 and M-3 showed growth rates of almost 9 percent, which were at the top end of the Federal Reserve's 6-to-9 percent target range. Reserve growth also was generous, far more so than in CY-83. Both total and nonborrowed reserves grew at double-digit rates. Borrowings at the Federal Reserve's discount window were often not much above frictional levels and free reserves in the banking system frequently exceeded $500 million—a very generous level.

Thus, from CY-83 to CY-86, considerable fears remained regarding the size of the budget deficit, the degree of ease of monetary policy, and their impact on inflation. Otherwise, the premium demanded by long-term bond investors would probably have declined from 8 percent in CY-83 to a more normal 3 or 4 percent instead of moving down to about 5 percent. Nevertheless, it was still a meaningful real interest rate decline.

Since Federal Reserve policy seemed more willing in CY-86 to tolerate moderate increases in inflation to stimulate real growth than it did in CY-83, this factor cannot explain the real interest rate reduction. Therefore, the reduced fears of an explosive budget deficit appear to be the primary reason for this real interest rate decline.

The analysis up to this point has concentrated upon three specific periods: calendar years 1974, 1983, and 1986. Yet, even if one looks at the 1974 through 1986 period as a whole, the importance of budget deficits as a determinant of interest rate levels is quite evident. Figure V-48.1 clearly points out this ongoing relationship. Real interest rates are shown on the left-hand scale. They are computed by taking yields on 20-year Treasury maturities (the only bond data available in earlier years) and subtracting the GNP deflator. On the right-hand scale, the deficit as a percentage of GNP is shown, and as the chart indicates, when this ratio rises, so do real interest rates. Thus, investors demand a higher real rate of return when the budget deficit increases relative to the size of GNP.

Most important, this analysis indicates if the United States wants to achieve substantially lower real interest rates (which would be a stimulant to economic growth), it must reduce the deficit as a percentage of GNP as it did in CY-87.

FIGURE V-48.1 Correlation Between Deficits and Interest Rates

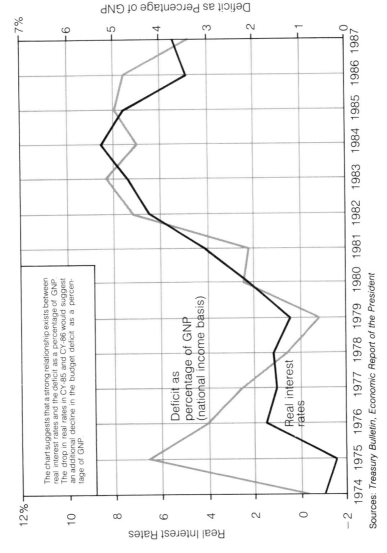

The chart suggests that a strong relationship exists between real interest rates and the deficit as a percentage of GNP. The drop in real rates in CY-85 and CY-86 would suggest an additional decline in the budget deficit as a percentage of GNP.

Deficit as percentage of GNP (national income basis)

Real interest rates

Sources: *Treasury Bulletin, Economic Report of the President*

217

FIGURE V-48.2 3-Month and 20-Year Treasury Issues (Average Annual Rates—Calendar Year)

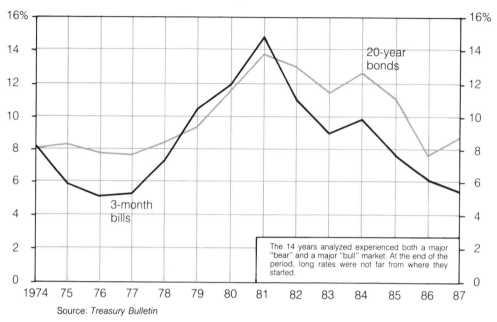

The 14 years analyzed experienced both a major "bear" and a major "bull" market. At the end of the period, long rates were not far from where they started.

Source: *Treasury Bulletin*

Calendar Year	3 Mo.*	6 Mo.*	1 Yr.	2 Yr.	3 Yr.	5 Yr.	7 Yr.	10 Yr.	20 Yr.	30 Yr.
1974	8.10%	8.39%	8.25%	—	7.82%	7.80%	7.71%	7.56%	8.05%	—
1975	5.96	6.38	6.76	—	7.49	7.77	7.90	7.99	8.19	—
1976	5.12	5.48	5.88	—	6.77	7.18	7.42	7.61	7.86	—
1977	5.42	5.70	6.09	6.45%	6.69	6.99	7.23	7.42	7.67	—
1978	7.42	7.97	8.34	8.34	8.29	8.32	8.36	8.41	8.48	8.49
1979	10.46	10.73	10.67	10.12	9.71	9.52	9.48	9.44	9.33	9.29
1980	11.96	12.20	12.05	11.77	11.55	11.48	11.43	11.46	11.39	11.30
1981	14.71	15.02	14.78	14.56	14.44	14.24	14.06	13.91	13.72	13.44
1982	11.06	11.90	12.27	12.80	12.92	13.01	13.06	13.00	12.92	12.76
1983	8.94	9.28	9.57	10.21	10.45	10.80	11.02	11.10	11.34	11.18
1984	9.89	10.41	10.89	11.65	11.89	12.24	12.40	12.44	12.48	12.39
1985	7.73	8.07	8.43	9.27	9.64	10.13	10.51	10.62	10.97	10.79
1986	6.15	6.30	6.46	6.87	7.06	7.31	7.55	7.68	7.85	7.80
1987	5.95	6.32	6.76	7.41	7.67	7.94	8.21	8.38	8.70	8.58

Interest Rate Levels—3-Month Through 30-Year Maturities

*Coupon equivalent

49. What are some important relationships to consider when forming budgetary policies?

A key comparison is whether the growth in savings has kept pace with the growth in Treasury financing. That has not been the case.

In CY-74, gross private savings amounted to $254 billion and marketable Treasury debt outstanding increased less than $4 billion, to a level of $267 billion. In CY-87, however, the story was much different. Savings for the year were less than $700 billion while marketable debt outstanding grew by over $100 billion, to almost $1.7 trillion. Thus, in CY-74 the annual increase in savings was over 60 times the increase in Treasury debt, while in CY-87 it was only about six times the increase. Figures V-49.1 and V-49.2 show this disparity.

The inability of savings to grow at an adequate rate creates problems. It puts upward pressure on interest rates and can lead to increased borrowing abroad. Moreover, if the circumstances are right, it can crowd-out or price-out some private sector needs. These factors, either directly or indirectly, can lead to subpar economic growth.

The analysis shows that increases in the deficit and its financing are not the sole causes of budgetary problems: the inability of the economy to create sufficient savings to finance the deficit is also of considerable importance. The savings rate is insufficient when measured against the growth of marketable Treasury debt outstanding. To rectify the situation, policies must be put in place which will add to the growth of private savings. Since it took about 12 years to create this situation, and since the deterioration may not be over, savings inducements, as they exist, appear insufficient to ameliorate the problem.

In support of this view, the 1986 Tax Reform Act is likely to be an impediment to an improved savings rate. It removed capital gains advantages, limited tax benefits for retirement accounts, eliminated investment tax credits, and reduced depreciation benefits. Not only is it unlikely to improve savings, there is a good possibility it will not add to total tax receipts in the years ahead.

A second comparison which can be made between the budget and the economy is to analyze their relative sizes (see Figure V-49.3). For example, in CY-74, federal government outlays (on a national income and products basis) were slightly more than 20 percent of nominal GNP. By CY-86, the ratio was more than 24 percent. These numbers indicate government spending for the period grew at a more rapid pace than the

FIGURE V-49.1 Important Budget Relationships

Year	Personal Income‡	Indiv. Income Taxes	2 ÷ 1	Corp. Profits*,‡	Corp. Income Taxes	5 ÷ 4	Nominal GNP	Govt. Receipts†,‡	8 ÷ 7
	1	2	3	4	5	6	7	8	9
1974	1,210.1	118.9	9.8%	101.7	38.6	38.0%	1,472.8	293.9	20.0%
1975	1,313.4	122.4	9.3	117.6	40.6	34.5	1,578.4	294.9	18.7
1976	1,451.4	131.6	9.1	145.2	41.4	28.5	1,782.8	340.1	19.1
1977	1,607.5	157.6	9.8	174.8	55.0	31.5	1,990.5	384.1	19.3
1978	1,812.4	181.0	10.0	197.2	60.0	30.4	2,249.7	441.4	19.6
1979	2,034.0	217.8	9.3	200.1	65.6	32.8	2,508.2	505.0	20.1
1980	2,258.5	244.0	9.3	177.2	64.6	36.5	2,732.0	553.8	20.3
1981	2,520.9	285.6	11.3	188.0	61.1	32.5	3,052.6	639.5	20.9
1982	2,670.8	298.1	9.0	150.0	49.2	32.8	3,166.0	635.3	20.1
1983	2,838.6	288.9	10.2	213.7	37.0	17.3	3,405.7	659.9	19.4
1984	3,108.7	295.9	9.5	266.9	56.9	21.3	3,772.2	726.0	19.2
1985	3,327.0	334.6	10.1	277.6	61.3	22.1	4,010.3	788.6	19.7
1986	3,534.3	349.0	10.0	284.4	63.1	22.2	4,235.0	827.4	19.5
1987	3,746.3	392.6	10.5	306.5p	83.9	27.4p	4,487.7	916.5	20.4

Nominal GNP	Govt. Outlayst,‡	11 ÷ 10	Nominal GNP	Deficitt,‡	14 ÷ 13	Gross Private Savings‡	Market- able Debt	17 ÷ 16	Year
10	11	12	13	14	15	16	17	18	
1,472.8	305.5	20.7%	1,472.8	− 11.6	.8%	254.3	266.6	104.8%	1974
1,578.4	364.2	22.8	1,578.4	− 69.4	4.3	303.6	315.6	104.0	1975
1,782.8	393.7	22.1	1,782.8	− 53.5	3.0	321.4	392.6	122.1	1976
1,990.5	430.1	21.6	1,990.5	− 46.0	2.3	354.5	443.5	125.1	1977
2,249.7	470.7	20.9	2,249.7	− 29.3	1.3	409.0	485.2	118.6	1978
2,508.2	521.1	20.8	2,508.2	− 16.1	.6	445.8	506.7	113.7	1979
2,732.0	615.1	22.5	2,732.0	− 61.3	2.2	478.4	594.5	124.3	1980
3,052.6	703.3	23.0	3,052.6	−63.8	2.1	550.5	683.2	124.1	1981
3,166.0	781.2	24.7	3,166.0	−145.9	4.6	557.1	824.4	148.0	1982
3,405.7	835.9	24.5	3,405.7	−176.0	5.2	592.2	1,024.0	173.0	1983
3,772.2	895.6	23.8	3,772.2	−169.6	4.5	673.5	1,176.6	174.7	1984
4,010.3	984.6	24.6	4,010.3	−196.0	5.0	664.2	1,360.2	204.8	1985
4,235.0	1,032.0	24.3	4,235.0	−204.7	4.9	679.8	1,564.3	230.1	1986
4,487.7	1,069.1	23.8	4,487.7	−152.6	3.4	673.6	1,676.0	248.8	1987

*With inventory valuation and capital consumption adjustments.

†National income and product accounts.

‡Calendar year.

The tax-take from individuals and corporations is quite low. It explains why tax receipts as a percentage of GNP are only about 20 percent. With outlays close to 24 percent of GNP, it should not be surprising that the budget deficit is an unacceptably high percentage of GNP.

Sources: Economic Report of the President, Economic Indicators, Monthly Treasury Statement of Receipts and Outlays of the U.S. Government

221

FIGURE V-49.2 Gross Private Savings Compared with Marketable Treasury Debt (Billions of Dollars)

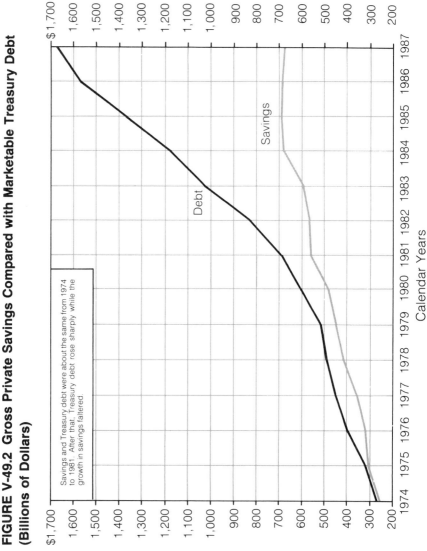

Savings and Treasury debt were about the same from 1974 to 1981. After that, Treasury debt rose sharply while the growth in savings faltered.

Source: *Economic Report of the President*

222

advance in the economy. An increase of more than 3 percent is huge in dollar terms given the size of nominal GNP. That helps explain why the deficit as a percentage of GNP rose to almost 5 percent in FY-86, from less than 1 percent in FY-74.

Yet, the budget/economy story is not all on the expenditure side. There is a tax receipts story to tell. Receipts as a percentage of GNP started a significant decline in CY-82. Moreover, the gross over-estimation of receipts by the executive branch (especially in FY-82 and FY-83) led to a higher rate of spending than otherwise would have been the case.

The various relationships cited indicate specific goals need to be established to reduce the deficit and its accompanying problems.

First, the economy must grow more rapidly. Real growth of close to 3 percent, which was the case from late CY-84 to mid-CY-87, is inadequate to reduce the deficit substantially. The average growth rate should be between 3 and 4 percent, and to achieve such an advance over a business cycle, in some years growth must be 4 percent or more.

From CY-74 to mid-CY-87, there were only two periods when real growth met these standards—CY-76 through CY-78 and CY-83 through CY-84. In only five of the years studied did real growth exceed 3 percent.

Second, the savings rate for individuals must increase to facilitate domestic financing of the deficit. From CY-74 through CY-87, individual savings as a percentage of disposable income dropped from over 7 percent to less than 4 percent. The goal should be to push this savings rate back to near 7 percent. With disposable personal income in CY-87 at almost $3.2 trillion, a 7 percent savings rate would have meant $223 billion in savings instead of $120 billion. The $103 billion difference was roughly the amount of all net foreign acquisitions of Treasury issues in CY-86 and CY-87 combined.

Third, the growth in government spending must be held to less than the rate of advance in nominal GNP. A reasonable target would be about a 1 percent differential for several years. Thus, if nominal GNP advances 5 percent, the growth target for government spending should be held to 4 percent. The advantage of this approach compared with more drastic measures is that the slowing in spending can be sustained and the economy would not be buffeted by sharp swings in outlays.

Finally, the tax-take as a percentage of GNP must improve. Individuals on average pay about 10 percent of their personal income in

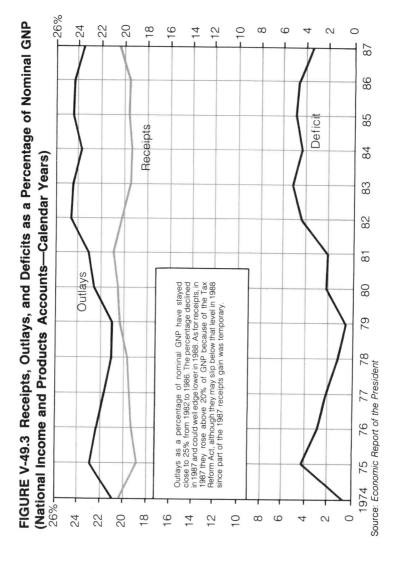

FIGURE V-49.3 Receipts, Outlays, and Deficits as a Percentage of Nominal GNP (National Income and Products Accounts—Calendar Years)

Outlays as a percentage of nominal GNP have stayed close to 25% from 1982 to 1986. The percentage declined in 1987 and could well edge lower in 1988. As for receipts, in 1987 they rose above 20% of GNP because of the Tax Reform Act, although they may slip below that level in 1988 since part of the 1987 receipts gain was temporary.

Source: Economic Report of the President

224

federal income taxes, which seems unduly low. Corporations are currently paying 27 percent, which was a sharp increase as a result of the 1986 Tax Reform Act. A mere 1 percent increase in the tax-take from individuals would have amounted to $39 billion in CY-87.

These four objectives are necessary because of the size of the deficit and the amount which is being financed abroad. Yet, there will be periods when one or more of these four objectives will not be met. That means improvement will not occur in a straight line. It is a long and painful road back to fiscal responsibility—no one should expect it to be easy.

50. Is there a direct relationship between the United States' budget and trade deficits?

There is no direct cause-and-effect relationship between the two deficits. What can be said is that both have grown substantially since the mid-1970s, and some factors causing increased budget deficits also have had an adverse impact on the trade numbers.

Figure V-50.1 illustrates both the rapid deficit growth and the pattern changes in both these areas. Most notable is that the budget deficit moved substantially higher beginning in 1980, but the sharp deterioration in the trade numbers did not start until 1983. Also, increases in the budget deficit in FY-82 and FY-83 were due in large part to the receipts shortfall resulting from the Tax Reform Act of 1981 and the recession. As for the trade deficit, the big increases took place in calendar years 1984, 1985, and 1986, and were due primarily to a large increase in imports, especially in the manufactured goods area.

A number of factors have adversely affected both the budget and foreign trade. A substandard advance in U.S. productivity has meant disappointing economic growth and, therefore, a reduction in tax receipts. It has also made the United States less competitive in its exports. Weakness in agriculture has not only resulted in substantial budget outlays and reduced tax receipts, but also has had an adverse impact on American exports. The increased strength of the dollar in the first half of the decade was in part responsible for the weakness in exports and to some degree limited U.S. corporate profits and therefore business taxes.

Since common forces contributed to the deterioration of both the budget and trade numbers, a turnaround in common forces can bring about an improvement in both. The decline in the budget deficit in FY-87 and the likely reduction in the trade deficit in CY-88 are a reflection of some changes in common forces. One final thought in this comparison: The budget problem can be solved through political courage, and it can be solved quickly if some of the untouchables are touched. The trade problem is more economics than politics; its resolution requires considerable economic courage on the part of the private sector. A quick fix is impossible.

In a related topic, large trade deficits have provided foreigners with more dollars to buy U.S. government securities. However, availability and impact are not synonymous. These funds may not all be held in dollars, and those which are may not all be invested in the U.S.

FIGURE V-50.1 U.S. Budget and Trade Deficits (Billions of Dollars)

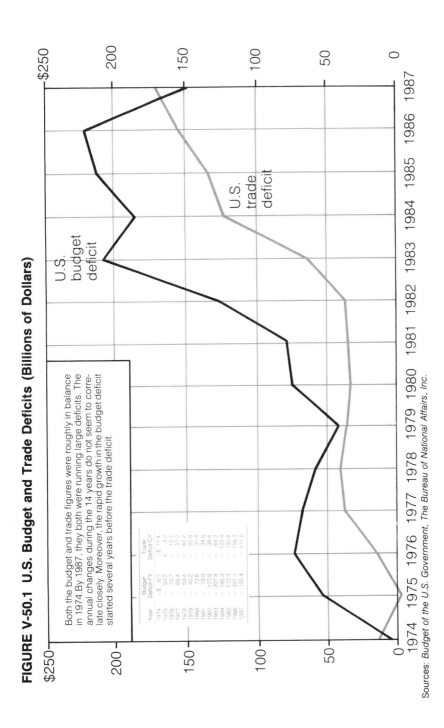

Both the budget and trade figures were roughly in balance in 1974. By 1987, they both were running large deficits. The annual changes during the 14 years do not seem to correlate closely. Moreover, the rapid growth in the budget deficit started several years before the trade deficit.

Year	Budget Deficit-FY	Trade Deficit-CY
1974	$ 6.1	– $ 11.4
1975	53.2	+ 3.0
1976	73.7	15.7
1977	68.4	37.2
1978	59.4	40.2
1979	40.2	35.9
1980	73.8	31.4
1981	78.9	34.6
1982	127.9	38.4
1983	207.8	64.2
1984	185.3	122.4
1985	212.3	130.6
1986	221.1	156.2
1987	150.4	171.0

U.S. budget deficit

U.S. trade deficit

Sources: Budget of the U.S. Government, The Bureau of National Affairs, Inc.

government market. Moreover, funds invested in short-term instruments are in an area where there is no shortage of domestic funds.

While a much-reduced trade deficit would mean considerably less in the way of foreign purchases of U.S. money market instruments, it could actually prove to be an inducement for foreigners to buy long-term Treasury obligations. In this regard, a smaller trade deficit would be a positive force for the dollar, and a stable dollar should attract more long-term foreign money to the United States.

APPENDIX

Since 1963, this author has co-written with William N. Griggs various weekly financial reports.[1] These weekly commentaries have concentrated on analyzing financial markets, monetary policy, the federal budget, and Treasury financing. Forecasts have frequently been made. In this section, excerpts are taken from weekly reports written during the two periods of budget deterioration (FY-75/FY-76 and FY-82/FY-83). Also included are budget comments for the period before the troubles began and for the period when the sharp deterioration ended. Important phrases have been italicized for emphasis and some paragraphing changes have been made to improve readability.

FY-75 AND FY-76. The table below shows the deficits for FY-75 and FY-76, and the original official estimates. It also shows the budget deficits for the year before and the year after the two-year period. The official estimating error for FY-75 was the largest and most embarrassing of the two years.

FIGURE A-1   Actuals and Estimates for Deficits, Fiscal Years 1975 and 1976

				Actuals (Billions of Dollars)				Estimates (Billions of Dollars)			
FY		Date		Rec.	Exp.	Def.		Date	Rec.	Exp.	Def.
1974	1	Jul	73	263.2	269.4	− 6.1					
	30	Jun	74								
1975	1	Jul	74	279.1	332.3	−53.2		Jan 74	295.0	304.4	− 9.4
	30	Jun	75								
1976	1	Jul	75	298.1	371.8	−73.7		Jan 75	297.5	349.4	−51.9
	30	Jun	76								
1977	1	Oct	76	355.6	409.2	−53.6					
	30	Sep	77								

FROM THE LEHMAN LETTER OF FEBRUARY 11, 1974.

The federal budget deficit for the current fiscal year (1974) should be around $3 billion and for the next fiscal year about $17 billion. Receipts in the current fiscal year should be about $269 billion and expenditures approximately $272 billion. For next fiscal year, receipts could come in about

[1]1963–1972:   The Lanston Letter
1972–1974:   The Lehman Letter
1974–1981:   The Schroder Report
1982–   :   The Griggs & Santow Report

$291 billion and expenditures should approximate $308 billion. If these receipt and expenditure flows are adjusted for seasonal factors, the resulting patterns show that the budget is currently in balance, that a modest deficit will have developed by the beginning of the new fiscal year, and that *a year from now the deficit will be substantial.*

FROM THE SCHRODER REPORT OF DECEMBER 23, 1974.

The federal budget, reflecting the effects of a weakening economy on receipts and expenditures, *is starting to deteriorate.* For the current fiscal year (1975), we estimate the deficit will be in the vicinity of $17 billion, with about $290 billion in receipts and $307 billion in expenditures. For the following fiscal year (1975-76), a deficit in the $25 billion to $30 billion area seems likely. This large deficit in the coming fiscal year could be due more to a shortfall in revenues than any explosion in expenditures.

FROM THE SCHRODER REPORT OF JULY 21, 1975.

The federal budget deficit for fiscal 1974-75 is estimated to have totaled about $45 billion and most forecasters are looking for the deficit to rise to between $60 billion and $70 billion in the current fiscal year (1976). . . . *Between now and the end of the calendar year though, the budget deterioration is likely to come to an end, although the plateau will be at a very sizable deficit level.*

However, in the January-March 1976 period we should begin to see an improvement in the receipts side, and the receipts picture in the April-June period should look significantly better. Thus, if the growth of expenditures does not get out of hand, the overall budget results should show a genuine improvement in the latter part of the fiscal year. This could well mean a deficit for fiscal 1975–76 that is larger than [that of] the fiscal year just ended but surprisingly less than most now expect. Moreover, unlike the current situation, we almost certainly will leave fiscal 1975–76 moving toward a much smaller deficit for the following fiscal year.

From the Schroder Report of November 24, 1975.

The budget picture for the current fiscal year (1976) does not look as ominous to us as it apparently does to other analysts. Our less pessimistic view is based on a number of factors. First, the deficit in the July–September quarter was $18 billion, about $4 billion of which was seasonal. Second, the deficit is largely due to a recession-related revenue shortfall rather than to an explosion in new spending programs. The importance of this lies in the fact that a deficit whose origins are on the revenue side is easier to deal with, since economic recovery will substantially increase revenues and thus reduce the deficit. (An expenditure explosion, which we currently do not have, is much more difficult to deal with, simply because spending, once it is built into the budget, is difficult to hold down, much less eliminate.)

Moreover, while the current recovery is likely to be moderate, it will almost certainly be sustained throughout the fiscal year, and corporate profits and personal income, which are the primary sources of tax receipts, have thus far performed better than expected. Therefore, budget revenues in the January–June period could be substantially higher than anyone is expecting. The major unknown in the budget outlook is, of course, the fate of the administration's tax and expenditure proposals. However, if the tax reduction for calendar 1976 is not much different from that which expires at the end of calendar 1975, and assuming that spending does not balloon, the deficit for the current fiscal year could be considerably smaller than public or private forecasters are currently projecting.

From the Schroder Report of January 26, 1976.

This budget (FY-77) presents assumptions and projections in a refreshing straightforward manner regardless of whether or not one agrees with all the various ideas, programs, etc. This surely makes the task of analyzing the budget much simpler than it has often been in the past. The expenditures estimate of $394 billion seems to fall more in the category of hope than estimate. Certainly it would not be a "best guess" of independent analysts who are trying to weigh all the various economic and political factors. An expenditure figure of $405 billion to $410 billion is probably more realistic. This higher range is largely accounted for by the expectation that the $10 billion expenditure reduction proposed by the administration will not be approved by Congress. It is worth noting in this regard that the higher spending figure still represents a definite slowdown (only about a 7 percent advance) in the rate of growth in government spending.

Receipts, like expenditures, appear to be understated. The administration's receipts estimate for fiscal 1977 is $351 billion, but we look for a figure in the vicinity of $365 billion to $370 billion. Two factors largely account for this difference—the additional $10 billion tax reduction, the passage of which is doubtful (although the social security tax increase seems to have a good chance of passage) and a belief that the receipts estimate for the current fiscal year (ending this June) is $5 billion to $7 billion too low. Since the administration's estimates on both corporate profits and personal income seem reasonable, much of this difference probably reflects differing assumptions on the tax-take per dollar of income.

If expenditures run between $405 billion and $410 billion, and receipts total between $365 and $370 billion, the deficit would be between $35 billion and $45 billion. In other words, despite considerably different receipts and expenditure estimates, the deficit range we envisage for fiscal 1977 encompasses the administration's estimate of $43 billion.

Looking at the longer-run economic forecast presented by the administration in its budget message through 1981, one is struck by the unbridled optimism it reflects. Unemployment and inflation head progressively downward and there is not even a hint of a business cycle except for a modest slowdown in real GNP in 1981. Such a performance would be truly remarkable in view of the fluctuations the economy has experienced since 1966. Indeed, it would turn Murphy's law on end, i.e., everything that could go right, would go right.

FY-82 AND FY-83. The following table presents the deficits for FY-82 and FY-83, and the initial official forecasts. It also displays the budget deficit for the year before and the year after the two-year period. The FY-82 estimating error was large, but all the adversity occurred in receipts. In FY-83, the estimating error was huge as both receipts and spending were responsible.

FIGURE A-2 Actuals and Estimates for Deficits, Fiscal Years 1982 and 1983

	Actuals (Billions of Dollars)				Estimates (Billions of Dollars)			
FY	Date	Rec.	Exp.	Def.	Date	Rec.	Exp.	Def.
1981	1 Oct 80	$599.3	$678.2	− $ 78.9				
	30 Sep 81							
1982	1 Oct 81	617.8	745.7	− 127.9	Jan 81	$711.8	$757.6	− $ 45.8
	30 Sep 82							
1983	1 Oct 82	600.6	808.3	− 207.8	Jan 82	666.1	773.3	− 102.2
	30 Sep 83							
1984	1 Oct 83	666.5	851.8	− 185.3				
	30 Sep 84							

FROM THE SCHRODER REPORT OF JULY 21, 1981.

One question which should be asked with respect to the 1982–83 budget is: Where is the greatest risk of error, and how would it affect the results? *The greatest risk of error is on the receipts side* because that estimate relies so heavily on the assumption that a meaningful recovery in the economy will occur and that the tax reduction program will be enacted in the specified amounts and terms. Because of this circumstance, actual receipts could vary by $10 billion to $15 billion from our estimate.

FROM THE SCHRODER REPORT OF AUGUST 31, 1981.

The catalyst for the market's plummeting on Monday was the *administration's public recognition that the federal budget deficit next fiscal year will be greater than had been officially estimated.* Moreover, the upward revision required is not just a few billion, which could easily be understood, but over $20 billion. This revision in thinking *takes the prospective deficit to near $60 billion, which is about where we indicated it would be last February* (see Schroder Report 2/9/81).

FROM THE SCHRODER REPORT OF OCTOBER 12, 1981.

In the July 27th Schroder Report we stated. . . at that time our receipts estimate (for FY-1982) was $664 billion. Since then, both the softness of the economy and the size of the tax reduction led us to believe that the likely receipts range is $650 billion to $660 billion. The lower end of the range could occur if there is no meaningful recovery in the economy between now and next fall and the administration does not find a way to raise additional revenues.

As for expenditures, we believe the statement made in the September 14th Schroder Report still holds true: Our analysis indicates spending in fiscal 1981–82 would be between $720 billion and $725 billion if no additional spending cuts were made. If there are cuts, and they are highly likely, a spending range of $715 billion to $720 billion would appear to be a better guess.

FROM THE SCHRODER REPORT OF NOVEMBER 2, 1981.

If the budget deficit in the current fiscal year should deteriorate to the $65 billion to $70 billion area, which at this point is a reasonable possibility, this deterioration would become particularly apparent in any year-over-year comparison during the second quarter of calendar 1982.

FROM THE SCHRODER REPORT OF NOVEMBER 20, 1981.

The budget outlook, reflecting the deterioration in the health of the economy, continues to worsen. While it is true that the decline in interest rates associated with the weakening economy will reduce interest expenses by several billion dollars, this savings will be dwarfed by lost revenues and additional expenditures associated with the sharply reduced growth of the economy. Interestingly, *this deterioration in the budget picture will not really become apparent until the second half of the fiscal year.* . . . on the assumption that the total budget deficit in the current fiscal year is $75 billion. . . .

FROM THE SCHRODER REPORT OF DECEMBER 14, 1981.

Government credibility is as fragile as it is important and in the economic policy sphere, the events of the last few months have done serious damage to that credibility. It could hardly be otherwise with the budget deficit estimate for the current fiscal year going from $42 billion to $109 billion in a matter of months (plus a budget that was projected to be in balance in fiscal year 1984 now projected to be in deficit by more than $150 billion). Events in the last several months have clearly not changed so drastically that the budget estimate for this year would require a revision of this magnitude.

What has happened is that a weaker-than-expected economy has reduced the likely volume of tax receipts to force an upward revision in the deficit of nearly $15 billion (and not $65 billion) for fiscal 1981–82. Thus, if one had had a realistic budget deficit estimate several months ago of $65 billion to $70 billion, that estimate would now be in the $80 billion to $85 billion range.

Whatever the reasons for the 180-degree shift. . . ., they certainly do nothing to add to one's confidence in current economic policy. Neither do comments by members of the Council of Economic Advisors that the deficit is not really all that important. Moreover, if the deficit were declining rather than rising, the Council's tune would be a much different one.

FROM THE SCHRODER REPORT OF FEBRUARY 1, 1982.

There is every reason to believe that the current budget picture will deteriorate sharply in the months ahead. Indeed, even assuming receipts run at higher levels than a credible model for the U.S. economy would suggest, the best that can be hoped for is receipts in the $635 billion to $640 billion range. With spending likely to be near $730 billion, a deficit of $90 billion to $95 billion now appears all but inevitable

(for FY-82). Equally disturbing, a deficit for the year between $90 billion and $95 billion implies that *the deficit will
be running at an annual rate well in excess of $100 billion as
we end the fiscal year.*

FROM THE SCHRODER REPORT OF FEBRUARY 15, 1982.

With spending and receipts both understated this year, the
$98 billion deficit for fiscal 1981–82 projected by the admin-
istration seems reasonable (the estimate, that is, not the
level). For fiscal 1982–83, the picture is quite different.
While receipts may again be somewhat underestimated, expenditures are underestimated by so much more (with the
core factors of military, social security, and interest costs
accounting for almost all of the growth), that *the administration's $92 billion estimated deficit for fiscal 1982–83 is
virtually out of the question.* The more likely result for fiscal
1982–83 is a budget deficit of at least $120 billion.

FROM THE SCHRODER REPORT OF MARCH 1, 1982.

The degree of fiscal stimulation (which we believe should be
viewed mainly by the change in the deficit rather than the
level itself) picks up substantially in the spring because of the
heavy refunds and then becomes even greater in the summer
when the tax reduction takes effect. Moreover, the 1983
fiscal year begins with the budget deficit running at an annual
rate of between $120 billion and $130 billion.

FROM THE SCHRODER REPORT OF APRIL 12, 1982.

In the current fiscal year (FY-82), the budget deficit will
probably fall between $90 billion and $100 billion and in
fiscal 1983, it will take sizable spending and tax changes to
hold the deficit under $120 billion. Moreover, *in the absence
of sizable budget adjustments the deficit can be expected to
grow even larger in 1984 and beyond.*

FROM THE SCHRODER REPORT OF MAY 10, 1982.

If one takes a very optimistic set of assumptions—a strong economic recovery throughout the fiscal year, a substantial decline in interest rates, and perhaps some modest upward adjustment in receipts and some modest downward adjustment in spending—the best that can be hoped for is a deficit of $120 billion to $130 billion (for FY-83). With a more neutral set of assumptions—a recovery that is moderate, interest rates that show little change, and only minimal changes in budget receipts and spending—the deficit would probably fall in the $130 billion to $150 billion range. A clearly pessimistic view of the future (though not necessarily an unrealistic one)—a recovery that is either disappointing or aborted, interest rates that move higher, and no adjustment in the current budget posture—would suggest that the deficit might well run as high as $150 billion to $160 billion.

FROM THE SCHRODER REPORT OF JUNE 28, 1982.

Despite the budget agreement reached between the two houses of Congress, it is still our view that *the deficit in fiscal 1983 is likely to turn out near $140 billion rather than the $104 billion officially targeted. If the budget picture unfolds as we expect, it will be disgraceful.*

FROM THE SCHRODER REPORT OF AUGUST 30, 1982.

The budget data published for July did not make for favorable reading. Especially disturbing was the poor receipts figure which also happened to be the case in June. Because of these soft receipts numbers, the deficit for the current fiscal year now appears likely to be between $105 billion and $110 billion. As for the next fiscal year (FY-83), if the disappointing receipts figures persist, it could easily wash out the beneficial effects on the budget from the recent fall in interest rates. Therefore, a budget deficit of about $140 billion for fiscal 1983 still seems likely.

FROM THE SCHRODER REPORT OF SEPTEMBER 6, 1982.

There have been a number of budget deficit estimates for fiscal 1983 published in the last week or so. They range from about $140 billion to somewhat over $160 billion and they all include the effects of the recent tax increase/expenditure reduction package, the large interest rate reductions, and expectations of a moderate economic expansion. The size of the deficit estimates suggests that the recent moves to reduce the deficit will achieve only limited dollar improvements.

FROM THE SCHRODER REPORT OF OCTOBER 25, 1982.

The budget deficit in fiscal 1982–83 will be substantially larger than that of fiscal 1981–82. However, the deficit posture for fiscal 1983–84 is not clear. As things stand now, the deficit for the next fiscal year (which begins October 1983) will be considerably larger than in the current fiscal year, although not by as much as would have been projected six months ago. The decline in interest costs and the improved chances for a meaningful recovery are largely responsible for the change.

FROM THE GRIGGS & SANTOW REPORT OF DECEMBER 6, 1982.

Net receipts totaled only $40.5 billion in October—$4.5 billion below the year-earlier number. Moreover, this is the sixth consecutive month in which net receipts have run under year-earlier numbers, with the October figures the weakest yet. Estimated individual income taxes in October were actually a minus and the receipts from the windfall profits tax are running $1 billion per month below last year. *These data confirm what every objective analyst of the budget has long known. The receipts side of the budget has been, and still is, its Achilles' heel because of the large and continuing tax reductions built into the system and the dependence of any receipts recovery on economic activity.*

Considering any significant economic recovery is months away at best, that November receipts also appear to have been quite weak, and that still further tax reductions are scheduled for July 1, 1983, there is every reason to wonder whether tax receipts for the year will equal the $618 billion total of last fiscal year. Such a receipts level is essential if there is to be any chance of holding the deficit for the current fiscal year to as low as $160 billion.

FROM THE GRIGGS & SANTOW REPORT OF FEBRUARY 7, 1983.

The administration's budget for this and the next fiscal year seems to be less a political document than has often been the case in the past. This is not to say that there are no questionable assumptions, only that they are not unreasonable. For example, our estimates for fiscal 1983 and 1984 show deficits for both years that fall in the $190 billion to $200 billion range, while administration projections assume a deficit this fiscal year ($208 billion) larger than in the coming fiscal year ($189 billion). . . . The official receipts figure for fiscal 1983 of $598 billion seems on the low side unless you assume that the recent improvement in the economy has little follow-through. A better estimate would be $600 billion to $605 billion.

On the expenditure side, the official estimate of $806 billion seems too high. It assumes that expenditures continue to rise at about an 11 percent rate—an unlikely development, we think. A range of $795 billion to $800 billion—9 percent to 10 percent growth—would seem a better guess. Looking to fiscal 1984, the bias in the official estimates appears to have shifted from assuming the worst to assuming the best possible outcome from the array of reasonable possibilities.

FROM THE GRIGGS & SANTOW REPORT OF MARCH 14, 1983.

The federal budget picture has shown some noticeable improvement in the last two months that is not fully appreciated but will almost certainly be reflected in the administration's much-discussed economic reassessment. (That reassessment, it is widely reported, will involve a more rapid pace of real growth for this year.) The administration's forecast of the deficit for fiscal 1982–83 is currently $208 billion. It appears, however, that the actual result could be about $190 billion or even somewhat less. . . . Receipts are still likely to fall short of last year's $618 billion total, but it appears that the shortfall will not be as great as previously feared. Our "best guess" at this point would call for receipts in fiscal 1982–83 of between $610 billion and $615 billion.

On the spending side, there has been a decided slow-down in the growth of monthly totals. Outlays averaged about $67 billion early in the fiscal year but currently seem to be rising only modestly, suggesting that the total for the year could be held in the vicinity of $800 billion.

FROM THE GRIGGS & SANTOW REPORT OF MAY 9, 1983.

Receipts must be increased substantially if we are to have any real chance of reducing the budget deficit significantly. To this end, a sustained economic recovery is essential—but not enough. To see the truth of this consider the following: Assume that in fiscal 1983 receipts are $605 billion, expenditures are $805 billion, and the deficit is $200 billion; the recovery is sustained at a moderate pace; inflation remains modest; there are no changes of law that significantly alter the future receipts picture from a legislative standpoint. Assume further that the percentage gain in both receipts and expenditures over the next few years is the same as in the 1976–79 period. On this basis, we would still be left with a deficit close to $150 billion in fiscal 1986.

FROM THE GRIGGS & SANTOW REPORT OF AUGUST 1, 1983.

While the recovery in economic activity will work to reduce the deficit from both the spending and receipts sides, and while budgets typically do better than projected in recovery periods, *a major budget imbalance still faces the United States in this and the next fiscal year (at least) with all the risks attendant thereto.*

Index

A

Actuality, versus economic assumptions, 50–51
Actuals/estimates
  budget figures, 3
  deficits, 6
    FY-75 and FY-76, 231
    FY-82 and FY-83, 235
  economic assumptions versus actuality, 50–51
  expenditures, 12
  GNP current dollar growth, 52
  health and human services (HHS), 31
  major expenditure categories, 28, 29
  receipts, 10
  tax refunds, 24
Administration and support activities, as mission category, 43, 201
Advance refunding technique, 87
Agricultural outlays, 25, 37–38
  growth rate, 37
    Commodity Credit Corporation (CCC) and, 38
    effect of foreign trade on, 37–38
  Reagan administration, 11
  spending cutbacks on, 40
Airlift/sealift, as mission category, 43, 201
Alcohol taxation, raising of, 75
Amtrak, sale of, 199
Assets, determining useful life of, 176

Asset sales, Reagan administration and, 199
Aubrey G. Lanston & Co., 128
Australia, foreign debt market investments by Japan, 137

B

Balanced-budget amendment (BBA), 79–80, 191–92
  Gramm-Rudman-Hollings (GRH) and, 79–80, 192
Bank of Japan (BOJ)
  investments in U.S. Treasury bills, 130
  portfolio approach and, 130–38
  maturities, 139
BBA, *See* Balanced-budget amendment (BBA).
BOJ, *See* Bank of Japan (BOJ).
Bond investors, effect of budget deficit on, 66
Budgetary policy, objective of, 192
Budget concepts
  federal budget document/process compared to corporate budgets, 207–9
  fiscal policy, 204–6
    used for countercyclical purposes, 210–12
  relationship between budget and trade deficits, 226–28
  relationship between large budget deficits and high interest rates, 213–16

243

Budget concepts (cont.)
  relationships to consider when forming
    policies, 219–25
Budget deficit
  avoiding deterioration of, 72
  causes of, 5–13
    expenditures increases, 5–8
    political environment, 8
    receipts shortfall, 8–13
  correlation between interest rates and, 217
  effect on bond investors, 63
  effect on confidence in government, 64
  effect on Federal Reserve policies, 62–63
  effect on foreign ownership of government
    securities, 63–64
  effect on international bargaining, 62
  effect on state/local government, 64–65
  future outlook of, 55–61
    deficit, 59–61
    expenditures, 55–57
    receipts, 57–59
  government credibility and, 237
  investor fears created by, 63
  party-in-power factor, 47–49, 53
  periods of, 5
  price U.S. is paying for, 62–65
  reduction of, 61, 72–73
    by raising receipts, 72, 74
  relationship between interest rates and,
    213–16
  relationship between trade deficit and,
    226–28
  stabilizing dollar amount of, 72
  trade deficit and, 227
Budget document/process, 176–201
  budget reporting, 196–201
  compared to corporate budget, 207–9
  deficit and the politician, 195
  devising a sensible budget amendment,
    191–192
  establishment of non-partisan estimation
    body, 184
  off-budget items, 196–98
    categories of, 196
    debt securities held by, 198
  official forecasts of appropriations/outlays,
    193
  placing expenditures off budget, 196–98
  quality of estimates/projections, 208
  responsibility for accuracy of estimates,
    208
  subdivision of budget outlays, 176–77
  submission period of budget, 180–82

  two-year versus one-year budget, 178–79
  use of president's line-item veto, 183
  using Gramm-Rudman-Hollings (GRH)
    approach, 185–89
    balanced-budget amendment versus, 190
    improving mandated expenditure
      reductions under, 190
Budget estimating errors, 56
Budget figures, actuals/estimates, 3
Budget outlays
  subdivision of, 176–77
    effect on government spending, 176
Budget receipts
  raising of, 69
  See also Receipts.
Budget relationships, 221–22
Budget reporting, 196–201
Budget submission information, 181

C

Canada, foreign debt market investments by
    Japan, 137
Capital gains tax
  Tax Reform Act (1986) and, 69–71
  See also Tax receipts.
Capital goods, as subdivision for budget
    outlays, 176–77
Carter administration
  defense spending during, 33–36
  deficit increase and, 49
  GNP deflator and, 34, 36
  GNP increase in, 49
  inflation during, 34
  political profile, 47
  underestimation of major spending
    categories, 25
Cash balance
  U.S. Treasury, 147–48
    limiting of, 160
    too large balances, 147–48
    too low balances, 148
    variability of, 148
Cash flow, suggestions for, 152–61
CBO, *See* Congressional Budget Office.
CCC, *See* Commodity Credit Corporation
    (CCC).
Central bank
  portfolio approach, 130–39
    maturities, 139
Central supply and maintenance, as mission
    category, 47, 201

Chief executive officer (CEO), role in
formulating corporate budgets, 207
China, foreign exchange reserves, 121
Commercial banks
as purchasers of U.S. Treasury debt,
105–7
U.S. Treasury tax and loan balance at,
156–57
Commodity Credit Corporation (CCC)
agricultural outlays and, 38
timing of payments, 151
Confidence in government, effect of budget
deficit on, 64
Congress, *See* U.S. Congress.
Congressional Budget Office (CBO) , 46,
53, 187
Gramm-Rudman-Hollings (GRH) and, 187
Conrail, sale of, 199
Consumer Price Index (CPI), 188
increases in HHS spending compared
with, 32
Corporate budgets
compared to federal budget
document/process, 207–9
responsibility for accuracy of estimates,
208
Corporate income taxes, 73
performance of, 21–23
collapse, 22
corporate profit growth rate, 21
receipt estimates, 22
tax rate reductions, 21
raising of, 74–75
timing of, 150, 154
Corporate profits, 73
Corporations
as domestic purchasers of U.S. Treasury
debt, 108
equity funds and, 70
as purchasers of U.S. Treasury debt, 108
Cost-of-living adjustments
government programs, 44
Medicare, 33
Council of Economic Advisors, 237
Countercyclical approach, arguments against,
210–11
Countercyclical policies, 210–12
Coupon issues, U.S. Treasury, 87
CPI, *See* Consumer Price Index (CPI).
Credibility of government, budget deficit
and, 237
Credit budget, 200
loans/loan guarantees and, 200

Crowding out, of private borrowers,
140–41
Cutbacks
areas for, 39–41
agricultural outlays, 40–41
federal disability insurance (FDI), 40
federal hospital insurance (FHI), 39–40
grants to states, 40
health and human services (HHS),
39–40
interest costs, 40

D

Daiwa Securities America Inc., 128
Debt ceiling, 2
abolishment of, 172
changes in, 173
end of each fiscal year (1974–1978), 174
excluding nonmarketable debt obligations
issued to trust funds, 173
improving applicability of, 173
U.S. Congress and, 172
usefulness of, 172–74
Debt management
U.S. Treasury, 87–97
size of debt, 87
Defense spending
competition between services for, 43
dividing budget into categories based on
missions, 200–1
during Carter administration, 33–34
increase in, 8, 11, 33
major expenditure categories, 42
cutbacks in, 42
operations and maintenance outlays, 42
personnel outlays, 42
procurement outlays, 42–43
research and development outlays, 42
major spending categories, 201
misestimates for major defense
components, 34–35
misleading aspect of, 200–1
mission categories, 47
Reagan administration, 11
spending estimates, 25
spending imbalances, 43
Deficit/GNP ratio, reduction of, 98
Deficits
FY-75 and FY-76, 252
FY-82 and FY-83, 235

Deficits (cont.)
  as percentage of gross national product,
    224
Democrats
  party-in-power factor of budget deficit
    and, 47–50, 52
  willingness to spend, 51–52
Deutsche mark, versus dollar, 132, 133
Domestic purchasers
  U.S. Treasury debt, 105–8
    commercial banks, 105–7
    corporations, 108
    individual investments, 107–8
    insurance companies, 107
    state/local governments, 107

E

Economic assumptions, versus actuality,
    50–51
Economic Recovery Tax Act (1981), 8
Economy, future outlook of, 59
Eighteen-month note
  Treasury issuance of, 144–45
  funds to be raised by, 145
Equity funds, corporations and, 70
Estimated appropriations/outlays, versus
    actual outlays, 180
Estimating errors, 5
  excise taxes, 22
Euro-market, foreign debt market
    investments by Japan, 137
Exchange Stabilization Fund, as off-budget
    category, 196
Excise taxes
  performance of
    estimating errors, 22
    receipts, 22–23
  raising of, 75
Expenditures
  actuals/estimates, 12
  budget expenditure components, 26–27
  Commodity Credit Corporation (CCC),
    timing of payments, 151
  future outlook of, 55–57
    agricultural outlays, 56
    defense spending, 56
    inflation impact in OASI, 55–56
    interest costs, 56
    relationship between government outlays

  and GNP, 57
  spending analysis, 57
  trends, 55
growth rate of, 72
increase in, 5–8
  health and human services (HHS), 5, 11
  interest cost, 8
  military outlays, 8, 11
  unemployment trust accounts, 5, 11
month-end expenditures, 152
rate of, 13
related to interest rates and CPI, 45
timing of, 151–52
  combined with receipts, 152
uncontrollability of, 204
underestimation of, 25
Export-Import Bank, as off-budget category,
    196
Exports
  Japanese exports, to U.S., 134
  West German exports
    to U.S., 134

F

FDI, *See* Federal disability insurance.
Federal disability insurance (FDI), spending
    cutbacks in, 40
Federal Farm Credit System, agricultural
    outlays and, 37
Federal Financing Bank (FFB), 197
  as off-budget category, 197
Federal hospital insurance (FHI), 30
  compared to social security, 39
  spending cutbacks in, 39–40
Federal Open Market Committee (FOMC),
    205
Federal Reserve, 44, 46
  effect of budget deficit on policies, 63
  fiscal policy and, 205–6
  move toward accommodative monetary
    policy, 140–41
  as primary agent for cyclical
    responsibility, 212
  stabilizing balance at, 147
  U.S. Treasury balance at, 158–59
  view of foreign institutions trading in
    government securities, 119

willingness to tolerate inflation increases, 216

Federal Reserve banks, U.S. Treasury funds and, 147

Federal Savings and Loan Corporation (FSLIC), 196

Financing, with long-term sources, 146

Fiscal policy, 204–6
priorities of, 210–12
improve equitability of policy, 210–12
maximize economic growth, 210
reduce budget deficit, 210
relationships to consider when forming, 219–25
used for countercyclical purposes, 210–12

Foreign holdings
breakout of Treasury securities holdings, 115
foreign exchange reserves, 121
future sales, 123–29
factors that influence investors, 128–29
Japan, 123–26
Middle East oil exporting countries, 127
Singapore, 127
Taiwan, 127
West Germany, 126–27
government securities, effect of budget deficit on, 63–64
marketable Treasury issues, 110
Treasury bills, 113, 114
Treasury bonds, 113, 114
breakout by countries of major holdings of, 117
by official/nonofficial institutions, 116–17
Treasury certificates, 113, 114
Treasury notes, 113, 114
breakout by countries of major holdings of, 117
by official/nonofficial institutions, 116–17

Foreign investors
U.S. Treasury debt, 109–22
increase in foreign holdings, 109
Japanese holdings, 109–16
West German holdings, 119–20

France
foreign exchange reserves, 121

holdings in U.S. Treasury debt, 116

FSLIC, *See* Federal Savings and Loan Corporation (FSLIC).

Future outlook, 55–61
agricultural outlays, 56
defense spending, 56
deficit, 59–61
expenditures, 55–57
inflation impact on OASI, 55–56
interest costs, 56
receipts, 57–59
relationship between government outlays and GNP, 55
spending analysis, 57
trends, 55

G

Gasoline taxes, raising of, 75

General Agreements on Tariffs and Trade (GATT), 69

General-purpose forces, as mission category, 43, 200–1

GNP, *See* Gross national product (GNP).

GNP deflator, 44
Carter administration and, 34, 36

Government bond yields
United States, 136
compared with other countries, 136

Government expenditures, *See* Expenditures.

Government revenues, 2

Government securities, foreign holdings of, 2, 113–15, 123–29

Gramm-Rudman-Hollings (GRH), 41, 46, 71, 79–80, 169, 183, 195
balanced-budget amendment (BBA), 79–80, 190
fail-safe mechanism of, 185–86
improving mandated expenditure reductions under, 188–89
Old Age and Survivors Insurance (OASI) and, 197
tax surcharge and, 79–80

Grants to states, spending cutbacks in, 40

Griggs & Santow Report, 240–42
on deterioration of budget, 240–42
on Reagan administration deficit forecast, 241–42
risk on expenditure side of budget, 241
risk on receipts side of budget, 240

Griggs, William N., 231
Gross national product (GNP), 169, 213
    current dollar growth, 52
    deficit/GNP ratio, 98
    FY-74, 2
    FY-86, 2–4
    growth rate, 72
    tax surcharge and, 78–80
    versus receipts shortfall, 8
Gross private savings, compared with
        marketable Treasury debt, 222
Growth rate
    agricultural outlays, 37
        Commodity Credit Corporation (CCC)
            and, 38
        effect of foreign trade on, 37–38
    interest costs, 37
Growth in trading, 168–69
Guard and reserves, as mission category, 43,
        200

H

Health and human services (HHS)
    actuals/estimates, 31
    break out of, 201
    changes in components of, 30
    increased spending in, 5, 11
    increases in spending compared to
        Consumer Price Index (CPI)
        advances, 32
    Medicare expenditures, 30–33
    political sensitivity of, 30
    social security outlays, 30
    spending estimates, 25
Helium Operations, sale of, 199
HHS, *See* Health and human services
        (HHS).
Hospital insurance, Medicare, 30
House of Representatives, political profile,
        48
Housing for the Elderly or Handicapped
        Fund, as off-budget category, 196

I

Implementation, receipt-raising measures,
        74–77

Improved trade balance, 70
Income tax refunds, as form of negative tax
        receipts, 148
Independent budget estimating organization
    establishment of, 184
    scope of, 184
Individual income taxes
    tax rates, raising of, 74
        political considerations, 74
    tax surcharge, 70, 78–80
    See also Nonwithheld individual income
        taxes; Withheld individual income
        taxes.
Individual investors
    as purchasers of U.S. Treasury debt,
        107–8
    role in financing deficit, 142–43
Individual income, 73
Individual retirement accounts (IRAs), Tax
        Reform Act (1986) and, 69
Inflation, 4
    deficit financing and, 213
    overestimation of, 11
Insurance companies, as purchasers of U.S.
        Treasury debt, 107
Intelligence and communications, as mission
        category, 43, 201
Interest costs
    growth of, 36–37
        factors affecting, 36
        high interest rates, 36
        importance of interest rate levels, 36–37
    increases in, 8, 11–12
    spending cutbacks in, 40
    underestimation of rate levels/size of
        deficit, 25
Interest payments
    contribution to budget deficit, 63
    tax deductibility of, 70
Interest rates
    correlation between deficits and, 217
    federal expenditures related to, 45
    relationship between budget deficits and,
        213–16
Internal Revenue Service (IRS), tax amnesty
        and, 81–83
International bargaining, effect of budget
        deficit on, 64
Investor fears, created by budget deficit, 63
Italy, foreign exchange reserves, 121

J

Japan
   exports to U.S., 134
   foreign debt market investments by
      country, 137
   foreign exchange reserves, 121
   foreign holdings of
      brokerage/dealer firms, 128
      future sales, 123–26
   government bond yields, 136
   holdings in U.S. Treasury debt, 109–16,
      120
      acquisitions, 109
      intermediate/longer-term obligations,
         112
      private investors, 112–17
      redemptions/refunds, 109–10
      short-term Treasury issues, 109
      Treasury coupon issues, 111
      underestimation of Japanese purchases,
         110
Japanese Treasury bonds, 135
   sense of investing in U.S. Treasury bills,
      130
   suggested investment program for, 130

L

Aubrey G. Lanston & Co., 128
Large cash balances, U.S. Treasury,
      disadvantages of, 147–48
Lehman letter, 231–32
Line-item veto, 183
Loans/loan guarantees, 200
   credit budget and, 200
   potential adversity caused by, 200
Local governments
   effect of U.S. budget deficit on, 64–65
   as purchasers of U.S. Treasury debt, 107
   See also State governments.
Low balances, U.S. Treasury, 148

M

Major spending categories
   actuals/estimates, 28–29
   See also Expenditures.
Marginal income tax rates, reduction in, 69
Marketable Treasury debt, 87
   held by private investors, 89

Marketable Treasury financing, 162–63
   gross amounts announced, 162
   net amount raised, 163
Medicare expenditures, 30–33
   cost-of-living adjustments, 33
   hospital insurance, 30
   supplemental medical insurance, 30
Middle East oil exporting countries
   foreign holdings of, future sales, 127
   holdings in U.S. Treasury debt, 119
Military outlays, *See* Defense spending.
Military pensions, defense budget and, 201
Mission categories, 47, 201
   for defense budget, 201
Money market funds, 108, 142
Month-end expenditures, 152

N

National sales tax, institution of, 76
Naval Petroleum Reserves, sale of, 199
Negative outlays, importance to Reagan
      administration, 199
Negative tax receipts, income tax refunds as
      form of, 148
Nikko Securities Co. International Inc., 128
Nomura Securities International Inc., 128
Nondeductible value-added tax, 76
   See also Value-added tax.
Nondefense area cutbacks, 39–41
   agriculture, 40–41
   health and human services (HHS), 39–40
   interest costs, 40
Nonmarketable obligations
   purchase of by individual investors, 143
   advantages of, 143
Nonmarketable Treasury debt, 96–97
Nonmonetary international organizations,
      120
Nonofficial institutions
   foreign holdings of Treasury notes/bonds
      by, 116–17
   short-term Treasury obligations owned
      by, 118
Nonwithheld income tax payment pattern
   current system, 149
   proposed system, 150
Nonwithheld individual income taxes
   payment of
      at beginning of January, 15
      avoiding month with overlap, 153
      on first of month, 153

Nonwithheld individual income taxes (cont.)
  performance of, 19–21
    dollar amount, 19–21
    estimating errors, 21
    rate of growth, 19
    underestimation, 21
  timing of, 148, 152
  See also Tax receipts.
Norway, foreign exchange reserves, 121

O

Off-budget items, 196–98
  categories of, 196
  debt securities held by, 198
Office of Management and Budget (OMB),
    185, 188
Official institutions
  foreign holdings of Treasury notes/bonds
    by, 116–17
  short-term Treasury obligations owned
    by, 118
Oil import taxes
  raising of, 75–76
  See also Tax receipts.
Old Age and Survivors Insurance (OASI)
    outlays, *See* Social security outlays.
OMB, *See* Office of Management and
    Budget (OMB).
One-year budget, versus two-year budget,
    178–79
OPEC, *See* Organization of Petroleum
    Exporting Countries (OPEC).
Operations, as subdivision for budget
    outlays, 176–77
Operations and maintenance outlays, defense
    spending, 42, 200
Organization of Petroleum Exporting
    Countries (OPEC), 2, 4
Outlays, as percentage of gross national
    product, 224

P

Party-in-power factor, budget deficit and,
    47–53
Pension Benefit Guaranty Corporation, as
    off-budget category, 196
Personal income, *See* Individual
    income.
Personnel outlays, defense spending, 42, 200
Plant/equipment expenditures, private sector,
    141
Political environment, as cause of budget
    deficit, 8
Political profile, 48
Portfolio approach
  Bank of Japan (BOJ) and, 130–38
    maturities, 139
  central banks, 130–38
    maturities, 139
Postal Service Fund, as off-budget category,
    196, 197
Power Marketing Administration, sale of,
    199
President's line-item veto, use of, 183
Private borrowers, crowding out of, 140–41
Privatization of budget, 199
Procurement outlays
  changing process of, 42–43
  defense spending, 42–43, 200

R

Reagan administration
  agricultural outlays, 11
  asset sales and, 199
  as beneficiary of lower inflation, 36
  competition between services for defense
    budget, 43
  cutbacks in outlays, 211
  defense outlays, 11
  defense spending during, 34
  deficit increase and, 47–53
  loans/loan guarantees, 200
  lowering of income tax rates, 61
  opposition to tax increases, 77
  political profile, 48
  privatization of budget and, 199
  receipts shortfall and, 49
    effect of tax reductions/tax reforms on,
      49
  role in slowing growth of government
    outlays, 44–46
  unemployment outlays, 11
    interest costs, 11–13
Receipt-raising measures
  alcohol taxation, 75, 77
  corporate income taxes, 75
  gasoline taxes, 75, 77
  implementation of, 74–77
  individual income taxes, 77
  individual income tax rates, 74
  oil import taxes, 75–77

reasons for lack of implementation, 74
political unpopularity of measures, 74
Reagan administration resistance to
raising taxes, 74
tax amnesty, 81–83
tax surcharge, 78–80
tobacco taxation, 75, 77
value-added tax, 76–77
Receipts
actuals/estimates, 10
analysis of, 72–73
as percentage of gross national product
(GNP), 224
excise taxes, 22–23
tax receipts, 57–59
future outlook of, 57–59
timing of, 148
trust account receipts, 18–19
See also Tax receipts; Undistributed
offsetting receipts.
Receipts shortfall
as cause of budget deficit, 8–13
amount of, 9–11
Reagan administration and, 49
effect of tax reductions/tax reforms on,
49
Regulation Q limitations, 142
Reporting dealers
daily dealer transaction increases, 166
dealer positions and transactions, 167
definition of, 165
increase in, 165–69
on January 1, 1974, 170
on January 6, 1988, 171
number of, 169
compared with 30-year bond
performance, 166
Republicans
party-in-power factor of budget deficit
and, 47–53
willingness to spend, 49
Research and development
defense spending, 42, 200
as mission category, 43, 201
Revenue neutrality, Tax Reform Act (1986)
and, 69
Revenue-raising measures, tax surcharge,
78–80
Rights technique, 87
Rural Electrification and Telephone
Revolving Fund, as off-budget
category, 196

Rural Telephone Bank, as off-budget
category, 196

S

Saudi Arabia, foreign exchange reserves,
121
SCA, *See* Spending-control amendment
(SCA).
Schroder Report, 232–40
on deterioration of budget, 232–40
on optimism of Carter administration, 234
risk on receipts side of budget, 235
Sealift, as mission category, 43, 201
Senate, *See* U.S. Senate.
Singapore
foreign exchange reserves, 121
foreign holdings of, future sales, 127
holdings in U.S. Treasury debt, 119, 120
Six-week bill
U.S. Treasury, 160–61
advantages of, 160
approximate sales of, 160
argument against, 161
SLUGS, *See* State and Local Government
Series (SLUGS) issues.
Social security, as off-budget entity, 197
Social Security Amendments of 1983, 197
Social security outlays, 30
argument for spending cutbacks in, 39
Spain, foreign exchange reserves, 121
Spending-control amendment (SCA), 191–92
advantages of, 191–92
basis of, 191
reenforcing proposals, 192
transition adjustments, 191
Spending cutbacks
agricultural outlays, 40–41
federal disability insurance (FDI), 40
federal hospital insurance (FHI), 39–40
grants to states, 40
health and human services (HHS), 39–40
interest costs, 40
State governments
effect of U.S. budget deficit on, 65
as purchasers of U.S. Treasury debt, 107
See also Local governments.
State grants, spending cutbacks in, 40
State and Local Government Series (SLUGS)
issues, 96
money raised by, 96

Strategic forces, as mission category, 43, 201
Subdivision of budget outlays, 176–77
Submission of budget, timing of, 180–82
Submission period of budget, 180–82
Supplemental medical insurance, Medicare, 30
Supply-side economics, 9
Support of other nations, as mission category, 43, 201
Surcharge, individual income tax, 70
Switzerland
    foreign exchange reserves, 121
    holdings in U.S. Treasury debt, 116
    Treasury bill yields, 136
Synthetic Fuels Corporation, as off-budget category, 197

T

Taiwan
    foreign holdings of, future sales, 127
    holdings in U.S. Treasury debt, 120
Targeting technique, 195
Tax amnesty, 81–83
    revenue inflow from, 81
Tax inflows, timing of, 148, 152
Tax and loan accounts, U.S. Treasury funds and, 147
Tax receipts
    future outlook of, 57–59
        cutting taxes, 61
        effect of inflation on, 58–59
        effect of Tax Reform Act on, 57–58
        increasing taxes, 61
        time periods involved, 57–58
    income tax refunds, 148
    performance of, 14–23
        corporate income taxes, 21–23
        excise taxes, 22–23
        nonwithheld individual income taxes, 19–21
        tax refunds, 23
        trust account receipts, 18–19
        withheld individual income taxes, 14–18
    See also Capital gains tax; Corporate income taxes; Nonwithheld individual income taxes; Receipts; Tax surcharge; Value-added tax; Withheld individual income taxes.
Tax Reform Act (1981), 204, 226

Tax Reform Act (1986), 71, 75, 77
    capital gains tax and, 69–70
    design prerequisites, 69–71
    as impediment to improved savings rate, 219
    improvements on
        capital gains tax benefits, 69–70
        individual income tax surcharge, 70
        individual retirement accounts (IRAs), 69
        interest payments, tax deductibility of, 70
        marginal income tax rates, reduction in, 69
        revenue neutrality, 69
    one-time receipts benefit, 72
    results of, 205
    tax receipts from, 9
Tax refunds
    actuals/estimates, 24
    effect of 1981 tax act on, 23
    growth in, 23
Tax surcharge, 78–80
    administration of, 79
    compatibility with
        Gramm-Rudman-Hollings (GRH), 79–80
    dollar amounts, 78, 80
    equitability of, 79
    See also Tax receipts.
Tax-take
    increase in tax-take, 73
    Tax Reform Act (1986) and, 69–71
    tax-take table, 60
    See also Tax receipts.
Three-month Treasury issues, 218
Tobacco taxation, raising of, 75
Trade balance, improving of, 70
Trade deficit, U.S. budget and, 227
Training, medical, and other general personnel activities, as mission category, 43, 201
Treasury, See U.S. Treasury.
Treasury bill/bond yields, 136
Trust account receipts
    performance of, 18–19
        contribution laws and, 18–19
    See also Receipts.
Twenty-year bond
    Treasury discontinuation of, 95
    Treasury issuance of, 144–5, 218

arguments supporting, 144
   funds to be raised by, 145
Two-year budget, 178–79
   advantages of, 178
   impact of, 178
   popularity of, 178–79
   versus one-year budget, 178–79

U

Undistributed offsetting receipts, 199
   adding receipts to revenue, 199
   treatment of, 199
   See also Receipts.
Unemployment outlays
   Reagan administration, 11
   interest costs, 11–13
Unemployment trust accounts, increased
   spending in, 5, 11
United Kingdom
   foreign debt market investments by Japan,
     137
   foreign exchange reserves, 121
   government bond yields, 136
   holdings in U.S. Treasury debt, 119
   Treasury bill yields, 136
U.S. Congress
   political profile, 48
   timing of budget submission and, 180–82
   two-year budget proposal and, 178–9
Useful life, of assets, determination of, 176
U.S. government
   confidence in, 64
   Congress
     Congressional Budget Office estimates,
      46
     discussing budget topics in, 53
     nondefense outlays and, 51
     political profile, 48
     role in slowing growth of government
      outlays, 44–46
     See also Congressional Budget Office
      (CBO).
   economic growth in, 62
   financing of budget from abroad, 140, 142
   government bond yields, 136
   resistance to tax amnesty, 81

Treasury bill yields, 136
   See also U.S. Treasury.
U.S. petroleum industry, oil import taxes
   and, 76
U.S. Railway Association, as off-budget
   category, 196, 197
U.S. Senate, political profile, 48
U.S. Treasury
   chronology of deficit need financing,
     87–89
   CY-74, 87–89
   CY-75/CY-76, 89–94
   CY-77, 94
   CY-78, 94
   CY-79, 94
   CY-80, 94
   CY-81, 94
   CY-82, 94–95
   CY-83, 95
   CY-84, 95
   CY-85, 95
   CY-86, 95
   CY-87, 95
   coupon issues, 87
   crowding out of private investors, 140–41
   debt management, 87–141
     approach to, 87–97
   discontinuation of twenty-year bond
     offerings, 95
   effect of tax amnesty on, 81–83
   future financing
     coupon notes, 100
     estimation approaches, 98
     marketable note and bond maturities,
      99–101, 102–4
     offerings, maturities and net increases in
      notes/bonds, 100–101
   future financings, 98–104
   improving cash flow, 147–59
   large cash balances and, 147–48
   marketable Treasury debt outstanding, 88
   maturity distribution of marketable debt
     held by private investors, 89
   1987 cash balance, 155–56
   nonmarketable debt outstanding, 96, 97
   offerings of notes and bonds for cash,
     90–93
   tax and loan balance at commercial banks,
     156–57
   techniques in adding to outstanding debt,
     87

U.S. Treasury (cont.)
  Treasury bills
    bill financing, 146
    timing recommendations, 164
  Treasury bonds
    compared to Japanese Treasury bonds, 135
    compared to West German Treasury bonds, 135
    U.S. yields compared with other countries, 137
  Treasury notes, timing recommendations, 164
  types of fund accounts, 147

V

Value-added tax
  institution of, 76–77
    arguments against, 76–77
  nondeductible, 77
  See also Tax receipts.
Veterans Benefits and Services, defense budget and, 200
Volcker, Paul, 63

W

West Germany
  exports to U.S. 132
  foreign exchange reserves, 121
  foreign holdings of, future sales, 126–127
  government bond yields, 136
  holdings in U.S. Treasury debt, 119–20
  purchases of U.S. Treasury notes and bonds, 132
  Treasury bill yields, 136
  West German Treasury bonds, 135
Withheld individual income taxes
  performance of, 14–18
    estimates, 18
    percentages, 14–18
  timing of, 148, 152
  See also Tax receipts.

Y

Yamaichi International, 128
Yen, versus dollar, 132